Alexander Maclaren

The Gospel of St. Matthew

Alexander Maclaren

The Gospel of St. Matthew

ISBN/EAN: 9783743329775

Manufactured in Europe, USA, Canada, Australia, Japa

Cover: Foto ©ninafisch / pixelio.de

Manufactured and distributed by brebook publishing software (www.brebook.com)

Alexander Maclaren

The Gospel of St. Matthew

Bible Class Expositions.

THE GOSPEL OF ST. MATTHEW.

WORKS BY THE SAME AUTHOR.

COLOSSIANS AND PHILEMON
(*Expositor's Bible*). Fifth Edition. Crown 8vo, cloth, 7s. 6d.

THE LIFE OF DAVID AS REFLECTED IN HIS PSALMS (*Household Library of Exposition*). Seventh Edition. Crown 8vo, cloth, 3s. 6d.

LONDON:
HODDER & STOUGHTON, 27, PATERNOSTER ROW.

THE
GOSPEL OF ST. MATTHEW

BY

ALEXANDER MACLAREN, D.D

VOLUME I

London
HODDER AND STOUGHTON
27, PATERNOSTER ROW

MDCCCXCII

Printed by Hazell, Watson, & Viney, Ld., London and Aylesbury.

CONTENTS.

LESSON I.
THE FIRST-FRUITS OF THE GENTILES . . . . PAGE 1

LESSON II.
THE KING IN EXILE 12

LESSON III.
THE HERALD OF THE KING 22

LESSON IV.
THE CORONATION OF THE KING 34

LESSON V.
THE VICTORY OF THE KING 43

LESSON VI.
THE EARLY WELCOME AND THE FIRST MINISTERS OF THE KING 54

LESSON VII.
THE NEW SINAI 63

Contents.

LESSON VIII.
THE NEW FORM OF THE OLD LAW 76

LESSON IX.
TRUMPETS AND STREET CORNERS 86

LESSON X.
WITHOUT CAREFULNESS 98

LESSON XI.
JUDGING, ASKING, AND GIVING 106

LESSON XII.
CLOSING WARNINGS 117

LESSON XIII.
THE CENTURION AND THE CAPTAIN OF THE LORD'S HOST 126

LESSON XIV.
THE PEACE-BRINGER IN THE WORLD OF NATURE . 136

LESSON XV.
THE PEACE-BRINGER IN THE WORLD OF CONSCIENCE . 144

LESSON XVI.
THE TOUCH OF FAITH AND THE TOUCH OF CHRIST . 152

LESSON XVII.
THE KING'S AMBASSADORS 164

Contents.

LESSON XVIII.
THE KING'S CHARGE TO HIS AMBASSADORS . 174

LESSON XIX.
JOHN'S DOUBTS OF JESUS, AND JESUS' PRAISE OF JOHN 185

LESSON XX.
CHRIST'S VOICE OF JUDGMENT, THANKSGIVING, SELF-ATTESTATION, AND INVITATION 196

LESSON XXI.
THE PHARISEES' SABBATH AND CHRIST'S . . . 207

LESSON XXII.
FOUR SOWINGS AND ONE RIPENING 217

LESSON XXIII.
VARIOUS ASPECTS OF THE KINGDOM . . . 228

LESSON XXIV.
MINGLED IN GROWTH, SEPARATED IN MATURITY . 238

LESSON XXV.
THE MARTYRDOM OF JOHN 248

INDEX OF SCRIPTURES.

	PAGE		PAGE
Matt. ii. 1-12	1	Matt. viii. 18-27	136
—— ii. 13-23	12	—— ix. 1-8	144
—— iii. 1-12	22	—— ix. 18-31	152
—— iii. 13-17	34	—— ix. 35-38; x. 1-8	164
—— iv. 1-11	43	—— x. 32-42	174
—— iv. 17-25	54	—— xi. 2-15	185
—— v. 1-16	63	—— xi. 20-30	196
—— v. 17-26	76	—— xii. 1-14	207
—— vi. 1-15	86	—— xiii. 1-9	217
—— vi. 24-34	98	—— xiii. 31-33, 44-52	228
—— vii. 1-12	106	—— xiii. 24-30	238
—— vii. 13-29	117	—— xiv. 1-12	248
—— viii. 5-13	126		

LESSON I.

The First-fruits of the Gentiles.

MATTHEW ii. 1-12.

1. "Now when Jesus was born in Bethlehem of Judæa in the days of Herod the king, behold, there came wise men from the east to Jerusalem,

2. Saying, Where is He that is born King of the Jews? for we have seen His star in the east, and are come to worship Him.

3. When Herod the king had heard these things, he was troubled, and all Jerusalem with him.

4. And when he had gathered all the chief priests and scribes of the people together, he demanded of them where Christ should be born.

5. And they said unto him, In Bethlehem of Judæa: for thus it is written by the prophet,

6. And thou Bethlehem, in the land of Juda, art not the least among the princes of Juda: for out of thee shall come a Governor, that shall rule my people Israel.

7. Then Herod, when he had privily called the wise men, enquired of them diligently what time the star appeared.

8. And he sent them to Bethlehem, and said, Go and search diligently for the young Child; and when ye have found Him, bring me word again, that I may come and worship Him also.

9. When they had heard the king, they departed; and, lo, the star, which they saw in the east, went before them, till it came and stood over where the young Child was.

10. When they saw the star, they rejoiced with exceeding great joy.

11. And when they were come into the house, they saw the young Child with Mary His mother, and fell down, and worshipped Him: and when they had opened their treasures, they presented unto Him gifts; gold, frankincense, and myrrh.

12. And being warned of God in a dream that they should not return to Herod, they departed into their own country another way."

MATTHEW'S Gospel is the gospel of the King. It has a distinctly Jewish colouring. All the more remarkable, therefore, is this narrative, which we should rather have looked for in Luke, the evangelist who delights to emphasise the universality of Christ's work. But the gathering of the Gentiles to the light of Israel was an essential part of true Judaism, and could not but be represented in the Gospel which set forth the glories of the King. There is something extremely striking and stimulating to the imagination in the vagueness of the description of these Eastern pilgrims. Where they came from, how long they had been in travelling, how many they were, what was their rank, whence they went,—all these questions are left unsolved. They glide into the story, present their silent adoration, "and as silently steal away." The tasteless mediæval tradition knows all about them: they were three; they were kings. It knows their names; and, if we choose to pay the fee, we can see their bones to-day in the shrine behind the high altar in Cologne Cathedral. How much more impressive is the indefiniteness of our narrative! How much more the half sometimes is than the whole!

I. We see here heathen wisdom led by God to the cradle of Christ. It is futile to attempt to determine the nationality of the wise men. Possibly they were Persian magi, whose astronomy was half astrology and wholly observation, or they may have travelled from some place even deeper in the mysterious East; but, in any case, they were led by God through their science, such as it was. The great lesson which they teach remains the same, however subordinate questions about the nature of the star and the like may be settled. The sign in the heavens and its explanation were both of God, whether the one was a natural astronomical phenomenon or a supernatural light, and the other the conclusions of their science or the inbreathing of His wisdom. So they stand as representatives of the great truth that, outside the limits of the people of revelation, God moved on hearts and led seeking souls to the light in divers manners. These silent strangers at the cradle carry on the line of recipients of Divine messages outside of Israel which is headed by the mysterious Melchizedek, and includes that seer who saw a Star arise out of Jacob, and which, in a wider sense, includes many a "poet of their own" and many a patient seeker after truth. Human wisdom, as it is called, is God's gift. In itself, it is incomplete. It raises more questions than it solves. Its highest function is to lead to Jesus. He is Lord of the sciences, as of all that belongs to man; and notwithstanding all the appearances to the contrary at present, we may be sure that the true scope of all science, and its certain end, is to lead to the recognition of Him.

May we not see in these magi, too, a type of the inmost meaning of heathen religions? These faiths have in them points of contact with Christianity. Besides their falsehoods and abhorrent dark cruelties and lustfulnesses, they enshrine confessions of wants which the King in the cradle alone can supply. Modern unbelieving teachers tell us that Christianity and they are alike products of man's own religious faculty. But the truth is that they are confessions of need, and Christianity is the supply of the need. At bottom, their language is the question of the wise men, "Where is He?" Their sacrifices proclaim man's need of reconciliation. Their stories of the gods coming down in the likeness of men speak of his longing for a manifestation of God in the flesh. The cradle and the cross are Heaven's answer to their sad questions.

II. The contrast of these Gentiles' joyful eagerness to worship the King of Israel, with the alarm of His own people at the whisper of His name, is a prelude of the tragedy of His rejection, and the passing over of the kingdom to the Gentiles. Notice the bitter and scornful emphasis of that "Herod the *king*," coming twice in the story in immediate connection with the mention of the true King. He is a usurper, caricaturing the true Monarch. Like most kings who have had "great" tacked to their names, his greatness consisted in supreme wickedness. Fierce, lustful, cunning, he had ruled without mercy; and now he was passing through the last stages of an old age without love, and ringed round by the fears born of his misdeeds. He trembles for his throne, as well he may, when he hears of these strangers. Probably he does not suppose them mixed up with any attempt to unseat him, or he would have made short work of them; unless, indeed, his craft led him to dissemble until he had sucked them dry, and had used them to lead him to the infant rival, after which he may have meant to murder them too. But he recognises in their question the familiar tones of the Messianic hope, which he knew was ever lying like glowing embers in the breast of the nation, ready to be blown into a flame. His creatures in the capital might disown it, but he knew in his secret heart that he was a usurper, and that at any moment that smouldering hatred and hope might burn up him and his upstart monarchy. An evil conscience is full of fears, and shrinks from the good news that the King of all is at hand. His coming should be joy, as the bursting spring or the rosy dawn; but our own sin makes the day of the Lord darkness, and not light, and sends us cowering into our corners to escape these searching eyes.

Nor less tragic and perverted is the trouble which "all Jerusalem" shared with Herod. The magi had naturally made straight for the capital, expecting to find the new-born King there, and His city jubilant at His birth. But they traverse its streets only to find none who knows anything about Him. They must have felt like men who see, gleaming from far on some hillside, a brightness which has all vanished when they reach the spot; or like some of our mission converts brought to our "Christian country," and seeing how little our people care for the Christ whom they have learned to know. Their question indicates utter bewilderment at the contrast between what they had seen in the East and what they found in Jerusalem. They must have been still more perplexed if they observed its effect. Nobody in Jerusalem knew anything about their King. That was strange enough. But nobody wanted Him. That was stranger still. A prophet had long ago called on "Zion" to "rejoice greatly" because "thy King cometh"; but now anxiety and terror cloud all faces. It was partly because personal ends bound many to Herod, and partly because they all feared that any outburst of Messianic hopes would lead to fresh cruelties inflicted by the relentless, trembling tyrant. So the magi, who represented the eagerness of Gentile hearts grasping the new hopes, and claiming some share in Israel's Messiah, saw his own people careless and, if moved from their apathy, alarmed at the unwelcome tidings that the promise which had shone as a great light through dreary centuries was at last on the eve of fulfilment. So the first page on the gospel history anticipates the sad issue, "They shall come from the east, and from the west," and you yourselves shall be thrust out.

III. Then comes the council of the theologians, with its solemn teaching of the difference between orthodoxy and life, and of the utter hollowness of mere knowledge, however accurate, of the letter of Scripture. The questions as to the composition of this gathering of authorities, and of the variations between the quotation of Micah in the text and its form in the Hebrew, will not be discussed at this time. We may remark on the evident purpose of God to draw forth the distinct testimony of the ecclesiastical rulers to the place of Messiah's birth, and on the fact that this, the most ancient interpretation of the prophecy, is vouched to us by existing Jewish sources as having been the traditional one until the exigencies of controversy with Christians pushed it aside. Notice the different conduct of Herod, the magi, and the scribes. The first is entangled in a ludicrous contradiction. He believes that Messiah is to be born in Bethlehem, and yet he determines to set himself against the carrying out of what he must, in some sense, believe to be God's purpose. "If this Infant is God's Messiah, I will kill Him," is surely as strange a piece of policy gone mad as ever the world heard of. But it is perhaps not more insane than much of our own action, when we set ourselves against what we know to be God's will, and consciously seek to thwart it. A child trying to stop a train by pushing against the locomotive has as much chance of success. The scribes, again, are quite sure where Messiah is to be born; but they do not care to go and see if He is born. These strangers, to whom the hope of Israel is new, may rush away, in their enthusiasm, to Bethlehem; but they, to whom it had lost all gloss, and become a commonplace, would take no such trouble. Does not familiarity with the gospel produce much the same effect on many of us? Might not the joy and the devotion, however ignorant if compared with our better knowledge of the letter which marks converts from heathenism, shame the tepid zeal and unruffled composure of us, who have heard all about Christ, till it has become wearisome? Here on the very threshold of the gospel story is the first instance of the lesson taught over and over again in it, namely, the worthlessness of head knowledge, and the constant temptation of substituting it for the submission of the will and the trust of the heart, which alone make religion. The most impenetrable armour against the gospel is the familiar and life-long knowledge of the gospel.

The magi, on their part, accept with implicit confidence the information. They have followed the star; they have now a more sure word, and they will follow that. They were led by their science to contact with the true guide. He that is faithful in his use of the dimmest light will find the light grow. The office of science is not to lead to Christ by a road discovered by itself, but to lead to the Word of God, which guides to Him. Not by accident, nor without profound meaning, did both methods of direction unite to point these earnest seekers, who were ready to follow every form of guidance, to the Monarch whom they sought.

IV. Herod's crafty counsel need not detain us. We

have already remarked on its absurdity. If the Child were not Messiah, he need not have been alarmed; if it were, his efforts were fruitless. But he does not see this, and so plots and works underground in the approved fashion of king-craft. His reason for questioning the magi as to the time was, of course, to get an approximate age of the Infant, that he might know how widely to fling his net. He did it privately, so as to keep any inkling of his plot secret till he had got the further information which he hoped to delude them into bringing. Like other students and recluses fed upon great thoughts, the magi were very easily deceived. Good, simple people, they were no match for Herod, and told him all without suspicion, and set off to look for the Child, quite convinced of his good faith; while he, no doubt, breathed more freely when he had got them out of Jerusalem, and congratulated himself on having done a good stroke of business in making them his spies. He was probably within a few months of his death. The world was already beginning to slip from him. But before he passes to his account, he too is brought within sight of the Christ, and summoned to yield his usurped dominion to the true King. How different this old man's reception of the tidings of the nativity from Simeon's! His hostility, in its cruelty, its blundering cunning and its impotence, is a type of the relations of the world-power to Christ. "The rulers take counse together, . . . against His anointed. . . . He that sitteth in the heavens shall laugh."

V. We have next the discovery of the king. The reappearing star becomes the guide to the humble house. It cannot have been an ordinary star, for no such could have pointed the precise house among all the homes of Bethlehem. The burst of joy at its reappearance vividly suggests the perplexity of the recent days, and the support given by it to the faith which had accepted, not perhaps without some misgivings caused by the indifference of the teachers, the teaching of the prophecy. Surely that faith would be more than ever tried by the humble poverty in which they found the King. The great paradox of Christianity, the manifestation of divinest power in uttermost weakness, was forced upon them in its most startling form. "This Child on His mother's lap with none to do Him homage, and in poverty which makes our costly gifts seem out of place,—this is the King, whose coming set stars ablaze and drew us hither. Is this all?" Their Eastern religions were not unfamiliar with the idea of incarnation. Their Eastern monarchies were splendid. They must have felt a shock at the contrast between what they expected and what they found. They learned the lesson which all have to learn, that Christ disappoints as well as fulfils the expectations of men, that the mightiest power is robed in lowliness, and the highest manifestation of God begins with a helpless Infant on His mother's knee. These wise men were not repelled. Our modern "wise men" are not all as wise as they.

VI. Adoration and offering follow discovery. The "worship" of the magi cannot have been adoration in the strict sense. We attribute too much to them if we suppose them aware of Christ's divinity. But it was clearly more than mere reverence for an earthly king. It hovered on the border line, and meant an indefinite submission and homage to a partially discerned superiority, in which the presence of God was in some sort special. The old mediæval interpretation of the offered gold as signifying recognition of His kingship, the frankincense of His deity, and the myrrh of His death, is so beautiful that one would fain wish it true. But it cannot pretend to be more than a fancy. We are on surer ground when we see in the gifts the choicest products of the land of the magi, and learn the lesson that the true recognition of Christ will ever be attended by the spontaneous surrender to Him of our best. These gifts would not be of much use to Mary. If there had been a "practical man" among the magi, he might have said, "What is the use of giving such things to such a household?" And it would have been difficult to have answered. But love does not calculate, and the impulse which leads to consecrate the best we have to Him is acceptable in His sight. This earliest page in the gospel history is a prophecy of the latest. These are the firstfruits of the Gentiles unto Christ. They bear "in their hands a glass which showeth many more," who at last will come like them to the King of the whole earth. "'They shall bring gold and incense; and they shall show forth the praises of the Lord." There were Gentiles at the cradle and at the cross. The magi learned the lessons which the East especially needed, of power in weakness, royalty in lowliness, incarnation not in monstrous forms, or with destructive attributes, but in feeble infancy, which pass through the ordinary stages of development. The Greeks who sought to see Jesus near the hour of His death, learned the lesson for want of which their nation's culture rotted away, "except a corn of wheat fall into the ground and die, it abideth alone."

So these two groups, one at the beginning, the other at the end, one from the mysterious East, the other from the progressive and cultured West, received each a half of the completed truth, the gospel of incarnation and sacrifice, and witness to the sufficiency of Christ for all human needs, and to the coming of the time when all the races of men shall gather round the throne to which cradle and cross have exalted Him, and shall recognise in Him the Prince of all the kings of the earth, and the Lamb slain for the sins of the world.

LESSON II.

The King in Exile.

MATT. ii. 13-23.

13. "And when they were departed, behold, the angel of the Lord appeareth to Joseph in a dream, saying, Arise, and take the young Child and His mother, and flee into Egypt, and be thou there until I bring thee word: for Herod will seek the young Child to destroy Him.

14. When he arose, he took the young Child and His mother by night, and departed into Egypt:

15. And was there until the death of Herod: that it might be fulfilled which was spoken of the Lord by the prophet, saying, Out of Egypt have I called My Son.

16. Then Herod, when he saw that he was mocked of the wise men, was exceeding wroth, and sent forth, and slew all the children that were in Bethlehem, and in all the coasts thereof, from two years old and under, according to the time which he had diligently enquired of the wise men.

17. Then was fulfilled that which was spoken by Jeremy the prophet, saying,

18. In Rama was there a voice heard, lamentation, and weeping, and great mourning, Rachel weeping for her children, and would not be comforted, because they are not.

19. But when Herod was dead, behold, an angel of the Lord appeareth in a dream to Joseph in Egypt,

20. Saying, Arise, and take the young Child and His mother, and go into the land of Israel: for they are dead which sought the young Child's life.

21. And he arose, and took the young Child and His mother, and came into the land of Israel.

22. But when he heard that Archelaus did reign in Judæa in the room of his father Herod, he was afraid to go thither: notwithstanding, being warned of God in a dream, he turned aside into the parts of Galilee:

23. And he came and dwelt in a city called Nazareth: that it might be fulfilled which was spoken by the prophets, He shall be called a Nazarene."

DR. DELITZSCH, in his "New Investigations into the Origin and Plan of the Canonical Gospels," tries to show that Matthew is constructed on the plan of the Pentateuch. The analogy is somewhat strained, but there are some striking points of correspondence. He regards Matthew i. to ii. 15 as answering to Genesis. It begins with the "genesis of Jesus," and, as the Old Testament book ends with the migration of Israel to Egypt, so this section of the Gospel ends with the flight of the Holy Family to the same land. The section from ii. 15 to the end of the Sermon on the Mount answers to Exodus, and here the parallels are striking. The murder of the innocents at Bethlehem by Herod answers to Pharaoh's slaughter of Hebrew children; the Exodus to the return to Nazareth; the call of Moses at the bush to the baptism of Jesus; the forty years in the wilderness to the forty days' desert hunger and temptation; and the giving of the law from Sinai to the Sermon on the Mount, which contains the new law for the kingdom of God. Without supposing that the evangelist moulded his gospel on the plan of the Pentateuch, we cannot but see that there is a real parallel between the beginnings of the national life of Israel and the commencement of the life of Christ. Our present lesson brings this parallel into great prominence. It is divided into three sections, each of which has for its centre an Old Testament prophecy.

I. We have first the flight into Egypt and the prophecy fulfilled therein. The appearance of the angel seems to have followed immediately on the departure of the magi. They were succeeded by a loftier visitor from a more distant land, coming to lay richer gifts and a more absolute homage at the Infant's feet. The angel of the Lord who had already eased Joseph's honest and troubled heart by disclosing the secret of Mary's Child, comes again. To Mary he had appeared waking; her meek eyes could look on him, and her obedient ears hear his voice. But Joseph, who stood on a lower spiritual level, needed the lower form of revelation by dream, which augurs less susceptibility in the recipient, and less importance in the communication. It is the only form appropriate to his power of receiving, and four times it is mentioned as granted to him. The warning to the wise men was also conveyed in a dream. We can scarcely help recalling the similar prominence of dreams in the history of the earlier Joseph, whose life was moulded in order to bring Israel into Egypt.

The angel speaks of "the young Child and His mother," reversing the order of nature, as if he bowed before the Infant, "Lord of men as well as angels," and would deepen the lesson which so many signs gathering round the cradle were teaching the silent Joseph,—that Mary and he were but humble ministers of His. The partial instruction given, and the darkness left lying over the future, are in accordance with the methods of God's leading, which always gives light enough for the next duty, and never for the one after that. The prompt and precise obedience of Joseph to the heavenly vision is emphatically expressed by the verbal repetition of the command in the account of its fulfilment. There was no hesitation, no reluctance, no delay. On the very night, as it appears, of the dream, he rose up; the simple preparations were quickly made; the wise men's gifts would help to sustain their modest wants, and before the day broke they were on their road. How strangely blended in our Lord's life, from the very dawning, are dignity and lowliness, glory and reproach! How soon

His brows are crowned with thorns! The adoration of the magi witnesses to Him as the King of Israel and the hope of the world. The flight of which that adoration was the direct cause witnesses no less clearly to Him as despised and rejected, tasting sorrow in His earliest food, and not having where to lay His head.

But the most important part of the story is the connection which Matthew discerns between it and Hosea's words. In their original place they are not a prophecy at all, but simply a part of a tender historical *résumé* of God's dealings with Israel, by which the prophet would touch his contemporaries' hearts into penitence and trust. How, then, is the evangelist justified in regarding them as prophetic, and in looking on Christ's flight as their fulfilment? The answer is to be found in that analogy between the national and the personal Israel which runs through all the Old Testament, and reaches its highest clearness in the second part of Isaiah's prophecies. Jesus Christ was what Israel was destined and failed to be, the true servant of God, His Anointed, His Son, the medium of conveying His Name to the world. The ideal of the nation was realised in Him. His brief stay in Egypt served the very same purpose in His life which their four hundred years there did in theirs,—it sheltered Him from enemies, and gave Him room to grow. Just as the infant nation was unawares fostered in the very lap of the country which was the symbol of the world hostile to God, so the infant Christ was guarded and grew there. The prophecy is a prophecy just because it is history; for the history was all a shadow of the future, and He is the true Israel and the Son of God. It would have been fulfilled quite as really,—that is to say, the parallel between Christ and the nation would have been as fully carried out,—if His place of refuge had been in some other land; but the precise outward identity helps to point the parallel to unobservant eyes. The great truth taught by it of the typical relation between the nation and the person is the key to large regions of Old Testament history and prophecy. Rightly, therefore, does Matthew call our attention to this pregnant thought, and bid us see in the Divine selection of the place where the young life of God manifest in the flesh was sheltered, a fulfilment of prophecy. Egypt was the natural asylum of every fugitive from Palestine, but a deeper reason bent the steps of the Holy Family to the shelter of its palms and temples.

II. The slaughter of the innocents, and the prophecy fulfilled therein. Herod's fierce rage, inflamed by the dim suspicion that these wily Easterns have gone away laughing in their sleeves at having tricked him, and by the dread that they may be stirring up armed defenders of their infant King, is in full accord with all that we know of him. The critics who find the story of the massacre "unhistorical," because Josephus does not mention it, must surely be very anxious to discredit the evangelist, and very hard pressed for grounds to do so, or they would not commit themselves to the extraordinary assumption that nothing is to be believed outside of the pages of Josephus. A splash or two of "blood of poor innocents," more or less, found on the Idumean tyrant's bloody skirts could be of little consequence in the eyes of those who knew what a long saturnalia of horrors his reign had been; and the number of the infants under two years old in such a tiny place as Bethlehem would be small, so that their feeble wail might well fail to reach the ears even of contemporaries. But there is no reason for questioning the simple truth of a story so like the frantic cruelty and sleepless suspicion of the grey-headed tyrant, who was stirred to more ferocity as the shades of death gathered about him, and power slipped from his rotting hands. Of all the tragic pictures which Scripture gives of a godless old age, burning with unquenchable hatred to goodness, and condemned to failure in all its antagonism, none is touched with more lurid hues than this. What a contrast between the king *de jure*, the cradled infant, and the king *de facto*, going down to his loathsome death, which all but he longed for! He may well stand as a symbol of the futility of all opposition to Christ the King.

The fate of these few infants is a strange one. In their brief lives they have won immortal fame. They died for the Christ whom they never knew. These lambs were slain for the sake of the Lamb who lived while they died, that by His death they might live for ever. These

> "Little flowers of martyrdom,
> Roses by the whirlwind shorn,"

head the long procession as martyrs, if not in intent, yet in fact, and, we may be sure, are amongst the palm-bearing crowd, "being the first-fruits to God and the Lamb." "O happy little ones!" says St. Augustine, "but just born, not yet tempted, not yet struggling, already crowned." Even in His infancy Christ came to bring not peace, but a sword, and the shadow of suffering for Him already attended the brightness of His rising.

But even in His infancy His coming abolished death, and made all who partook, even by anticipation, of His sufferings sharers in His glory. The weeping mothers of Bethlehem might have taken for their own the comfort which the prophet addresses to the weeping Rachel, in the context of the words quoted by Matthew, "Refrain thy voice from weeping, and thine eyes from tears. . . . Thy children shall come again to their own border."

That quotation, from Jeremiah xxxi. 15, requires a brief consideration. The original is still less a prophecy than was the passage in Hosea. It is a highly imaginative and grandly weird personification of the mighty mother of three of the tribes, stirring in her tomb, and lifting up the shrill lamentation of Eastern grief over her children carried away to captivity. That hopeless wail from the grave by Bethlehem is heard as far north as Ramah, beyond Jerusalem. Once again, says Matthew, the same imaginative grief might have been heard from the long-silent tomb so near the scene of this pitiful tragedy. And the second ancestral weeping was fuller of woe than the bitterness of that first lament; for this bewailed the actual slaughter of innocents, and wept the miseries that so soon gathered round the coming of the King, so long waited for. Seeing that the prophet's words do not describe a fact, but are a poetical personification to convey simply the idea of calamity, which might make the dead mother weep, the word "fulfilled" can obviously be applied to them only in a modified and somewhat elastic sense, and is sufficiently defended if we recognise in the slaughter of these children a woe which, though small in itself, yet, when considered in reference to its inflicter, a usurping king of the Jews, and in reference to its occasion, the desire to slay the God-sent King, and in reference to its innocent victims, and in reference to its place as first of the tragic series of martyrdoms for Messiah, was heavy with a sorer burden of national disaster, when seen by eyes made wise by death, than even the captivity which seemed to falsify the promises of God and the hopes of a thousand years.

III. The return to Nazareth, and the prophecy fulfilled therein. They who patiently wait for guidance, and move not till the cloud moves, are never disappointed, nor left undirected. Joseph is a pattern of self-abnegating submission, and an example of its rewards. The angel ever comes again to those who have once obeyed and continue to wait. This third appearance is described in the same words as the former. His coming was the appearance of a familiar presence. His command begins by a verbal repetition of the former summons, "Arise, and take the young Child and His mother, and go," and then passes to a singular allusion to the command to Moses which was the first step towards the former calling of God's Son—the nation—out of Egypt. "All the men are dead which sought thy life," was the encouragement to Moses to go back. "'They are dead that sought the young Child's life," is the encouragement to Joseph. It sums up in one sentence the failure of the first attempt, and is like an epitaph cut on a tombstone for a man yet living,—a prophecy of the end of all succeeding efforts to crush Christ and thwart His work. "The dreaded infant's hand" is mightier than all mailed fists, or fingers that hold a pen. Christ lives and grows; Herod rots and dies.

Apparently Joseph's intention was to return to Bethlehem. He may have thought that Nazareth would scarcely satisfy the angel's injunction to go to the "land of Israel," or that David's city was the right home for David's heir. At all events, his perplexity appeals to Heaven for direction; and, for the fourth time, his course is marked for him by a dream, whether through the instrumentality of the angel, who knew the way to his couch so well, we are not told. Archelaus, Herod's son, who had received Judæa on the partition at his father's death, was a smaller Herod, as cruel and less able. There was more security in the obscurity of Nazareth, under the less sanguinary sway of Antipas, whose share of his father's vices was his lust, rather than his ferocity. So, after so many wanderings, and with such strange new experience and thoughts, the silent, steadfast Joseph and the meek mother bring back their mysterious Charge and secret to the humble old home. Matthew does not seem to have known that it had been their home, but his account is no contradiction of Luke's.

Again he is reminded of a prophecy, or perhaps, rather, of many prophecies, for he uses the plural "prophets," as if he were summing up the tenor of more than one utterance. The words which he gives are not found in any prophet. But we know that to call a man "a Nazarene" was the same thing as to call him lowly and despised. The scoff of the Pharisee to Nicodemus' timid appeal on Christ's behalf, and the guileless Nathanael's question, show that. The fact that Christ by His residence in Nazareth became known as the Nazarene, and so shared in the contempt attaching to all Galileans, and especially to the inhabitants of that village, is a kind of concentration of all the obscurity and ignominy of His lot. The name was nailed over His head on the cross as a scornful *reductio ad absurdum* of His claims to be King of Israel. This explanation of the evangelist's meaning does not exclude a reference in his mind to the prophecy in Isaiah xi. 1, where Messiah is called "a branch," or, more properly "a shoot," for which the Hebrew word is *netzer*, connected with the name Nazareth. The little village was probably so called to express its insignificance. The meaning of the prophecy is that the offspring of David, who should come when the Davidic house was in the lowest depths of obscurity, like a tree of which only the stump is left, should not appear in royal pomp, or in a lofty condition, but as insignificant, feeble, and of no account. Such prophecy was fulfilled in the very fact that He was all His life known as "of Nazareth," and the verbal assonance between that name, "the shoot," and the word "Nazarene," is a finger-post pointing to the meaning of the place of abode chosen for Him. The mere fact of residence there, and the consequent contempt, do not exhaust the prophecies to which reference is made. These might have been fulfilled without such a literal and external fulfilment. But it serves, like the literal riding upon an ass, and many other instances in Christ's life, to lead dull apprehensions to perceive more plainly that He is the theme of all prophecy, and that in His life the trivial is significant and nothing accidental.

LESSON III.

The Herald of the King.

MATT. iii. 1-12.

1. "In those days came John the Baptist, preaching in the wilderness of Judæa,
2. And saying, Repent ye: for the kingdom of heaven is at hand.
3. For this is He that was spoken of by the prophet Esaias, saying, The voice of one crying in the wilderness, Prepare ye the way of the Lord, make His paths straight.
4. And the same John had his raiment of camel's hair, and a leathern girdle about his loins; and his meat was locusts and wild honey.
5. Then went out to him Jerusalem, and all Judæa, and all the region round about Jordan,
6. And were baptized of him in Jordan, confessing their sins.
7. But when he saw many of the Pharisees and Sadducees come to his baptism, he said unto them, O generation of vipers, who hath warned you to flee from the wrath to come?
8. Bring forth therefore fruits meet for repentance:
9. And think not to say within yourselves, We have Abraham to our father: for I say unto you, that God is able of these stones to raise up children unto Abraham.
10. And now also the axe is laid unto the root of the trees: therefore every tree which bringeth not forth good fruit is hewn down, and cast into the fire.
11. I indeed baptize you with water unto repentance: but He that cometh after me is mightier than I, whose shoes I am not worthy to bear: He shall baptize you with the Holy Ghost, and with fire:
12. Whose fan is in His hand, and He will throughly purge His floor, and gather His wheat into the garner; but He will burn up the chaff with unquenchable fire."

MATTHEW'S Gospel is emphatically the Gospel of the kingdom. The key-note sounded in the story of the magi dominates the whole. We have stood

The Herald of the King.

by the cradle of the King, and seen the homage and the dread which surrounded it. We have seen the usurper's hatred and the Divine guardianship. Now we hear the voice of the herald of the King. This lesson may be conveniently treated as falling into two parts—the first, from verse 1 to verse 6, a general outline of the Baptist's person and work; the second, from verse 7 to end, a more detailed account of his preaching.

I. We have an outline sketch of the herald and of his work. The voice of prophecy had fallen silent for four hundred years. Now, when it is once more heard, it sounds in exactly the same key as when it ceased. Its last word had been the prediction of the day of the Lord, and of the coming of Elijah once more. John was Elijah over again. There were the same garb, the same isolation, the same fearlessness, the same grim, gaunt strength, the same fiery energy of rebuke, which bearded kings in the full fury of their self-will. Elijah, Ahab, and Jezebel have their doubles in John, Herod, and Herodias. The closing words of Malachi, which Matthew, singularly enough, does not quote, are the best explication of the character and work of the Baptist. His portrait is flung on the canvas with the same startling abruptness with which Elijah is introduced. Matthew makes no allusion to his relationship to Jesus, has nothing to say about his birth or long seclusion in the desert. He gives no hint that his vague expression "in these days" covers thirty years. John leaps, as it were, into the arena full grown and full armed. His work is described by one word,—"preaching"; out of which all modern associations, which have too often made it a synonym for long-winded tediousness and toothless platitudes, must be removed. It means proclaiming, or acting as a herald, and implies the uplifted voice and the brief, urgent message of one who runs before the chariot, and shouts, "The king! the king!"

His message is summed up in two sentences, two blasts of the trumpet,—the call to repentance, and the rousing proclamation that the kingdom of heaven is at hand. In the former he but reproduces the tone of earlier prophecy, when he insists on a thorough change of disposition and a true sorrow for sin. But he advances far beyond his precursors in the latter, which is the reason for the repentance. They had seen the vision of the kingdom and the King, "but not nigh." He has to peal into the drowsy ears of a generation that had almost forgotten the ancient hope, that it was at the very threshold. Like some solitary stern crag which catches the light of the sun, yet unrisen but hastening upwards, long before the shadowed valleys, John flamed above his generation, all aglow with the light, as the witness that in another moment it would spring above the eastern horizon. But he sees that this is no joyful message to them. Nothing is more remarkable in his preaching than the sombre hues with which his expectation of the day of the Lord is coloured. To what purpose is the day of the Lord to you? "It is darkness, and not light"; it is to be judgment, therefore repentance is the preparation.

The gleam and the purity of lofty spiritual ideas are soon darkened, as a film forms on quicksilver soon after its exposure. John's contemporaries thought that the kingdom of heaven meant exclusive privileges, and their rule over the heathen. They had all but lost the thought that it meant first God's rule over their wills, and their harmony with the glad obedience of heaven. They had to be rudely shaken out of their self-complacency, and taught that the livery of the King was purity, and the preparation for His coming penitence.

The next touch in this outline sketch is John's fulfilment of prophecy. Matthew probably knew that wonderfully touching and lowly answer of his to the deputation from the ecclesiastical authorities, which at once claimed prophetic authority and disclaimed personal importance, "I am the voice of one crying in the wilderness." The prophecy in its original application refers to the preparation of a path in the desert for Jehovah coming to redeem His people from captivity. The use made of it by Matthew, and endorsed by all the evangelists, rests on the principle, without which we have no clue to the significance of the Old Testament, that the history of Israel is prophetic, and that the bondage and deliverance are types of the sorer captivity from which Christ redeems.

Our evangelist gives a vivid picture of the asceticism of John, which was one secret, as our Lord pointed out, of his hold on the people. The more luxuriously self-indulgent men are, the more are they fascinated by religious self-denial. A man " clothed in soft raiment " would have drawn no crowds. A religious teacher must be clearly free from sensual appetites and love of ease, if he is to stir the multitude. John's rough garb and coarse food were not assumed by him to create an impression. He was no mere imitator of the old prophets, though he wore a robe like Elijah's. His asceticism was the expression of his severe, solitary spirit, detached from the delights of sense, and even from the softer play of loves, because that coming kingdom flamed ever before him, and his age seemed to him to be rotting and ready for the fire. There is no need to bring in irrelevant learning about Essenes to account for his mode of life. The thoughts which burned in him drove him into the wilderness. He who was possessed with them could not "come eating and drinking," and might well seem to sense-bound wonderers as if some demonic force, other than ordinary motives, tyrannized over him.

The last point in this brief *résumé* of John's work is the universal excitement which it produced. He did not come out of the desert with his message. If men would hear it, they must come to him. And they came. All the southern portion of the country seemed to empty itself into the wilderness. Sleeping national hopes revived, the awe of the coming judgment seized all classes. It was so long since a fiery soul had scattered flaming words; and religious teachers had for so many centuries been mumbling the old well-worn formulas, and splitting hairs, that it was an apocalypse to hear once more the accent of conviction from a man who really believed every word he said, and himself thrilled with the solemn truths which he thundered. Wherever a religious teacher shows that he has John's qualities, as our Lord in His eulogium analyzed them—namely, unalterable resolution, like an iron pillar, not a reed shaken with the wind, conspicuous superiority to considerations of ease and comfort, a direct vision of the unseen, and a message from God—the crowds will go out to see him; and even if the enthusiasm be shallow and transient, some spasm of conviction will pass across many a conscience, and some will be pointed by him to the King.

II. The second portion of this lesson is a more detailed account of John's preaching, which Matthew gives as addressed to the Pharisees and Sadducees. We are not to suppose that at any time John had a congregation exclusively made up of these; nor that these words were addressed to them only. What is emphasized is the fact that among the crowds were many of both these parties, the religious aristocracy who represented two tendencies of mind bitterly antagonistic, and each unlikely to be drawn to the prophet. Self-righteous pedants who had turned religion into a jumble of petty precepts, and very superior persons who keenly appreciated the good things of this world, and were too enlightened to have much belief in anything, and too comfortable to be enthusiasts, were not hopeful material. If they were drawn into the current, it must have run strong indeed. These representatives of the highest and coldest level of the national life got the very same red-hot words flung at them as the mob did. Luke tells us that the first words in this summary were spoken to the people. Both representations are true. All fared alike. So they should; and so they always will, if a real prophet has to talk to them. John's salutation is excessively rough and rude. Honeyed words were not in his line; he had not lived in the desert for all these years, and held converse with God and his own heart, without having learned that his business was to smite on conscience with a strong hand, and to tear away the masks which hid men from themselves. The whole spirit of the old prophets was revived in his brusque, almost fierce, address to such very learned, religious, and distinguished personages. Isaiah in his day had called their predecessors "rulers of Sodom";

John was not scolding when he called his hearers, "ye offspring of vipers," but charging them with moral corruption and creeping earthliness.

The summary of his preaching is like a succession of lightning flashes. We can but note in a word or two each flash as it flames and strikes. The remarkable thing about his teaching is that, in his hands, the great hope of Israel became a message of terror, the proclamation of the impending kingdom passes into a denunciation of "the wrath to come," set forth with a tremendous wealth of imagery as the axe lying at the root of the trees, the fan winnowing the wheat from the chaff, the destroying fire. That wrath was inseparable from the coming of the King; for His righteous reign necessarily meant punishment of unrighteousness. So all the older prophets had said, and John was but carrying on their testimony. So Christ has said. No more terrible warnings of the certain judgment of evil, involved in his merciful work, have ever been given, than fell from the lips into which grace is poured. We need to-day a clearer discernment of the truth which flamed before John's eyes, that the full proclamation of the kingdom of heaven must include the plain teaching of "the wrath to come."

Next comes the urgent demand for reformation of life as the sign of real repentance. His exhortation does not touch the deepest ground for repentance in the heart-softening love of God manifested in the sacrifice of the King, but is based wholly on the certainty of judgment. So far, it is incomplete; but the demand for righteous living as the only test of religious emotion is fully Christian, and needed in this generation as much as it ever was. All preachers and others concerned in "revivals" may well learn a lesson, and while they follow John in seeking to arouse torpid consciences by the terrors which are a part of the gospel, not forget to demand, not merely an emotional repentance, but the solid fruits which alone guarantee the worth of the emotion.

The next flash strikes the lofty structure of confidence in their descent. John knows that every man in that listening crowd believes that his birth secured him joy and dominion when Messiah came. So he wrenches away this shield against which his sharpest arrows were blunted. What a murmur of angry denial must have met his contemptuous, audacious denial of their trusted privilege! The pebbles on the Jordan beach, or the loose rocks scattered so plentifully over the desert, could be made as good sons of Abraham as they. A glimpse of the transference of the kingdom to the despised Gentiles passed across his vision. And in these far-reaching words lay the anticipation, not only of the destruction of all Jewish exclusiveness, but of the miracles of quickening to be wrought on the stony hearts of those beyond its pale.

Once more with a new emblem the immediate beginning of the judgment is proclaimed, and its principles and issues are declared. The sharp axe lies at the roots of the tree, ready to be lifted and buried in its bark. The woodman's eye is looking over the forest; he marks with the fatal red line the worthless ones, and at once the swinging blows come down, and the timber is carried away to be burned. The trees are men. The judgment is an individualizing one, and all-embracing. Nothing but actual righteousness of life will endure. All else will be destroyed.

The coming of the kingdom implied the coming of the King. John knew that the King was a man, and that He was at the door. So his sermon reaches its climax in the ringing proclamation of His advent. The first noticeable feature in it is the utter humility of the dauntless prophet before the yet veiled Sovereign. All the fiery force, the righteous scorn and anger, the unflinching bravery, melt into meek submission. He knows the limits of his own power, and gladly recognizes the infinite superiority of the coming One. He never moved from that lowly attitude. Even when his followers tried to stir up base jealousy in him at being distanced by the Christ, who, as they suggested, owed His first recognition to him, "He must increase; but I must decrease"; he was glad "to fade in the light of the" Sun that "he loved." What a wealth of suppressed emotion and lowly love there is in the words so pathetic from the lips of the lonely ascetic, whom no home joys had ever cheered, "He that hath the bride is the bridegroom. . . . My joy is fulfilled"!

Note, too, the grand conception of the gifts of the King. John knew that his baptism was, like the water in which he immersed, cold, and incapable of giving life. It symbolized, but did not effect, cleansing, any more than his preaching righteousness could produce righteousness. But the King would come, bringing with Him the gift of a mighty Spirit, whose quick energy, transforming all deadness into its own likeness, burning out the foul stains from character, and melting cold hearts into radiant warmth, should do all that his poor, cold, outward baptism only shadowed. Form and substance of this great promise gather up many Old Testament utterances. From of old fire had been the emblem of the Divine nature, not only, nor chiefly, as destructive, but rather as life-giving, cleansing, gladdening, fructifying, transforming. From of old the promise of a Divine Spirit poured out on all flesh had been connected with the kingdom of Messiah; and John but reiterates the uniform voice of prophecy, even as he anticipates the crowning gift of the gospel, in this saying.

Note, further, the renewed prophecy of judgment. There is something very solemn in the stern refrain at the end of each of three consecutive verses,—" with fire." The first and the last refer to the destructive fire; the second, to the cleansing Spirit. But the fire that destroys is not unconnected with that which purifies. And the very same Divine flame, if welcomed and yielded to, works purity, and if repelled and scorned, consumes. The rustic simplicity of the figures of the husbandman with his winnowing-shovel; the threshing-floor exposed to every wind; the stored wheat; the rootless, lifeless, worthless chaff, and the fierce fire in some corner of the autumn field where it is utterly burned up,—needs no comment. They add nothing but another vivid picture to the thoughts already dealt with. But the question arises as to the whole of the representation of judgment here,—does it look beyond the present world? I see no reason for supposing that John was speaking about anything but the sifting and destroying which would attend the coming of the looked-for kingdom on earth. The principles which he laid down are, no doubt, true for both worlds; but the application of them which his prophetic mission embraced lies on this side the grave.

Note, further, the limitations in John's knowledge of the King. His prophecy unites, as contemporaneous, events which, in fact, are widely separate,—the coming of Christ, and the judgments which He executes, whether on Israel or in the final "great day of the Lord." There is no perspective in prophecy. The future is foreshortened, and great gulfs of centuries are passed over, as, standing on a plain, we see it as continuous, though it may really be cleft by deep ravines. He did not know "what manner of time" the spirit which was in him did "signify." No doubt his expectations were correct, in so far as Christ's coming really sifted and separated, and was the rising and the falling of many; but it was not attended by such tokens as John inferred. Hence we can understand his doubts when in prison, and learn that a prophet was often mistaken as to the meaning of his message.

Again, while we have here a clear prediction of the Spirit as bestowed by Christ, we find no hint of His work as the sacrifice for sin, through whom the guilt, which no repentance and no outward baptism could touch, was taken away. The Gospel of John gives us later utterances of the Baptist's, by which we learn that he advanced beyond the point at which he stands here. "Behold the Lamb of God, which taketh away the sin of the world" was his message after Christ's baptism. It is the last, highest voice of prophecy. The proclamation of a kingdom of heaven, of a King mighty and righteous, whose coming kindled a fire of judgment, and a blessed fire of purifying, into one or other of which all men must be plunged, contained elements of terror, as well as of hope. It needed completion by that later word.

When John stretched out his forefinger, and with awestruck voice bade his hearers look at Jesus coming to him, prophecy had done its work. The promise had been gradually concentrated on the nation, the tribe, the house, and now it falls on the person. The dove narrows its circling flight till it lights on His head. The goal has been reached, too, in the clear declaration of Messiah's work. He is King, Giver of the Spirit, Judge, but He is before all else the Sacrifice for the world's sins. Therefore he to whom it was given to utter that great saying was a prophet, and more than a prophet; and when he had spoken it, there was nothing more for him to do but to decrease. He was like the breeze before sunrise, which springs up, as crying," The dawn ! the dawn ! " and dies away.

LESSON IV.

The Coronation of the King.

MATT. iii. 13-17.

13. "Then cometh Jesus from Galilee to Jordan unto John, to be baptized of him.

14. But John forbad Him, saying, I have need to be baptized of Thee, and comest Thou to me?

15. And Jesus answering said unto him, Suffer it to be so now: for thus it becometh us to fulfil all righteousness. Then he suffered Him.

16. And Jesus, when He was baptized, went up straightway out of the water: and lo, the heavens were opened unto Him, and He saw the Spirit of God descending like a dove, and lighting upon Him:

17. And lo a voice from heaven, saying, This is My beloved Son, in whom I am well pleased."

THE place where Jesus was baptized is uncertain, but the traditional site, near Jericho, is a mistake. Whether we read Bethabarah or Bethany in John i. 28, we must look for the scene somewhere much higher up the stream than Jericho, in order to satisfy the conditions of John's narrative, which allow only a day for reaching Cana from it. We are to think, then, of Jesus travelling a day's journey from Nazareth, probably alone, and not having declared His purpose to any. He

"Came as then obscure,
Unmarked, unknown,"

with thoughts which we can but faintly imagine filling His mind. A similar tension of spirit to that which set its mark on His face, and awed His disciples, as they followed Him up the rocky road on His last journey to Jerusalem, urged Him on His solitary path from the peaceful seclusion of Nazareth to His public life of conflict, sorrow, and rejection, with the cross closing the view. The baptism was, on His part, the assumption of His Messianic office; and on God's, His anointing or coronation as the King. There are three stages in this lesson: The preliminary dialogue, which explains the paradox of the baptism of the sinless by and with the sinful, the Divine anointing of the King, and the Divine proclamation.

I. The becomingness of the apparently unbecoming baptism. It was a baptism of repentance, in which the subjects confessed their sins. The stern preacher, who lowered his tone of denunciation before no rank, and refused to baptize the most religious Pharisees, not because they were too good, but because they were too bad for the rite, bows in lowliest abasement before his carpenter Cousin, and feels that his own character shows black against that lustrous whiteness. The Greek puts emphasis on the pronouns in the sentence, "I have need . . . of thee . . . thou to me." It is like "Dost thou wash my feet?" in its consciousness of unworthiness and sin, while so unlike that saying in its recognition of some cleansing virtue in Jesus, for which the preacher of righteousness yearned. Who would have thought, when John was flashing and thundering against sin, that such sense of his own evil underlay his boldness? He clearly feels that Jesus is his superior, and needs no baptism of repentance. How had he come to this conviction? Difficulties have been raised as to the consistency of these words with his declaration that he "knew Him not." But, not to dwell on the fact that anticipations and expectations are not knowledge, why should this insight into the character of Jesus not have then been granted to him by prophetic intuition, as he gazed on the gentle face? Why should not the Divine voice have then for the first time sounded in John's heart, "Arise, anoint Him: for this is He"? It is a pure assumption that John had previous knowledge of Jesus. The city in the hill country of Judæa, where his boyhood had possibly been passed, was far from Nazareth, and he had very early betaken himself to the desert and its isolation. The circumstances of the nativity may, or may not, have been known to him; but there is no reason to explain this conviction of the inappropriateness of his baptism of Jesus by previous knowledge. The other explanation seems to me both more probable and more accordant with his prophetic office. But, however that may be, the picture of the Baptist melting into humility before the only soul in which his keen eye had detected no impurity, and strenuously seeking to forbid (for the Greek gives the notion of earnest attempts to hinder) the incongruity of his polluted hands baptizing so pure a Being, is one of the most pathetic on the pages of Scripture.

Christ accepts without demur the place which John gives Him. He always accepted the highest place which any man put Him in, and never rebuked any estimate of Himself as enthusiastic or too lofty. Why did He not say, "I too have sins, and need repentance and remission"? An honest man would have said so, if he knew himself. It is a strange way for a "meek and lowly" teacher to begin his career by allowing unblamed the ascription to himself of freedom from all need of cleansing. If Jesus had not up till that moment lived a perfectly sinless life, He committed a black sin in tacitly endorsing this estimate of Him. If He had lived such a life, on what theory of His nature is it explicable? A sinless man must be more than man.

The same consciousness of blamelessness is put into plain words in His answer to John, which is Jesus' own explanation of His baptism. It was a temporary submission to an apparent inferiority, which was speedily and permanently to give place to a reversal of their relative positions, in which He would baptize the Baptist with cleansing fire. It was an act of obedience to a Divine appointment, and therefore it "became" Him. There we catch the first accents of that continual reference to a Divine "must" which sounds through His whole life. "Lo, I come . . . to do Thy will, O God." It was the fulfilment of "righteousness"; that is to say, Jesus did not confess sin, but professed sinlessness in His baptism, and submitted to it, not because He needed cleansing, but because it was appointed as the duty for the nation of which He was a member. Words could not more plainly assert that His past life had been the unbroken fulfilment of the law, or that, in submitting to the baptism of repentance, He was conscious that He "needs no repentance."

Why, then, was He baptized? For the same reason for which He was found in the likeness of the flesh of sin, and submitted to other requirements of the law from which, as Son, He was free, and bore the sorrows which were not the issue of His own sins, and went down at last to the other baptism with which He had to be baptized, though His pure life had for itself no need to pass through that awful submersion beneath the black, cold waters of death. The whole mystery of His identification of Himself with sinful men, and of His being "made sin . . . for us, who knew no sin," lies in germ in His baptism by John. No other conception of its meaning does justice to the facts.

II. We have next the Divine anointing or coronation. The language here leaves it doubtful whether the vision was for Jesus or John. "He saw" is most naturally referred to the former, but "He saw the Spirit . . . coming upon Him" most naturally means that John saw it falling upon Jesus, and the form of the Divine proclamation suggests that it was addressed to the Baptist. In Mark and Luke, on the contrary, it is spoken to Jesus. It appears from John i. 32-34, that the Baptist saw the dove, and both the visible and audible tokens were probably given to both Jesus and John. It is useless to ask whether others, if present, would have perceived either. We know too little of the external "realities" which occasioned prophetic visions, and of the real nature of "material realities," to dogmatize. The voice and the hovering dove were no less "real," though no coarse material impact set air or luminiferous ether vibrating, or even though ear and eye were not employed in producing the impression. It is enough that these were actual communications, having their source, not in the recipients, but in God's miraculous action.

The symbol of the dove seems to carry allusions to the grand image which represents the Spirit of God as "brooding" over chaos, and quickening life, as a bird in its nest by the warmth of its own soft breast; to the dove which bore the olive-branch, first messenger of hope to the prisoners in the ark; to the use of the dove as clean, in sacrifice; to the poetical attribution to it, common to many nations, of meek gentleness and faithful love. Set side by side with that, John's thought of the Holy Spirit as fire, and we get all the beauty of both emblems increased, and understand how much the stern ascetic, whose words burned and blistered, had to learn. He knew "what manner of spirit" the King possessed and bestowed. Meekness is throned now. Gentleness is stronger than force. The dove conquers Rome's eagles and every strong-taloned, sharp-beaked bird of prey. "The Prince of the kings of the earth" is anointed by the descending dove, and His second coronation is with thorns, and a reed is His sceptre; for His kingdom is based on purity and meekness, is won by suffering, and wielded in gentleness. As is the King, so are His subjects, whose only weapons He has assigned when He bids them be "harmless as doves."

The purpose of this descent of the Spirit on Jesus was twofold. In John's Gospel it is represented as principally meant to certify the Baptist of the identity of the Messiah. But we cannot exclude its effect on Jesus. For Him it was the Divine anointing for His official mediatorial work. A king is king before he is anointed or crowned. These are but the signs of what we may call the official assumption of His royalty. We are not to conceive that Jesus then began to be filled with the Spirit, or that absolutely new powers were given to Him then. No doubt the anointing did mark a stage in His human development, and the accession to His manhood of all that was needed to equip it for His work. But the Spirit of God had formed His pure manhood ere He was born, and had dwelt in growing measure in His growing Spirit, through all His sinless thirty years. Since He was a man, He needed the Divine Spirit. Since He was a sinless Man, He was capable of receiving it in perfect measure and unbroken continuity. Since His baptism began His public career, He needed then, and then received, the anointing which at once designated and fitted Him for His work of witnessing and atonement.

III. We have finally the Divine proclamation. God Himself takes the herald's office. The coronation ends with the solemn recitation of the style and title of the King. We need not stay to discuss what was the objective fact, how this "voice" was audible, whether it was meant for John, as Matthew represents, or for Jesus, as Mark and Luke suppose. Two Old Testament passages seem to be melted together in it: that in the second psalm, which says to the Messianic King, "Thou art my Son"; that in Isaiah xlii. 1, which calls on the nations to "behold . . . mine elect, in whom my soul delighteth." Thus the originals are addressed to the King, and to others, just as the varying reports of the evangelists represent the voice to have been. God speaks from heaven, and quotes a psalm and a prophet. Does that seem strange? Is it not natural that His utterances to men should be conditioned by their stage of knowledge, and should attach themselves to previous revelations? Why should He not speak from heaven an illuminating word, which interprets whole regions of the Old Testament? This Divine testimony touches first the mystery of our Lord's nature. "Son of God" is not merely a synonym of Messiah, but it includes the distinct conception of Divine origin and of consequent Divine nature. The name implies that the relation between Him and the Father is unique. It is not exhausted by reference to our Lord's supernatural birth, but goes back to eternal depths when "in the beginning the word was with God." His designation to His Messianic work, His supernatural entrance into humanity, are consequences of that ante-temporal and extra-creatural relation. Jesus is "the King of glory" because He is the everlasting "Son of the Father."

The voice attests the Divine complacency in Him. The form of the verb in the Greek implies a definite past delight of the Father in the Son, and carries back our thoughts to that wonderful intercourse of which Jesus lets us catch some faint glimpse when He says, "Thou lovedst Me before the foundation of the world." Silence is best in the presence of such words. From eternity the Father mirrored Himself in the eternal Son, and rejoiced in the perfect likeness, which was at once the beam from His brightness and the reflection of His beauty. From eternity the mysterious depths of the Divine nature moved in soft waves of love, and in its solitude there was society. These are heights where we cannot walk; but on the lower levels, such words teach us the absolute sinlessness of Jesus, and are the Divine attestation of the truth of His own claim, "the Father hath not left Me alone; because I do always the things that please Him."

Nor can we leave out of view the thought that the Father's delight in the Son is through the Son extended to all who love and trust the Son. In Jesus, God is well pleased towards us. That complacent delight embraces us too, if we become sons through faith in the only begotten Son. The dove that rested on His head will come and nestle in our hearts, and brood there, over their chaos, if we have faith in Christ. Sonship, Divine favour, the abiding Spirit, the share in His kingdom, the inheritance of His throne, may all be ours if we listen to that voice which on the Mount of Transfiguration renewed its witness to Jesus with the added exhortation, "Hear ye him." If we anoint Him King over our hearts we shall be quickened by His Spirit, and made sharers in His royalty.

LESSON V.

The Victory of the King.

Matt. iv. 1-11.

1. "Then was Jesus led up of the Spirit into the wilderness to be tempted of the devil.
2. And when He had fasted forty days and forty nights, He was afterward an hungred.
3. And when the tempter came to Him, he said, If Thou be the Son of God, command that these stones be made bread.
4. But He answered and said, It is written, Man shall not live by bread alone, but by every word that proceedeth out of the mouth of God.
5. Then the devil taketh Him up into the holy city, and setteth Him on a pinnacle of the temple,
6. And saith unto Him, If Thou be the Son of God, cast Thyself down: for it is written, He shall give His angels charge concerning Thee: and in their hands they shall bear Thee up, lest at any time Thou dash Thy foot against a stone.
7. Jesus said unto him, It is written again, Thou shalt not tempt the Lord thy God.
8. Again, the devil taketh Him up into an exceeding high mountain, and shewed Him all the kingdoms of the world, and the glory of them;
9. And saith unto Him, All these things will I give Thee, if Thou wilt fall down and worship me.
10. Then saith Jesus unto him, Get thee hence, Satan: for it is written, Thou shalt worship the Lord thy God, and Him only shalt thou serve.
11. Then the devil leaveth Him, and, behold, angels came and ministered unto Him."

EVERY word of the first verses of this narrative is full of meaning. "Then" marks the immediate connection, not only in time but in causation, between the baptism and the temptation. The latter followed necessarily on the former. "Of the Spirit"—then God does lead His Son into temptation. For us all, as for Christ, it is true that, though God does not tempt as wishing us to fall, He does so order our lives that they carry us into places where the metal of our religion is tried. "To be tempted"—then a pure, sinless human nature is capable of temptation, and the King has to begin His career by a battle. "Of the devil"—then there is a dark kingdom of evil, and a personal head of it, the prince of darkness. He knows his rival, and yet he knows Him but partially. He strides out to meet Him in desperate duel, as Goliath did the stripling whom he despised; and both hosts pause and gaze. To a sinless nature no temptation can arise from within, but must be presented from without.

We leave untouched the question as to the manner of this temptation, which remains equally real, whether we conceive that the tempter appeared in bodily form, and actually carried the body of our Lord from place to place, or whether we suppose that, during it all, Christ sat silent, and apparently alone in the wilderness. We only divert attention from the true importance of the incident by giving prominence to picturesque or questionable externals of it.

I. The first assault and repulse, in the desert.

Unlike John the Baptist, whose austere spirit was unfolded in the desert, Jesus grew up among men, passing through and sanctifying childhood and youth, home duties, and innocent pleasures. But ere He enters on His work, the need which every soul appointed to high and hard tasks has felt, namely, the need for seclusion and communion with God in solitude, was felt by Him. Like Moses and Elijah, the wilderness was His school; and as the collective Israel, so the personal Son of God, has to be led into the wilderness, that there God may "speak to His heart." So deep and rapt was the communion, that, for forty days, spirit so mastered flesh that the need and desire for food were suspended. But when He touched earth again, the pinch of hunger began. Analogous cases of the power of high emotion to hold physical wants in abeyance are sufficiently familiar to make so extreme an instance explicable.

We have to distinguish in the first temptation between the sphere in which it moves, the act suggested, and the true nature of the act as dragged to light in Christ's answer. The sphere is that of the physical nature. Hunger has nothing to do with right or wrong. It asserts itself independent of all considerations. In itself neutral, it may, like all physical cravings, lead to sin. Most men are most tempted by fleshly desires. Satan had tried the same bait before on the first Adam. It had answered so well then, that he thinks himself wise in bringing it out once more. Adam, in his garden, surrounded by all that sense needed, had yielded, and thereby had turned the garden into desert; Christ, in the desert, pressed by hunger, does not yield, and thereby turns the desert into a garden again. At the beginning of His course He is tempted by the innocent desire to secure physical support; at its close He is tempted by the innocent desire to avoid physical pain. He overcomes both, and by His victories in the wilderness so unlike the garden, and in Gethsemane, another garden, so unlike the first, He brings "a statelier Eden back to man."

The act suggested seems not only innocent, but in accordance with His dignity. It was a strange anomaly for "the Son of God," on whose head the dove had descended, and in whose ears the voice had sounded, to be at the point of starving. What more unbecoming than that One possessed of His mysterious closeness to God should be suffering from such ignoble necessities? What more foolish than to continue to hunger, when a word could spread a table in the wilderness? John had said that God could make children of Abraham out of these stones. Could He not make bread out of them? The suggestion sounds benevolent, sensible, almost religious. The need is real, the remedy possible and easy; the result desirable as preserving valuable life, and putting an end to an anomaly, and the objections apparently *nil*. The bait is skilfully wound over the barbed hook.

Christ's answer tears it away, and discloses the sharp points. He will not discuss with Satan whether He is Son of God or no. To the Jews He was wont to answer, "I say unto you"; to Satan He answers, "It is written." He puts honour on "the sword of the Spirit, which is the Word of God," and sets us an example of how to wield it. The words quoted are found in the account of Israel's miraculous sustenance in the desert by the manna, and are applied by Christ to Himself, not as Son of God, but as simple man. They contain the great truth that God can feed men, in their physical life, by bread or without bread. When He does it by bread or other ordinary means, it is even then not the material substance in itself, but His will operating through it, which feeds. He can abolish all the outward means, and still keep a man alive. There is no reference to the truth which is sometimes forcibly inserted into this saying, that man has a higher than his bodily life, which needs more than material bread to feed the hunger of the soul. The whole scope of them is to state the law of physical nourishment as dependent at last on the Divine will, and therefore equally capable of being accomplished with or without bread, by ordinary means or apart from these.

The bearing of the words on Christ's hunger is twofold: First, He will not use His miraculous power to provide food, for that would be to distrust God, and so to cast off His filial dependence; second, He will not separate Himself from His brethren, and provide for Himself by a way not open to them, for that would really be to reverse the very purpose of His incarnation and to defeat His whole work. He has come to bear all man's burdens, and shall He begin by separating Himself from them? Therefore He answers in words which declare the law for "man," and thereby merges all that was distinctive in His position in a loving participation in our lot. If the Captain of our Salvation had begun by refusing to share the privations of the rank and file, and had provided dainties for Himself, what would have become of His making common cause with them? The temptation addressed to Christ's physical nature was, to put it roughly, "Look out for Yourself." His answer was, "As Son of God, I hold by My filial dependence. As Man, I share My brethren's lot, and am content to live as they live."

II. The second assault and repulse, on the temple.

We need not touch on the questions as to whether

our Lord's body was really transported to the temple, and, if so, to what part of it. But we may point out that there is nothing in the narrative to warrant the usual interpretation of this temptation, as being addressed to the desire of recognition, and as equivalent to the suggestion that our Lord should show Himself, by a stupendous miracle before the multitude, as the Messiah. There is nothing about spectators, and no sign that the dread solitude wrapping these two was broken by others. We must seek for the point of the second temptation in another direction.

The very locality chosen for it helps us to the right understanding of it. There were plenty of cliffs in the desert, down which a fall would have been fatal. Why not choose one of them? The temple was God's house; the fitting scene for an attempt to work disaster by the abuse of religious ideas. The former temptation underlies this. That had sought to move Jesus to cast off His filial confidence; this seeks to pervert that confidence, and through it to lead Him to cast off filial obedience. Therefore "the devil quotes Scripture for his purpose." What could be more religious than an act of daring based upon faith, which again was based on a word which proceeded "out of the mouth of God?" It is not in the suppression of certain words in the quotation that Satan's error lies. The omitted words are not material. What did he hope to accomplish by this suggestion? If Jesus was, in bodily reality, standing on the summit of the temple, the tempter, profoundly disbelieving the promise, may have thought that the leap would end his anxieties by the death of his rival. But, at any rate, he sought to lead His faith into wrong paths, and to incite to what was really sinful self-will under the guise of absolute trust.

Our Lord's answer, again drawn from Deuteronomy, strips off the disguise from the action which seemed so trustful. He changes the plural verb of the original passage into the singular, thus at once taking as His own personal obligation the general command, and pointing a sharp arrow at his foe, who was now knowingly or unknowingly so flagrantly breaking that law. If God had bidden Jesus cast Himself down, to do it would have been right. As He had not, to do it was not faith, but self-will. To cast Himself into dangers needlessly, and then to trust God (whom He had not consulted about going into them) to get Him out, was to "tempt God." True faith is ever accompanied with true docility. He had come to do His Father's will. A Divine "must" ruled His life. Was He to begin His career by throwing off His allegiance on pretext of trust? If the Captain of our Salvation commences the campaign by rebellion, how can He lead the rank and file to that surrender of their own wills, which is victory?

The lessons for us from the second temptation are weighty. Faith may be perverted. It may even lead to abandoning filial submission. God's promised protection is available, not in paths of our own choosing, but only where He has sent us. If we take the leap without His command, we shall fall mangled on the very temple pavement. It is when we are "in the way" which He has prescribed, that "the angels of God" whom He has promised "meet" us. How many scandals in the falls of good men would have been avoided, and how many mad enterprises would have been unattempted, and how much more clearly would the relations of filial faith and filial obedience have been understood, if the teaching of this second temptation had been laid to heart!

III. The final assault and repulse, on the mountain.

Again the scene changes, because the stress of the temptation is different. The "exceeding high mountain" is not to be looked for in our atlases. The manner in which all the glories of the world's kingdoms were flashed in one dazzling panorama, like an instantaneous photograph, before Christ's eyes, is beyond our knowledge. We note that Satan has no more to say about "the Son of God." He has been foiled in both his assaults on Christ in that character. If He stood firm in filial trust and in filial submission, there was no more to be done. So the tempter tries new weapons, and seeks to pervert the desire for that dominion over the world which was a consequence of the Sonship. He has not been able to touch Him as Son; can he not spoil Him as King? They are rivals; can they not strike up a treaty? Jesus thinks that He is going to reign as God's viceroy; can He not be induced, as a much quicker way of getting to His end, to become Satan's? Such a scheme sounds very stupid; but Satan is very stupid, for all his wisdom, and the hopeless folly of his proposal is typical of the absurdities which lie in all sins. There is an old play the title of which would be profane if it were not so true, "The Devil is an Ass."

His boast, like all his wiles, is a little truth and a great lie. It is true that his servants do often manage to climb into thrones and other high places. It is true that beggars, and worse than beggars, ride on horseback, and that for princes, and better than princes, walking is often the rule. It is true that the crowned saints of the world might be counted on the fingers. But, for all that, the father of lies was like himself in this promise. He did not say that, if he gives a kingdom to one of his servants, he takes it from another. He did not say that his gifts are shams, and fade away when the daylight comes. He did not say that he and his are, after all, tools in God's hands.

What was it that he thought he was appealing to in Christ? Ambition? He knew that Jesus was destined to be King of the earth, and he blunders to the conclusion that His reign is to be such as he could help Him to. How impossible it is for Satan to penetrate the depths of that loving heart! How mole-blind evil is to the radiant light of goodness! How hate fails when it tries to fathom love! If all that Satan meant by "the glory" of the world had been Christ's, he would have been no nearer his heart's desire.

The temptation was not only to fling away the ideal of his kingdom, but to reverse the means for its establishment. Neither temptation could originate within Christ's heart, but both beset Him all His life. The cravings of His followers, the expectations of His race, the certainty of an enthusiastic response if He would put Himself at their head, and the equal certainty of death if He would not, were always urging Him to the very same thing.

"There is nothing weaker," says an old school-man, "than the devil stripped naked." The mask is thrown off at last, and swift and smiting comes the gesture and the word of abhorrence, "Get thee hence, Satan,"—now revealed in thy true colours. Jesus still couches His refusal in Scripture words, as if sheltering Himself behind its broad shield. It is safest to meet temptation, not by our own reasonings and thoughts, but by the words which cannot lie. As He had held unmoved, by His filial trust and his filial submission, now He clings to the foundation principle of all religion,—the exclusive worship and service of God. His kingdom is to be a kingdom of priests; therefore to begin it by such an act would be suicide. It is to be the victorious antagonist of Satan's kingdom, because it is to lead all men to worship God alone; therefore enmity, not alliance, is to be between these two. Christ's last words are not only His final refusal of all the baits, but the ringing proclamation of war to the death, and that a war which will end in victory. The enemy's quiver is empty. He feels that he has met more than his match, so he skulks from the field, beaten for the first time by having encountered a heart which all his fiery darts failed to inflame, and presaging yet more utter defeat.

The last temptation teaches us both the nature of Christ's kingdom and the means of its establishment. It is the rule over men's hearts and wills, swaying them to goodness, and the exclusive worship and service of God. That being so, the way to found it follows of course. It can only be set up by suffering, utter self-sacrifice, gentleness, and goodness. Christ is King of all because He is Servant of all. His cross is His throne. His realm is hearts softened, cleansed, made gladly obedient, and growingly like Himself. For such a King, weapons of force are impossible, and for His subjects the same law holds. They have often tried to fight for Christ with the devil's weapons, to make compliance with him for ends which they thought good, to keep terms with evil, or to adopt worldly policy, craft, or force. They have never succeeded, and, thank God! they never will.

That duel was fought for us. There we all conquered, if we will hold fast by Him who conquered then, and then taught our "hands to war" and our "fingers to fight." The strong man is bound. The spoiling of his house follows of course, and is but a question of time.

LESSON VI.

The Early Welcome and the First Ministers of the King.

MATTHEW iv. 17-25.

17. "From that time Jesus began to preach, and to say, Repent: for the kingdom of heaven is at hand.

18. And Jesus, walking by the sea of Galilee, saw two brethren, Simon called Peter, and Andrew his brother, casting a net into the sea: for they were fishers.

19. And He saith unto them, Follow Me, and I will make you fishers of men.

20. And they straightway left their nets, and followed Him.

21. And going on from thence, He saw other two brethren, James the son of Zebedee, and John his brother, in a ship with Zebedee their father, mending their nets; and He called them.

22. And they immediately left the ship and their father, and followed Him.

23. And Jesus went about all Galilee, teaching in their synagogues, and preaching the gospel of the kingdom, and healing all manner of sickness and all manner of disease among the people.

24. And His fame went throughout all Syria: and they brought unto Him all sick people that were taken with divers diseases and torments, and those which were possessed with devils, and those which were lunatick, and those that had the palsy: and He healed them.

25. And there followed Him great multitudes of people from Galilee, and from Decapolis, and from Jerusalem, and from Judæa, and from beyond Jordan."

IN these verses we have a summary of our Lord's early Galilean ministry. The events are so presented and combined as to give an impression as of a triumphal progress of the newly anointed Monarch. He sweeps through the northern regions, everywhere exercising the twofold office of teaching and healing, and everywhere followed by eager crowds. This joyous burst of the new power, like some strong spring leaping into the sunshine, and this rush of popular enthusiasm, are meant to heighten the impression of the subsequent hostility of the people. The King welcomed at first is crucified at last. It was "roses, roses, all the way" in these early days, but they withered soon. There are three points in these verses, —the King acting as His own herald; the King calling His first servants; and the King wielding His power and welcomed by His subjects.

I. In verse 17 we have a striking picture of the King as His own herald. The word rendered "preach" of course means, literally, proclaiming as a herald. It is remarkable that this earliest phase of our Lord's teaching is described in the same words as John's preaching. The stern voice was silenced. Instead of the free wilderness, John had now the gloomy walls of Machærus for the bound of his activity. But Jesus takes up his message, though with a difference. The severe imagery of the axe, the fan, the fire, is not repeated, as it would seem. Sterner words than John's could fall hot from the lips into which grace was poured; but the time for these was not yet come. It may seem singular that Christ should have spoken of the kingdom, and been silent concerning the King. But such silence was only of a piece with the reticence which marked His whole teaching, and was a sign of His wise adaption of His words to the capacity of His hearers, as well as of His lowliness. He veils His royalty by deigning to be His own herald; by substituting the proclamation of the abstract, the kingdom, for the concrete, the King; by seeming to careless hearers to be but the prolongation of the forerunner's message; by the simple, remote region which He chose for His earliest work. The belief that the kingdom was at hand was equally necessary, and repentance equally indispensable as preparation for it, whoever the King might be. The same law of congruity between message and hearers, which He enjoined on His followers, when He bade them be careful where they flung their pearls, and which governed His own fullest final revelations to His most trusted friends, when He said, "I have yet many things to say unto you, but ye cannot carry them now," moulded His first words to the excited but ignorant crowds.

II. The King's mandate summoning His servants. The call of the first four disciples is so told as to make prominent these points,—the brotherhood of the two pairs, their occupation at the moment of their call, the brief, authoritative word of Christ, His investiture of them with new functions, which yet in some sense were the prolongation of the old, their unhesitating instantaneous obedience, and willing abandonment of their all. These things all help the impression of regal power, and do something to explain the nature of the kingdom, and the heart of the King. Matthew does not seem to have known of the previous intercourse of the four with Jesus, as recorded in John 1. His narrative, taken alone, would lay stress on the strange influence wielded by Jesus over these busy fishermen. But that influence is no less remarkable, and is more explicable, by taking John's supplemental account into consideration. It tells us that one brother of each pair—namely Andrew, and probably John,—had sought Jesus on the Baptist's testimony, and in that never-to-be-forgotten night had acquired the conviction that He was the King of Israel. It tells us, too, that Andrew first found his own brother, Simon; from which we may infer that the other one of the two next found his brother James, and that each brought his own brother to Jesus. The bond of discipleship was then riveted. But apparently, when Jesus went up to Jerusalem on that first journey recorded only by John's Gospel, they went back to their fishing, and waited for His further call. It comes in the manner which Matthew describes. The background, which John enables us to fill in, shows us that their following was no sudden blind impulse, but the deliberate surrender of men who knew well what they were doing, though they had not fathomed the whole truth as to His kingdom, and their place in it. They knew, at any rate, that He was the Messiah, and that they were called by a voice, which they ought to obey, to be His soldiers and partisans. They could not but know that the call meant danger, hardship, conflict. They rallied to the call, as soldiers might when the commander honours them by reading out their names, as picked for leaders of the storming party.

Was this the same incident which St. Luke narrates as following the first miraculous draught of fishes? That is one of the difficulties in harmonizing the synoptic narratives which will always divide opinions. On the whole, I incline to think it most natural to answer "no." The reasons would take us too far afield. But accepting that view, we may note how many stages Jesus led this group of His disciples through before they were fully recognized as apostles. First there was their attachment to Him as disciples, which in no degree interfered with their trade.

Then came this call to more close attendance on Him, which, however, was probably still somewhat intermittent. Then followed the call recorded by Luke, which finally tore them from their homes; and, last of all, their appointment as apostles. At each stage they "might have had opportunity to have returned." Their vocation in the kingdom dawns on them slowly. They and we are led on, by little and little and little, to posts and tasks of which we do not dream at the beginning. Duty opens before the docile heart bit by bit. Abram is led to Haran, and only there learns his ultimate destination. Obedience is rewarded by the summons to more complete surrender, which is also fuller possession of him for whom the surrender is made.

"The word of a king is with power." Christ's call is authoritative in its brevity. All duty lies in "Come ye after Me." He does not need to use arguments. From the very first this meek and lowly Man assumes a tone which in other lips we call arrogant. His style is royal. His mouth is autocratic. He knows that He has the right to command. And, strangely enough, the world admits the right, and finds nothing unworthy of His meekness—a meekness of which He was fully conscious, which is another paradox—in this unconditional claim of absolute submission to His curt orders. What is the explanation of this tone of authority? How comes it that the kingdom which is liberty is, from its very foundation, an absolute despotism? That same peremptory summons reaches beyond these four fishermen to us all. They were the first to hear it, and continued to hold pre-eminence among the disciples. For they make up the first group of the three quaternions into which the list of the apostles is always divided. But the very same voice speaks to us, and we are as truly summoned by the King to be His servants and soldiers as were they.

Their prompt self-surrendering response is the witness of the power over their hearts which Jesus had won. The one pair of brothers left their net floating in the water; the other left their father with the mesh and the twine in his old hands. It was not much wealth to leave. But he surrenders much who surrenders all, however little that all may be; and he surrenders nothing who keeps back anything. One sweet portion of their earthly happiness He left them to enjoy, heightened by discipleship, for each had his brother by his side, and the natural affection was ennobled by common faith and service. If Zebedee was left, John still had James. True, Herod's sword cut their union asunder, and James died first, and John last of the twelve; but years of happy brotherhood were to come before then. So both the surrender which outwardly gives up possessions or friends, and that which keeps them, sanctified by being held and used as for and from him, were exemplified in the swift obedience of these four to the call of the King.

"I will make you fishers of men." That shows a kindly wish to make as little as may be of the change of occupation. Their old craft is to be theirs still, only in nobler form. The patience, the brave facing of the storm and the night, the observance of the indications which taught where to cast, the perseverance which toiled all night, though not a fin glistened in the net, would all find place in their new career. Nor are these words less royal than was the call. They contain profound hints as to the nature of the kingdom which could scarcely be apprehended at first. But this at least would be clear, that Jesus summoned them to service, to gather in men out of the dreary waves of worldly care and toil, into a kingdom of stable rest, and that by summoning them to service He endowed them with power. So He does still. All whom He summons to follow Him are meant by Him to be fishers of men. It was not as apostles, but as simple disciples, that these four received this charge and ability. The same command and fitness are given to all Christians. Following Christ, surrender, the obligation of effort to win others, capacity to do so, belong to all the subjects of Christ's kingdom.

III. The triumphal progress of the King. Our evangelist evidently masses together, without regard to chronological order, the broad features of the early Galilean ministry. He paints it as a time of joyful activity, of universal recognition, of swift and far-spreading fame. We do not exaggerate the impression of victorious publicity which they give, when we call these closing verses the record of the King's triumphal progress through His dominions. Observe the reiterated use of "all,"—all Galilee, all manner of sickness and all manner of disease, all Syria, all that were sick. Matthew labours to convey the feeling of universal stir and wide-reaching, all-embracing welcome. Observe, too, that the activity of Christ is confined to Galilee, but the fame of Him crosses the border into heathendom. The King stays on His own territory, but He conquers beyond the frontier. Syria, and the mostly heathen Decapolis, and Peræa ("beyond Jordan"), are moved. The odour of the ointment not only fills the house, but enriches the scentless outside air. The prophecy of the magi is beginning to be fulfilled. From its first preaching, the kingdom is diffusive. Note, too, the contrast between John's ministry and Christ's, in that the former stayed in one spot, and the crowds had to go out to him, while the very genius of Christ's mission expressed itself in that this shepherd King sought the sad and sick, and "went about in all Galilee." Observe, too, that He first teaches and preaches the good news of the kingdom, before He heals. John's proclamation of the kingdom had been so charged with threatenings and mingled with fire that it could scarcely be called a "gospel"; but here that joyous word, used for the first time, is in place. As the tidings came from Christ's lips, they were good tidings, and to proclaim them was His first task. The miracles of healing came after. They were not "the bell before the sermon," but the benediction after it. They flowed from Christ in rich abundance. The eager receptiveness of the people, ignorant as it was, was greater then than ever afterwards. Therefore the flow of miraculous power was more unimpeded. But it may be questioned whether we generally have an adequate notion of the immense number of Christ's miracles. Those recorded are but a small proportion of those done. There were more grapes in the vineyards of Eshcol than the messengers brought in evidence to the camp. Our Lord's miracles are told by units; they seem to have been wrought by scores. These early ones were not only attestations of His claim to be the King, but illustrations of the nature of His kingdom. He had conquered and bound the strong man, and now He was "spoiling His house." They were parables of His higher work on men's souls, which He comes to cleanse from the oppression of demons, from the foamings of epilepsy, from impotence to good. They were tokens of the inexhaustible fountain of power, and of the swift and equally inexhaustible treasures of sympathy which dwelt in Him. They were His first trophies in His holy war, His first gifts to His subjects.

Thus compassed with enthusiasm, and shedding on the wearied new hopes, and on the sick unwonted health, and stirring in sluggish souls some aspirations that greatened and inspired, the King appeared. But no illusions deceived His calm prescience. From the beginning He knew the path which stretched before Him; and while the transient loyalty of the ignorant shouted hosannas around His steps, He saw the cross at the end and the sight did not make Him falter.

LESSON VII.

The New Sinai.

MATTHEW v. 1-16.

1. "And seeing the multitudes, He went up into a mountain: and when He was set, His disciples came unto Him:

2. And He opened His mouth, and taught them, saying,

3. Blessed are the poor in spirit: for theirs is the kingdom of heaven.

4. Blessed are they that mourn: for they shall be comforted.

5. Blessed are the meek: for they shall inherit the earth.

6. Blessed are they which do hunger and thirst after righteousness: for they shall be filled.

7. Blessed are the merciful: for they shall obtain mercy.

8. Blessed are the pure in heart; for they shall see God.

9. Blessed are the peacemakers: for they shall be called the children of God.

10. Blessed are they which are persecuted for righteousness' sake: for theirs is the kingdom of heaven.

11. Blessed are ye, when men shall revile you, and persecute you, and shall say all manner of evil against you falsely, for my sake.

12. Rejoice, and be exceeding glad: for great is your reward in heaven: for so persecuted they the prophets which were before you.

13. Ye are the salt of the earth: but if the salt have lost his savour, wherewith shall it be salted? it is thenceforth good for nothing, but to be cast out, and to be trodden under foot of men.

14. Ye are the light of the world. A city that is set on an hill cannot be hid.

15. Neither do men light a candle, and put it under a bushel, but on a candlestick; and it giveth light unto all that are in the house.

16. Let your light so shine before men, that they may see your good works, and glorify your Father which is in heaven."

THE unnamed mountain somewhere on the sea of Galilee is the Sinai of the new covenant. The contrast between the savage desolation of the wilderness and the smiling beauty of the sunny slope near the haunts of men symbolizes the contrast in the genius of the two codes, given from each. There God came down in majesty, and the cloud hid Him from the people's gaze; here Jesus sits amidst His followers, God with us. The King proclaims the fundamental laws of His kingdom, and reveals much of its nature by the fact that He begins by describing the characteristics of its subjects, as well as by the fact that the description is cast in the form of beatitudes.

We must leave unsettled the question as to the relation between the Sermon on the Mount and the shorter edition of part of it given by Luke, only pointing out that in this first part of Matthew's Gospel we are evidently presented with general summaries; as, for example, the summary of the Galilean ministry in the previous verses, and the grand procession of miracles, which follows in chapters eight and nine. It is therefore no violent supposition that here too the evangelist has brought together, as specimens of our Lord's teaching, words which were not all spoken at the same time. His description of the Galilean ministry in Matthew iv. 23, as "teaching" and "healing," governs the arrangement of His materials from chapter five to the end of chapter nine. First comes the sermon, then the miracles follow.

The beatitudes, as a whole, are a set of paradoxes to the "mind of the flesh." They were meant to tear away the foolish illusions of the multitude as to the nature of the kingdom; and they must have disgusted and turned away many would-be sharers in it. They are like a dash of cold water on the fiery, impure enthusiasms which were eager for a kingdom of gross delights and vulgar conquest. And, no doubt, Jesus intended them to act like Gideon's test, and to sift out those whose appetite for carnal good was uppermost. But they were tests simply because they embodied everlasting truths as to the characters of His subjects. Our narrow space allows of only the most superficial treatment of these deep words.

I. The foundation of all is laid in poverty of spirit. The word rendered "poor" does not only signify one in a condition of want, but rather one who is aware of the condition, and seeks relief. If we may refer to Latin words here, it is *mendicus* rather than "pauper," a beggar rather than a poor man, who is meant. So that to be poor in spirit is to be in inmost reality conscious of need, of emptiness, of dependence on God, of demerit; the true estimate of self, as blind, evil, weak, is intended; the characteristic tone of feeling pointed to is self-abnegation, like that of the publican smiting his breast, or that of the disease-weakened, hunger-tortured prodigal, or that of the once self-righteous Paul, "O wretched man that I am!" People who do not like evangelical teaching sometimes say, "Give me the Sermon on the Mount." So say I. Only let us take all of it; and if we do, we shall come, as we shall have frequent occasion to point out in subsequent lessons, to something uncommonly like the evangelical theology to which it is sometimes set up as antithetic. For Christ begins His portraiture of a citizen of the kingdom with the consciousness of want and sin. All the rest of the morality of the sermon is founded on this. It is the root of all that is heavenly and divine in character. So this teaching is dead against the modern pagan doctrine of self-reliance, and really embodies the very principle for the supposed omission of which some folk like this sermon; namely, that our proud self-confidence must be broken down before God can do any good with us, or we can enter His kingdom. The promises attached to the beatitudes are in each case the results which flow from the quality, rather than the rewards arbitrarily given for it. So here, the possession of the kingdom comes by consequence from poverty of spirit. Of course, such a kingdom as could be so inherited was the opposite of that which the narrow and fleshly nationalism of the Jews wanted, and these first words must have cooled many incipient disciples. The "kingdom of heaven" is the rule of God through Christ. It is present wherever wills bow to Him; it is future in complete realisation in the heaven, from which it comes, and to which, like its King, it belongs, even while on earth. Obviously, its subjects can only be those who feel their dependence, and in poverty of spirit have cast off self-will and self-reliance. "Theirs is the kingdom" does not mean "they shall rule," but "of them shall be its subjects." True, they shall rule in the perfected form of it; but the first and, in a real sense, the only, blessedness is to obey God; and that blessedness can only come when we have learned poverty of spirit, because we see ourselves as in need of all things.

II. Each beatitude springs from the preceding, and all twined together make an ornament of grace upon the neck, a chain of jewels. The second sounds a more violent paradox than even the first. Sorrowing is blessed. This, of course, cannot mean mere sorrow as such. That may or may not be a blessing. Grief makes men worse quite as often as it makes them better. Its waves often flow over us like the sea over marshes, leaving them as salt and barren as it found them. Nor is sorrow always sure of comfort. We must necessarily understand the word here so as to bring it into harmony with the context, and link it with the former beatitude as flowing from it, as well as with the succeeding. The only intelligible explanation is that this sorrow arises from the contemplation of the same facts concerning self as lead to poverty of spirit, and is, in fact, the emotional side of the same disposition. He who takes the true measure of himself cannot but sorrow over the frightful gulf between what he should and might be, and what he is, for he knows that there is more than misfortune or unavoidable creatural weakness at work. The grim reality of sin has to be reckoned. Personal responsibility and guilt are facts. The soul that has once seen its own past as it is, and looked steadily down into the depths of its own being, cannot choose but "mourn." Such contrition underlies all moral progress. The ethical teaching of the Sermon on the Mount puts these two, poverty of spirit and tears for sin, at the foundation. Do its admirers lay that fact to heart? This is Christ's account of discipleship. We have to creep through a narrow gate, which we shall not pass but on our knees, and leaving all our treasures outside. But once through, we are in a great temple with far-reaching aisles and lofty roof. Such sorrow is sure of comfort. Other sorrow is not. The comfort it needs is the assurance of forgiveness and cleansing, and that assurance has never been sought from the King in vain. The comfort is filtered to us in drops here; it pours in a flood hereafter. Blessed the sorrow which leads to experience of the tender touch of the hand that wipes away tears from the face, and plucks evil from the heart! Blessed the mourning, which prepares for the festal garland and the oil of gladness and the robe of praise, instead of ashes on the head and sackcloth on the spirit!

III. Meekness here seems to be used principally as exercised to men, and thus constitutes the first of the social virtues, which henceforward alternate with those having exclusive reference to God. It is the grace which opposes patient gentleness to hatred, injury, or antagonism. The prominence given to it in Christ's teaching is one of the peculiarities of Christian morals, and is a standing condemnation of much so-called Christianity. Pride and anger and self-assertion and retaliation flaunt in fine names, and are called manly virtues. Meekness is smiled at, or trampled on, and the men who exercise it are called "Quakers," and "poor-spirited," and "chicken-hearted," and the like. Social life among us is in flagrant contradiction of this beatitude; and as for national life, all "Christian nations" agree that to apply Christ's precept to it would be absurd and suicidal. He said that the meek should inherit the earth; statesmen say that the only way to keep a country is to be armed to the teeth, and let no man insult its flag with impunity. There does not seem much room for "a spirited foreign policy" or for "proper regard to one's own dignity" inside this beatitude, does there? But notice that this meekness naturally follows the preceding dispositions. He who knows himself, and has learned the depth of his own evil, will not be swift to blaze up at slights or wrongs. The true meekness is not mere natural disposition, but the direct outcome of poverty of spirit and its consequent sorrow. So, it is a test of their reality. Many a man will indulge in confessions of sin, and crackle up in sputtering heat of indignation at some slight or offence. If he does, his lowly words have had little meaning, and the benediction of these promises will come scantily to his heart.

Does Christ mean merely to say that meek men will get landed property? Is there not a present inheritance of the earth by them, though they may not own a foot of it? They have the world who enjoy it, whom it helps nearer God, who see Him in it, to whom it is the field for service, and the means for growing character. But in the future the kingdom of heaven will be a kingdom of the earth, and the meek saints shall reign with the King who is meek and lowly of heart.

IV. Righteousness is conformity to the will of God, or moral perfection. Hunger and thirst are energetic metaphors for passionate desire, and imply that righteousness is the true nourishment of the Spirit. Every longing of the noble spirit is blessed. Aspiration after the unreached is the salt of all lofty life. It is better to be conscious of want than to be content. There are hungers which are all unblessed, greedy appetites for the swine's husks, which are misery when unsatisfied, and disgust when satiated. But we are meant to be righteous, and shall not desire it in vain. God never sends mouths but He sends meat to fill them. Such longings prophesy their fruition.

Notice that this hunger follows the experience of the former beatitudes. It is the issue of poverty of spirit, and of that blessed sorrow. Observe, too, that the desire after, and not the possession or achievement of, righteousness, is blessed. Is not this the first hint of the Christian teaching that we do not work out or win, but receive, it? God gives it. Our attitude towards that gift should be earnest longing. Such a blessed hungerer shall "receive . . . righteousness from the God of his salvation." The certainty that he will rests at last on the faithfulness of God, who cannot but respond to all desires which He inspires. They are premonitions of His purposes, like rosy clouds that run before the chariot of the sunrise. The desire to be righteous is already righteousness in heart and will, and reveals the true bent of the soul. The realisation in life is a question of time. The progressive fulfilment here points to completeness in heaven, when we shall behold His face in righteousness, and be satisfied when we awake in His likeness.

V. Again, we have a grace which is exercised to men. Mercy is more than meekness. That implied opposition, and was largely negative. This does not regard the conduct of others at all, and is really love in exercise to the needy, especially the unworthy. It embraces pity, charitable forbearance, beneficence, and is revealed in acts, in words, in tears. It is blessed in itself. A life of selfishness is hell; a life of mercy is sweet with some savour of heaven. It is the consequence of mercy received from God. Poverty of spirit, sorrow, hunger after righteousness, bring deep experiences of God's gentle forbearance and bestowing love, and will make us like Him in proportion as they are real. Our mercifulness, then, is a reflection from His. His ought to be the measure and pattern of ours in depth, scope, extent of self-sacrifice, and freeness of its gifts. A stringent requirement!

Our exercise of mercy is the condition of our receiving it. On the whole, the world gives us back, as a mirror does, the reflection of our own faces; and merciful men generally get what they give. But that is a law with many exceptions, and Jesus means more than that. Merciful men get mercy from God,—not, of course, that we deserve mercy by being merciful. That is a contradiction in terms; for mercy is what we do not deserve. The place of mercy in this series shows that Jesus regarded it as the consequence, not the cause, of our experience of God's mercy. But He teaches over and over again that a hard, unmerciful heart forfeits the Divine mercy. It does so, because such a disposition tends to obscure the very state of mind to which alone God's mercy can be given. Such a man must have forgotten his poverty and sorrow, his longings and their rich reward, and so must have, for the time, passed from the place where he can get God's gift. A life inconsistent with Christian motives will rob a Christian of Christian privileges. The hand on his brother's throat destroys the servant's own forgiveness. He cannot be at once a rapacious creditor and a discharged bankrupt.

VI. If detached from its connection, there is little blessedness in the next beatitude. What is the use of telling us how happy purity of heart will make us? It only provokes the despairing question, "And how am I to be pure?" But when we set this word in its place here, it does bring hope. For it teaches that purity is the result of all that has gone before, and comes from that purifying which is the sure answer of God to our poverty, mourning, and longing. Such purity is plainly progressive, and as it increases, so does the vision of God grow. The more the glasses of the telescope are cleansed, the brighter does the great star shine to the gazer. "No man hath seen God," nor can see Him either amid the mists of earth or in the cloudless sky of heaven, if by seeing we mean perceiving by sense, or full, direct comprehension by spirit. But seeing Him is possible even now, if by it we understand the knowledge of His character, the assurance of His presence, the sense of communion with Him. Our earthly consciousness of God may become so clear, direct, real, and certain that it deserves the name of vision. Such blessed intuition of Him is the prerogative of those whose hearts Christ has cleansed, and whose inward eye is therefore able to behold God, because it is like Him. "Unless the eye were sunlike, how could it see the sun?" We can blind ourselves to Him by wallowing in filth. Impurity unfits for seeing purity. Swedenborg profoundly said that the wicked see only blackness where the sun is.

Like all these beatitudes, this has a double fulfilment, as the kingdom has two stages of here and hereafter. Purity of heart is the condition of the vision of God in heaven. Without holiness, "no man shall see the Lord." The sight makes us pure, and purity makes us see. Thus heaven will be a state of ever-increasing, reciprocally acting sight and holiness. Like Him because we see Him, we shall see Him more because we have assimilated what we see, as the sunshine opens the petals, and tints the flower with its own colours the more deeply the wider it opens.

VII. Once more, we have the alternation of a grace exercised to men. If we give due weight to the order of these beatitudes, we shall feel that Christ's peacemaker must be something more than a mere composer of men's quarrels. For he is trained by all the preceding experiences, and has to be emptied of self, penitent, hungering for and filled with righteousness, and therefore pure in heart, as well as, in regard to men, meek and merciful, ere he can hope to fill this part. That apprenticeship deepens the conception of the peace which Christ's subjects are to diffuse. It is, first and chiefly, the peace which enters the soul that has traversed all these stages; that is to say, the Christian peacemaker is first to seek to bring about peace between men and God by beseeching them to be reconciled to Him, and then afterwards, as a consequence of this, is to seek to diffuse through all human relations the blessed unity and amity which flow most surely from the common possession of the peace of God. Of course, the relation which the subjects of the true King bear to all wars and fightings, to all discord and strife, is not excluded, but is grounded on this deeper meaning. The centuries that have passed since the words were spoken have not yet brought up the Christian conscience to the full perception of their meaning and obligation. Too many of us still believe that "great doors and effectual" can be blown open with gunpowder, and regard this beatitude as a counsel of perfection, rather than as one of the fundamental laws of the kingdom.

The Christian who moves thus among men seeking to diffuse everywhere the peace with God which fills his own soul, and the peace with all men, which they only who have the higher peace can preserve unbroken in their quiet, meek hearts, will be more or less recognized as God-like by men, and will have in his own heart the witness that he is called by God His child. He will bear visibly the image of his Father, and will hear the voice that speaks to him too as unto a son.

VIII. The last beatitude crowns all the paradoxes of the series with what sounds to flesh as a stark contradiction. The persecuted are blessed. The previous seven have perfected the portraiture of what a child of the kingdom is to be. This appends a calm prophecy, which must have shattered many a rosy dream among the listeners, of what his reception by the world will certainly turn out. Jesus is not summoning men to dominion, honour, and victory; but to scorn and suffering. His own crown, He knew, was first to be twisted of thorns, and copies of it were to wound His followers' brows. Yet even that fate was blessed; for to suffer for righteousness, which is to suffer for Him, brings elevation of spirit, a solemn joy, secret supplies of strength, and sweet intimacies of communion else unknown. The noble army of martyrs rose before His thoughts as He spoke; and now, eighteen hundred years after, heaven is crowded with those who by axe and stake and gibbet have entered there. "The glory dies not, and the grief is past." They stoop from their thrones to witness to us that Christ is true, and that the light affliction has wrought an eternal weight of glory.

These eight beatitudes complete the series. Verses 11 and 12 apply the last of them to the listening disciples. The remaining verses of the lesson describe the relation of His followers to the world, under the two figures of salt and light; the one of which works by contact, preserving from corruption, and in an inconspicuous way; the other illuminates, scatters darkness, and shines from afar. Space forbids my dealing with these two emblems, which beautifully supplement each other, and, taken together, give a complete exhibition of the Christian duty to the world, and the manner of discharging it.

LESSON VIII.

The New Form of the Old Law.

MATTHEW v. 17-26.

17. "Think not that I am come to destroy the law, or the prophets: I am not come to destroy, but to fulfil.

18. For verily I say unto you, Till heaven and earth pass, one jot or one tittle shall in no wise pass from the law, till all be fulfilled.

19. Whosoever therefore shall break one of these least commandments, and shall teach men so, he shall be called the least in the kingdom of heaven: but whosoever shall do and teach them, the same shall be called great in the kingdom of heaven.

20. For I say unto you, That except your righteousness shall exceed the righteousness of the scribes and Pharisees, ye shall in no case enter into the kingdom of heaven.

21. Ye have heard that it was said by them of old time, Thou shalt not kill; and whosoever shall kill shall be in danger of the judgment:

22. But I say unto you, That whosoever is angry with his brother without a cause shall be in danger of the judgment: and whosoever shall say to his brother, Raca, shall be in danger of the council: but whosoever shall say, Thou fool, shall be in danger of hell fire.

23. Therefore if thou bring thy gift to the altar, and there rememberest that thy brother hath ought against thee:

24. Leave there thy gift before the altar, and go thy way; first be reconciled to thy brother, and then come and offer thy gift.

25. Agree with thine adversary quickly, whiles thou art in the way with him; lest at any time the adversary deliver thee to the judge, and the judge deliver thee to the officer, and thou be cast into prison.

26. Verily I say unto thee, Thou shalt by no means come out thence, till thou hast paid the uttermost farthing."

THIS lesson falls naturally into two parts—the former extending from verse 17 to 20 inclusive; the latter, from verse 21 to the end. In the former, the King of the true kingdom lays down the general principles of the relation between its laws and the earlier revelation of the Divine will; in the latter He exemplifies this relation in one case, which is followed, in the remainder of the chapter, by three other illustrative examples.

I. The King laying down the law of His kingdom in its relation to the older law of God.

The four verses included in this section give a regular sequence of thought: verse 17 declaring our Lord's personal relation to the former revelation as fulfilling it; verse 18 basing that statement of the purpose of His coming on the essential permanence of the old law; verses 19 and 20 deducing thence the relation of His disciples to that law, and that in such a way that verse 19 corresponds to verse 18, and affirms that this permanent law is binding in its minutest details on His subjects, while verse 20 corresponds to verse 17, and requires their deepened righteousness as answering to His fulfilment of the law.

The first thing that strikes one in looking at these verses is their authoritative tone. There may, even thus early in Christ's career, have been some murmurs that He was taking up a position of antagonism to Mosaism, which may account for the "think not" which introduces the section. But however that may be, the swift transition from the beatitudes to speak of Himself and the meaning of His work is all of a piece with His whole manner; for certainly never did religious teacher open his mouth, who spoke so perpetually about Himself as did the meek Jesus. "I came" declares that He is "the coming One," and is really a claim to have voluntarily appeared among men, as well as to be the long-expected

Messiah. With absolute decisiveness He states the purpose of His coming. He knows the meaning of His own work, which so few of us do, and it is safe to take His own account of what He intends, as it so seldom is. His opening declaration is singularly composed of blended humility and majesty. Its humility lies in His placing Himself, as it were, in line with previous messengers, and representing Himself as carrying on the sequence of Divine revelation. It would not have been humble for anybody but Him to say that, but it was so for Him. Its majesty lies in His claim to "fulfil" all former utterances from God. His fulfillment of the law properly so called is twofold: first, in His own proper person and life, He completes obedience to it, realises its ideal; second, in His exposition of it, both by lip and life, He deepens and intensifies its meaning, changing it from a letter which regulates the actions, to a spirit which moves the inward man.

So these first words point to the peculiarity of His coming as His own act, and make two daring assertions as to His character, which He claims to be sinless, and as to His teaching, which He claims to be an advance upon all the former Divine revelation. To the former, He speaks here as He did to John, "thus it becometh us to fulfil all righteousness." No trace of consciousness of sin or defect appears in any words or acts of His. The calmest conviction that He was perfectly righteous is always manifest. How comes it that we are not repelled by such a tone? We do not usually admire self-complacent religious teachers. Why has nobody ever given Christ the lie, or pointed to His unconsciousness of faults as itself the gravest fault? Strange in-

The New Form of the Old Law.

augural discourse for a humble sage and saint to assert his own immaculate perfection, stranger still that a listening world has said, "Amen!" Note, too, the royal style here. In this division of the lesson our Lord twice uses the phrase, "I say unto you," which He once introduces with His characteristic "verily." Once He employs it to give solemnity to the asseveration which stretches forward to the end of this solid-seeming world, and once He introduces by it the stringent demand for His followers' loftier righteousness. His unsupported word is given us as our surest light in the dark future, His bare command as the most imperative authority. This style goes kingly; it calls for absolute credence and unhesitating submission. When He speaks, even if we have nothing but His word, it is ours neither "to make reply" nor "to reason why," but simply to believe, and swiftly to do. Rabbis might split hairs and quote other rabbis by the hour; philosophers may argue and base their teachings on elaborate demonstrations; moralists may seek to sway the conscience through reason; legislators to appeal to fear and hope. He speaks, and it is done; He commands, and it stands fast! There is nothing else in the world the least like the superb and mysterious authority with which He fronts the world, and, as Fountain of knowledge and Source of obligation, summons us all to submit and believe by that "Verily, I say unto you."

Verse 18. Next we have to notice the exuberant testimony to the permanence of the law. Not the smallest of its letters, not even the little marks which distinguished some of them, or the flourishes at the top of some of them, should pass,—as we might say, not even the stroke across a written "t," which shows that it is not "l." The law shall last as long as the world. It shall last till it be accomplished. And what then? The righteousness which it requires can never be so realised that we shall not need to realise it any more, and in the new heavens righteousness dwelleth. But law shall cease when fulfilled in a very real sense. There is no law to him who can say, "Thy law is within my heart." When law has become both law and impulse, it has ceased to be law, inasmuch as it no longer stands over against the doer as an external constraint.

Verse 19. On this permanence of the law, Christ builds its imperative authority in His kingdom. Obviously, the "kingdom of heaven" in verse 19 means the earthly form of that kingdom. The King republishes, as it were, the old code, and adopts it as the basis of His law. He thus assumes the absolute right of determining precedence and dignity in that kingdom. The sovereign is the "fountain of honour," whose word ennobles. Observe the merciful accuracy of the language. The breach of the commandments either in theory or in practice does not exclude from the kingdom, for it is, while realised on earth, a kingdom of sinful men aiming after holiness; but the smallest deflection from the law of right, in theory or in practice, does lower a man's standing therein, inasmuch as it makes him less capable of that conformity to the King, and consequent nearness to Him, which determines greatness and smallness there. Dignity in the kingdom depends on Christ-likeness, and Christ-likeness depends on fulfilling, as He did, all righteousness. Small flaws are most dangerous because least noticeable. More Christian men lose their chance of promotion in the kingdom by a multitude of little sins than by single great ones.

Verse 20. As the King has Himself by His perfect obedience fulfilled the law, His subjects likewise must, in their obedience, transcend the righteousness of those who best knew and most punctiliously kept it. The Scribes and Pharisees are not here regarded as hypocrites, but taken as types of the highest conformity with the law which the old dispensation afforded. The new kingdom demands a higher, namely a more spiritual and inward righteousness, one corresponding to the profounder meaning which the King gives to the old commandment. And this loftier fulfilment is not merely the condition of dignity in, but of entrance at all into, the kingdom. Inward holiness is the essence of the character of all its subjects. How that holiness is to be ours is not here told, except in so far as it is hinted by the fact that it is regarded as the issue of the King's fulfilling the law. These last words would have been terrible and excluding if they had stood alone. When they follow " I am come to fulfil," they are a veiled gospel, implying that by His fulfilment the righteousness of the law is fulfilled in us.

II. The illustrative example in the case of the old commandment against murder. This part of our lesson falls into three—each occupying two verses. First we have the deepening and expansion of the commandment. This part begins with the royal style again. " What was said to them of old" is left in its full authority. " But I say unto you," represents Jesus as possessing co-ordinate authority with that law of which the speaker is unnamed, perhaps because the same word of God which now spoke in Him had spoken it. We shall not refer here to the Jewish courts and Sanhedrim, and to that valley of Hinnom, where the offal of Jerusalem and the corpses of criminals were burned. Nor need we discuss the precise force of "Raca" and "thou fool." The main points to be observed are, the distinct extension of the conception of "killing" to embrace malevolent anger, whether it find vent or is kept close in the heart; the clear recognition that, whilst the emotion which is the source of the overt act is of the same nature as the act, and that therefore he who "hateth his brother is a murderer," there are degrees in criminality, according as the anger remains unexpressed, or finds utterance in more or less bitter and contemptuous language; that consequently there are degrees in the severity of the punishment which is administered by no earthly tribunal; and that, finally, this stern sentence has hidden in it the possibility of forgiveness, inasmuch as the consequence of the sin is liability to punishment, but not necessarily suffering of it. The old law had no such mitigation of its sentence.

Verses 23, 24. The second part of this illustration intensifies the command by putting obedience to it before acts of external worship. The language is vividly picturesque. We see a worshipper standing at the very altar while the priest is offering his sacrifice. In that sacred moment, while he is confessing his sins, a flash across his memory shows him a brother offended,—rightly or wrongly it matters not. The solemn sacrifice is to pause while he seeks the offended one, and, whatever the other man's reception of his advances may be, he cleanses his own bosom of its perilous stuff; then he may come back and go on with the interrupted worship. Nothing could put in a clearer light the prime importance of the command than this setting aside of sacred religious acts for its sake. "Obedience is better than sacrifice." And the little word "therefore," at the beginning of verse 23, points to the terrible penalties as the reason for this urgency. If such destruction may light on the angry man, nothing should come between him and the conquest of his anger. Such self-conquest, which will often seem like degradation, is more acceptable service to the King, and truer worship, than all words or ceremonial acts. Deep truths as to the relations between worship, strictly so called, and life, lie in these words, which may well be taken to heart by those whose altar is Calvary, and their gift the thank-offering of themselves.

Verses 25, 26. The third part is a further exhortation to the same swiftness in casting out anger from the heart, thrown into a parabolic form. When you quarrel with a man, says Christ in effect, prudence enjoins to make it up as soon as possible, before he sets the law in motion. If once he, as plaintiff, has brought you before the judge, the law will go on mechanically through the stages of trial, condemnation, surrender to the prison authorities, and confinement till the last farthing has been paid. So, if you are conscious that you have an adversary,—and any man that you hate is your adversary, for he will appear against you at that solemn judgment to come,— agree with him, put away the anger out of your heart at once. In the special case in hand, the "adversary" is the man with whom we are angry. In the general application of the precept to the whole series of offences against the law, the adversary may be regarded as the law itself. In either interpretation, the stages of appearing before the judge and so on up till the shutting up in prison are the stages of the judgment before the tribunal, not of earth, but of the kingdom of heaven. They point to the same dread realities as are presented in the previous verses under the imagery of the Jewish courts and the foul fires of the valley of Hinnom. Christ closes the grave parable with His solemn " Verily I say unto thee "—as looking on the future judgment, and telling us what His eyes saw. The words have no bearing on the question of the duration of the imprisonment, for He does not tell us whether the last farthing could ever be paid or not; but they do teach this lesson, that, if once we fall under the punishments of the kingdom, there is no end to them until the last tittle of the consequences of our breach of its law has been paid. To delay obedience, and still more to delay abandoning disobedience, is madness, in view of the storm that may at any moment burst on the heads of the rebels.

Thus He deepens and fulfils one precept of the old law by extending the sweep of its prohibition from acts to thoughts, by setting obedience to it above sacrifice and worship, and by picturing in solemn tones of parabolic warning the consequences of having the disobeyed precept as our unreconciled adversary. In this one case we have a specimen of His mode of dealing with the whole law, every jot of which He expanded in His teaching, and perfectly observed in His life.

A gospel is hidden even in these warnings, for it is distinctly taught that the offended law may cease to be our adversary, and that we may be reconciled with it, ere yet it has accused us to the judge. It was not yet time to proclaim that the King "fulfilled" the law, not only by life, but by death, and that therefore all His believing subjects "are justified from all things, from which ye could not be justified by the law," as well as endowed with the righteousness by which they fulfil that law in deeper reality, and fairer completeness, than did those "of old time," who loved it most.

LESSON IX.

Trumpets and Street Corners.

MATTHEW vi. 1-15.

1. "Take heed that ye do not your alms before men, to be seen of them: otherwise ye have no reward of your Father which is in heaven.

2. Therefore when thou doest thine alms, do not sound a trumpet before thee, as the hypocrites do in the synagogues and in the streets, that they may have glory of men. Verily I say unto you, They have their reward.

3. But when thou doest alms, let not thy left hand know what thy right hand doeth:

4. That thine alms may be in secret: and thy Father which seeth in secret Himself shall reward thee openly.

5. And when thou prayest, thou shalt not be as the hypocrites are: for they love to pray standing in the synagogues and in the corners of the streets, that they may be seen of men. Verily I say unto you, They have their reward.

6. But thou, when thou prayest, enter into thy closet, and when thou hast shut thy door, pray to thy Father which is in secret; and thy Father which seeth in secret shall reward thee openly.

7. But when ye pray, use not vain repetitions, as the heathen do: for they think that they shall be heard for their much speaking.

8. Be not ye therefore like unto them: for your Father knoweth what things ye have need of, before ye ask Him.

9. After this manner therefore pray ye: Our Father which art in heaven, Hallowed be Thy name.

10. Thy kingdom come. Thy will be done in earth, as it is in heaven.

11. Give us this day our daily bread.

12. And forgive us our debts, as we forgive our debtors.

13. And lead us not into temptation, but deliver us from evil: For Thine is the kingdom, and the power, and the glory, for ever. Amen.

14. For if ye forgive men their trespasses, your heavenly Father will also forgive you:

15. But if ye forgive not men their trespasses, neither will your Father forgive your trespasses."

OUR Lord follows His exposition of the deepened sense which the old law assumes in His kingdom, by a warning against the most subtle foes of true rightceousness. He first gives the warning in general terms in verse 1, and then flashes its light into three dark corners, and shows how hankering after men's praise corrupts the beneficence which is our duty to our neighbour, the devotion which is our duty to God, and the abstinence which is our duty to ourselves. Our lesson includes the two former, and certain other teachings which are loosely appended to the condemnation of ostentation in prayer.

We have first the general warning, given out like the text of a sermon, or the musical phrase which underlies the various harmonies of some concerto. The first word implies that the evil is a subtle and seducing one. "Take heed" as of something which may steal into and mar the noblest lives. The serpent lies coiled under the leaves, and may sting and poison the unwary hand. The generality of the warning, and the logical propriety of the whole section, require the adoption of the reading of the Revised Version, namely, "righteousness." The thing to be taken heed of is not the doing it "before men," which will often be obligatory, often necessary, and never in itself wrong, but the doing it "to be seen of them." Not the number of spectators, but the furtive glance of our eyes to see if they are looking at us, makes the sin. We are to let our good works shine, that men may glorify our Father. Pious souls are to shine, and yet to be hid,— a paradox which can be easily solved by the obedient. If our motive is to make God's glory more visible, we shall not be seeking to be ourselves admired. The harpstring's swift vibrations, as it gives out its note, make it unseen.

The reason for the warning goes on two principles:

one that righteousness is to be rewarded, over and above its own inherent blessedness; another, that the prospect of the reward is a legitimate stimulus, over and above the prime reason for righteousness, namely, that it is righteous. The New Testament morality is not good enough for some very superfine people, who are pleased to call it selfish because it lets a martyr brace himself in the fire by the vision of the crown athwart the smoke. Somehow or other, however, that selfish morality gets itself put in practice, and turns out more unselfish people than its assailants manage to produce. Perhaps the motive which they attack may be part of the reason.

The mingling of regard for man's approbation with apparently righteous acts absolutely disqualifies them for receiving God's reward, for it changes their whole character, and they are no longer what they seem. Charity given from that motive is not charity, nor prayer devotion.

I. The general warning is applied to three cases, of which we have to deal with two. Our Lord speaks first of ostentatious alms-giving. Note that we are not to take "blowing the trumpets" as actual fact. Nobody would do that in a synagogue. The meaning of all attempts, however concealed, to draw attention to one's beneficence, is just what the ear-splitting blast would be; and the incongruity of startling the worshippers with the harsh notes is like the incongruity of doing good and trying to attract notice. I think Christ's ear catches the screech of the brazen abomination in a good many of the ways of raising and giving money, which find favour in the Church to-day. This is an advertising age, and flowers that used to blush unseen are forced now under glass for exhibition. Nobody needs to blow his own trumpet nowadays. We have improved on the ruder methods of the Pharisees and newspapers and collectors will blow lustily and loud for us, and defend the noise on the ground that a good example stimulates others. Perhaps so, though it may be a question what it stimulates to, and whether B's gift, drawn out in imitation or emulation of A's, is any liker Christ's idea of gifts than was A's, given that B might hear of it. To a very large extent, the money getting and giving arrangements of the modern Church are neither more nor less than the attempt to draw Christ's chariot with the devil's traces. Christ condemned ostentation. His followers too often try to make use of it.

"They have their reward." Observe that *have* means *have received in full*, and note the emphasis of that *their*. It is all the reward they will ever get, and all that they are capable of. The pure and lasting crown, which is a fuller possession of God Himself, has no charms for them, and could not be given. And what a poor thing it is which they seek—the praise of men!—a breath, as unsubstantial and short-lived as the blast of the trumpet which they blew before their selfish benevolence. Their charity was no charity, for what they did was not to give, but to buy. Their gift was a speculation. They invested in charity, and looked for a profit of praise. How can they get God's reward? The true benevolence will even hide the giving right hand from the idle left, and, as far as may be, will dismiss the deed from the doer's consciousness. Such alms, given wholly out of pity and desire to be like the all-giving Father, can be rewarded, and will be, with that richer acquaintance with Him, and more complete victory over self, which is the heaven of heaven, and the foretaste of it now.

In its coarsest forms, this ostentation is out and out hypocrisy, which consciously assumes a virtue which it has not. But far more common and dangerous is the subtle, unconscious mingling of it with real charity,— the eye wandering from the poor, whom the hand is helping, to the bystanders,—and it is this mingling which we have therefore to take most heed to avoid. One drop of this sour stuff will curdle whole gallons of the milk of human kindness. The hypocrisy which hoodwinks ourselves is more common and perilous than that which blinds others.

II. We need not dwell at length on the second application of the general warning—to prayer; as the words are almost, and the thoughts entirely, identical with those of the former verses. If there be any action of the spirit which requires the complete exclusion of thoughts of men, it is prayer, which is the communion of the soul alone with God. It is as impossible to pray, and at the same time to think of men, as to look up and down at once. If we think of prayer, as formalists in all times have done, as so many words, then it will not seem incongruous to choose the places where men are thickest for "saying our prayers," and we shall do it with all the more spirit if we have spectators. That accounts for a great deal of the "devotion" in Mohammedan and Roman Catholic countries which travellers with no love for Protestant Christianity are so fond of praising. But if we think of prayer as Christ did, as being the yearning of the soul to God, we shall feel that the inmost chamber and the closed door are its fitting accompaniments. Of course, our Lord is not forbidding united prayer; for each of the worshippers may be holding communion with God, which is none the less solitary though shared by the others, and none the less united though in it each is alone with God.

III. Our Lord passes for a time from the more immediate subject of ostentation to add other teaching about prayer, which still farther unfolds its true conception. Another corruption arising from the error of thinking that prayer is an outward act, is "vain repetition," characteristic of all heathen religion, and resting upon a profound disbelief in the loving willingness of God to help. Of course, earnest, reiterated prayer is not vain repetition. Jesus is not condemning His own agony in Gethsemane when He thrice "said the same words." The persistence in prayer, which is the child of faith, is no relation to the parrot-like repetition which is the child of disbelief, nor does the condemnation of the one touch the other. The frenzied priests who yelled, "O Baal, hear us!" all the long day; the Buddhists who repeat the sacred invocation till they are stupefied; the poor devotee who thinks merit is acquired by the number of paternosters and aves, are all instances of this gross mechanical conception of prayer. Are there no similar superstitions nearer home? Are there no ministers or congregations that we ever heard of, who have a regulation length for their prayers, and would scarcely think they had prayed at all if their devotions were as short as most of the prayers in the Bible? Are we in no danger of believing what Christ tells us here is pure heathenism,—that many words may move God?

The only real remedy against such degradation of the very idea of prayer lies in the deeper conceptions of God and of it which Christ here gives. He knows our needs before we ask. Then what is prayer for? Not to inform Him, nor to move Him, unwilling, to have mercy, as if, like some proud prince, He required a certain amount of recognition of His greatness as the price of His favours. But to fit our own hearts by conscious need, and true desire and dependence, to receive the gifts which He is ever willing to give, but we are not always fit to receive. As St. Augustine has it, the empty vessel is by prayer carried to the full fountain.

We cannot pretend to treat the prayer which teaches how to pray in our limited space, but must content ourselves with the slightest touch. "After this manner" may or may not imply that Christ meant this prayer to be a form, but He certainly meant it for a model. And they who drink in its spirit, and pray seeking God's glory before their own satisfaction, and, while trustfully asking from His hand their daily bread, rise quickly to implore the supply of their spiritual hunger, do pray "after this manner," whether they use these words or no.

We may briefly point out the structure of the prayer, although we cannot dwell on the separate petitions. All begins with the recognition of the fatherhood of God. The clear and fixed contemplation of God is the beginning of all true prayer, and that contemplation does not fasten on His remote and partially intelligible attributes, nor strive to climb to behold Him as in Himself, but grasps Him as related to us. The fatherhood of God implies His communication of life, His tenderness, and our kindred. This is a prayer for the children of the kingdom, and can only be truly offered by those who, by faith in the Son, have received the adoption of sons. It gathers all such into a family, so delivering their prayer from selfish absorption in their own joys or needs. As our Father "in Heaven," He is lifted clear above earth's limitations, changes, and imperfections. So child-like familiarity is sublimed into reverence, our hearts are drawn upward, and delivered from the oppressive and narrowing attachment to earth and sense.

The perfect sevenfold petitions of the prayer fall into two halves, corresponding roughly to the first and second tables of the decalogue. The first half consists of three petitions, which refer to God and His kingdom. They are three, in accordance with the symbolism of numbers, which, in the Old Testament, always regards three as the sacred number of completeness and of divinity. The second half consists of four petitions, which refer to ourselves. They are four,—the number which symbolizes the creature. The lessons taught by the order in which these two halves occur do not need to be dwelt upon. God first and man second, His glory before our wants,— that is the true order. For how few of us is it the spontaneous order? Do we first rise to God, and only second descend to ourselves?

Note, too, the sequence in each of these halves. In the first we may say that we begin from above and come down, or from within and come outwards. In the second, the process is the opposite. We begin on the lowest level with the external needs, and go upwards and inwards to removal of sin, exemption from temptation, and complete deliverance from evil. The first half gives us the beginning, middle, and end of God's purposes for the world. The recognition of His name is the basis of His kingdom, and His kingdom is the sphere in which alone His will is done. The second half, in like manner, gives us the beginning, middle, and end of His dealings with the individual, the common mercies of daily bread, forgiveness, guidance, protection in conflict, and final deliverance.

The "name" of God is His revealed character. He hallows it when He so acts as to make His holiness manifest. We hallow it when we regard it as the holy thing which it is. That petition is first, because the knowledge of God as He is self-revealed is the deepest want of men, and the spread of that knowledge and reverence the way by which His kingdom comes.

God's kingdom is His rule over men's hearts. Christ began His ministry by proclaiming its near approach, and in effect brought it to earth. But it spread slowly in the individual heart, and in the world. Therefore, this second petition is ever in place, until the consummation. God's rule is established through the hallowing of His name; for it is a rule which works on men through their understandings, and seeks no ignorant submission.

The sum of this first half is, "Thy will be done, as in Heaven, so on earth." Obedience to that will is the end of God's self-revelation. It makes all the difference whether we begin with the thought of the name or of the will. In the latter case, religion will be slavish and submission sullen. There is no more horrible and paralyzing conception of God than that of mere sovereign will. But if we think of Him as desiring that we should know His name, and gathering all its syllables into the one perfect "word of God"; then we are sure that His will must be intelligible and good. Obedience becomes delight, and the surrender of our wills to His the glad expression of love. He who begins with "Thy will be done" is a slave, and never really does the will at all: he who begins with "Our Father, hallowed be Thy name" is a son, and his will, gladly yielding, is free in surrender, strong in self-abnegation, and restful in putting the reins into God's hands.

The two halves make a whole. The second, which deals with our needs, starts with the cry for bread, and climbs up slowly through the ills of life, from bodily hunger to trespasses and human unkindness and personal weakness, and a world of temptation, and the double evil of sin and of sorrow, and so regains at last the starting-point of the first half, Heaven and God. The probable meaning of the difficult word rendered "daily" seems to be "sufficient for our need." The lessons of the petition are that God's children have a claim for the supply of their wants, since He is bound, as a faithful Creator, not to send mouths without sending meat to fill them, but that our desires should be limited to our actual necessities, and our cravings, as well as our efforts for the bread that perishes, made into prayers. Such a prayer rightly used would put an end to much wicked luxury among Christians, and to many questionable ways of getting wealth. "Bless my cheating, my sharp practice, my half lies!" If we dare not pray this prayer over what we do in "earning our living," we had better ask ourselves whether we are not rather earning our death.

Sin is debt incurred to God. . So Christ taught in the previous lesson by His parable of agreeing with the adversary; and in the other parables of the two debtors (Luke vii. 41) and of the unmerciful servant (Matt. xviii. 23). As universal as the need for bread is the need for pardon It is the first want of the spiritual nature, but it is a constantly recurring want, as this petition teaches us. Forgiveness is the cancelling of a debt; but we must not forget that it is a Father's forgiveness, and therefore does not merely, or even chiefly, imply the removal of penalty, but much rather the unimpeded flow of the Father's love, and consequently the removal of the miserable consciousness of separation from Him. The appended comparison "as we have forgiven" does not mean that our forgiveness is the reason for God's forgiveness of us. The ground of our pardon is Christ's work, the condition of it our faith; but, as we saw in considering the beatitudes, the condition on which the children of the kingdom can retain the blessing of the Divine pardon is their imitation of it.

The next petition is the expression of conscious weakness. The forgiven man, though in his deepest soul hating sin, is still surrounded with sparks which may fire the combustibles in his heart. If we ask not to be led into temptation, because we want a smooth and easy road, we are wrong. If we do so from self-distrust and fear lest we fall, then it is allowable. But perhaps we may draw a distinction between being tempted and being led into temptation. The former may mean the presentation of the inducement to do evil which we cannot hope to escape, and which it is not well that we should escape. The latter may mean the further step of embracing or being entangled in it by consenting to it.

We do not need to dread the entrance into the Valley of the Shadow of Death, for if the Lord be with us we shall pass through it. Our prayer may mean, lead us, not into, but through, the trial. It is the plaint of conscious weakness, the recognition of God as ordering our path, the cry of a heart which desires holiness most of all, and which trusts in God's upholding hand in the hour of trial.

Deliver us from evil is a petition which, in its width, fits the close of the prayer better than the translation of the Revised Version. There seems an echo of the words in Paul's noble confidence while the headsman's axe was so near, "The Lord will deliver me from every evil work." Entire exemption from evil of every sort, whether sin or sorrow, is the true end of our prayers, as it is the crown of God's purpose. Nothing less can satisfy our yearnings; nothing less can fulfil the Divine desire for us. Nothing less should be the goal of our faith and hope. To that height of meek assurance, and that reaching out of our souls in desire which is the pledge of its own fulfilment, Christ would have us attain on the wings of prayer. They can have no narrower bounds to the horizon of their hopes, nor any lesser blessing for the satisfaction of their longings, whose prayer begins with, "Our Father which art in heaven"; for where the Father is, the child must wish to be, and some day will be, to go no more out.

LESSON X.

"Without Carefulness."

MATTHEW vi. 24-34.

24. "No man can serve two masters: for either he will hate the one, and love the other; or else he will hold to the one, and despise the other. Ye cannot serve God and mammon.

25. Therefore I say unto you, <u>Take no thought for your life</u>, what ye shall eat, or what ye shall drink; nor yet for your body, what ye shall put on. Is not the life more than meat, and the body than raiment?

26. Behold the fowls of the air: for they sow not, neither do they reap, nor gather into barns; yet your heavenly Father feedeth them. Are ye not much better than they?

27. Which of you by taking thought can add one cubit unto his stature?

28. And why take ye thought for raiment? Consider the lilies of the field, how they grow; they toil not, neither do they spin:

29. And yet I say unto you, That even Solomon in all his glory was not arrayed like one of these.

30. Wherefore, if God so clothe the grass of the field, which to day is, and to morrow is cast into the oven, shall He not much more clothe you, O ye of little faith?

31. <u>Therefore take no thought, saying</u>, What shall we eat? or, What shall we drink? or, Wherewithal shall we be clothed?

32. (For after all these things do the Gentiles seek:) for your heavenly Father knoweth that ye have need of all these things.

33. But seek ye first <u>the kingdom of God, and His righteousness</u>; and all these things shall be added unto you.

34. Take therefore no thought for <u>the morrow</u>: for the morrow shall take thought for the things of itself. Sufficient unto the day is the evil thereof."

WE have here first a plain maxim of common experience applied to a religious purpose. We cannot serve—in the deepest reality of that word—two masters. A servant must at bottom have one voice from which he takes orders. If there be two who have control over him, one will have the real sway of his will. That would be true, even if the two pulled the same way and gave parallel orders. What if one forbids all that the other commands, and commands all that the other forbids? A joint service will be a hopeless attempt then. So is it, says Jesus, with God and this world's goods. God's servant may have these, but he must be their master, not they his. If they are, he cannot serve God.

This sharp denial of the possibility of serving both comes into view mainly as the foundation of the exhortations which fill the remainder of the chapter. They are Christ's warnings against anxiety about material good. Such anxiety, then, is one form of mammon-worship. The man who thinks that it is the supreme good, and the man who dreads the loss of it as the supreme evil, are the same man. We have then chiefly to consider the sweet persuasions with which Christ would here win our timid hearts to bold trust. The whole section falls into three parts of unequal length, marked off by the repetition of the command "Be not anxious." It occurs at verses 25, 31, and 34, and on each occasion introduces a fresh set of reasons against anxious care. If we look closely at these, we shall see that they may be briefly stated thus: anxiety is opposed to the teaching of nature, as seen in the lower creation, which shows it to be needless; to the teaching of revelation, which shows it to be heathenism; and to the teaching of providence, which condemns it as useless.

1. This anxiety, which is a form of mammon-worship, and therefore inconsistent with true devotion, is dead

against the teaching of nature. Our Lord puts three facts of nature before us,—our compelled dependence on God for bodily life at all; the way in which the birds of the air are fed; and that in which the lilies grow,—and bids us see if these do not condemn our anxieties.

Take that first thought, "Is not the life more than meat, and the body than raiment?" That is in effect equivalent to saying, You have to trust God, whether you will or no, for your body, its form, its growth, its duration. You are obliged to trust Him to give you it, and to keep you in its possession; trust Him to clothe and feed it. You cannot help being dependent. All that you can do, with all your carking care, is but to adorn a little more or less beautifully the allotted span. What is the use of being careful for food and raiment, when below these lies the question for the answer to which you have to hang in implicit dependence on God,—shall I live, or die? Your anxiety does not go very deep, after all, but is like a passing shower, that softens an inch of the hard-baked ground, and never gets near the seeds that lie feet below the reach of its useless moisture. You must trust Him for the greater; you may as well trust Him for the less. God gives the greater, and that binds Him to give the less. He gives royally and liberally, logically and completely. When He bestows life, you may be sure that He will not stultify His gift.

Then follow the exquisite illustrations of the fowls of the air and the lilies of the field, which people who know little else of the Bible know by heart. I need not linger over their beauty, which appeals to all. Our Lord points to them as specimens in the lower creation of the working of the loving care to which we ought to trust.

"Solomon in all his glory was not arrayed like one of these,"—there is an instance of God's giving more than barely enough; He lavishes beauty, He touches the flower into grace, and decks waste places with fairness, and "so" clothes the grass of the field that we may learn that a fair spirit, who delights in a fair creation, a bountiful spirit who gives with both hands, presides over all things, and divides His gifts to men.

Much of the force of our Lord's words here depends on the inferiority of these creatures. Observe the points of inferiority. One is that they do not need to toil. "They sow not, neither do they reap"; and that is no privileged exemption, but one of the particulars in which we are "much better than they." We have the privilege of work, and so can influence to-morrow, therefore we need not fret about it. We have hands that can grasp the tool or the pen. They labour not, and yet are fed. Much more will He feed us, whom He has made capable of toil. Again, "Your heavenly Father feedeth them"; they cannot say "father," yet they are cared for. Shame on us if we are anxious! for every lily blows and every bird carols its song without foreboding, and yet there is no Father in heaven to them.

Again, they are inferior in their brief duration. "To-day it is, and to-morrow it is cast into the oven." They are blessed in the present. The oven to-morrow saddens not the blossoming of to-day. We have nobler and more lasting needs, and are in so far better. The same hand which supplies the more transient necessities will not grudge or forget to supply the wants which wander through eternity.

II. Verses 31-33 lead us to another line of thought,

which tends to dispel anxious care. It is contrary to the lessons of revelation, which show it to be at bottom heathenism. "After all these things do the Gentiles seek." It is the very characteristic of the Gentile, that is to say, of the heathen, that earth should bound his horizon and contain all his desires. If a Christian is living in the anxious foreboding of some worldly disaster, or is unable to leave to-morrow in God's hands, is not the very root of such a temper heathenish worldly-mindedness?

Again, this anxiety rests upon a misunderstanding or lack of trust in the character of God. "Your Heavenly Father knoweth that ye have need of all these things"; the heathen thought of God is that He is far removed from our perplexities, ignorant of our struggles, or careless about them. The Christian has the double armour against anxiety,—the name of Father, and the conviction that His knowledge is co-extensive with His love. He who calls us His children thoroughly understands and sympathizes with our wants.

Further, anxious care can only be stilled by true religion. "Seek ye first the kingdom of God!" It is of no use to tell men that they ought to trust, and to point them for teachers to birds and flowers; nor is it enough to preach to them that distrust is heathenism. The heart must be filled with a supreme and transcendent desire after one supreme object; and then there will be no room for anxious care about lesser good. If our souls are stretching out towards that state of complete and joyful submission to God's loving will which is the kingdom of God within us, "the cares that infest the day" will steal away from out of the sacred pavilion of your believing spirit. If we could live on the heights, sure that we have God, and sure that He is enough, come what darkness of sorrow may come, then we should not be anxious about the complexion of to-morrow, for we should be calm in the possession of what nothing that has power over the changeable goods of life can touch or take away.

III. Finally, Christ here tells us that anxiety for to-morrow is contrary to the scheme of providence, which shows it to be vain.

"The morrow shall take thought for the things of itself." It will have anxieties enough of its own, after and in spite of all the anxieties about it to-day, by which you try to free it from care when it comes. Every day, to the end of the days, will have its own evil, and the day's portion which you cannot get rid of will be enough for all the strength which you have to cope with it. And anxiety about the future is vain. After all our careful watching of the heaven, the clouds will rise in an unwatched quarter. After all our fortifying of the citadel, there will be some little postern left unguarded, some weak place uncommanded by a battery, and there, where we never looked for him, the inevitable assailant will make his entrance. After all the dipping of the hero in the waters that gave invulnerability, there was the little spot on the heel, and the arrow found its way there. Nothing is certain but the unexpected. To-morrow will have its cares in spite of all that anxious care and foreboding can do. It is God's law of providence that we shall be disciplined by sorrow, and to try to escape from that law by forecasting prudence is hopeless.

And what does our anxiety do? It does not empty

to-morrow of its sorrows, but it empties to-day of its strength. It does not give escape from evil, but it makes us unfit to cope with it when it bursts on us. It does not bless to-morrow, and it robs to-day. For every day has its own burden, which is quite heavy enough for the day's strength. Sufficient for each day is the evil which properly belongs to it. We shall be wise if we do not add to-morrow's weight to to-day's load, nor drag the future, wrongly conceived as it will be sure to be, into the present, where there is no place for it. The present has enough to do in looking after its own concerns.

We have always, or we can always get, strength enough to bear the evil when it comes. We have not strength to bear the foreboding of it. "As thy days, so shall thy strength be." In strict proportion to the God-appointed existing exigency will be the God-given power. But if we crowd both the sorrows of to-day, which we actually feel, and those of to-morrow which we anticipate, into the narrow room of four-and-twenty hours, there is no promise that our strength will be as that day. God gives us power to bear all the sorrows and cares of His making; but He does not bind Himself to give us power to bear those which we manufacture with perverse industry for ourselves by being "over-exquisite to cast the fashion of uncertain evils."

Thus, then, our Lord would teach us that the exercise of that anxious care, which is the misuse of the great faculty of looking forward and picturing things to come, is contrary to nature, revelation, and providence; that it weakens and distracts; that it takes the sunshine out of every landscape, and flings a shadow over all good. Surely God gave us that wonderful faculty for better purposes than that we might by it torment ourselves, and suffer every evil twice over. Why should we exercise our power of imagining the future chiefly in regard to to-morrow's possible evils, when we might by its aid fill the winter of our earthly life with the glorious summer of eternity, and bring assurance of things hoped for to lighten the dark present? We cannot but look forward; but we may choose whether we shall look but a little way ahead on the low level, or beyond and above all the trifles at hand to "that one far-off divine event to which the whole creation moves."

LESSON XI.

Judging, Asking, and Giving.

MATTHEW vii. 1-12.

1. "Judge not, that ye be not judged.
2. For with what judgment ye judge, ye shall be judged: and with what measure ye mete, it shall be measured to you again.
3. And why beholdest thou the mote that is in thy brother's eye, but considerest not the beam that is in thine own eye?
4. Or how wilt thou say to thy brother, Let me pull out the mote out of thine eye; and, behold, a beam is in thine own eye?
5. Thou hypocrite, first cast out the beam out of thine own eye; and then shalt thou see clearly to cast out the mote out of thy brother's eye.
6. Give not that which is holy unto the dogs, neither cast ye your pearls before swine, lest they trample them under their feet, and turn again and rend you.
7. Ask, and it shall be given you; seek, and ye shall find; knock, and it shall be opened unto you:
8. For every one that asketh receiveth; and he that seeketh findeth; and to him that knocketh it shall be opened.
9. Or what man is there of you, whom if his son ask bread, will he give him a stone?
10. Or if he ask a fish, will he give him a serpent?
11. If ye then, being evil, know how to give good gifts unto your children, how much more shall your Father which is in heaven give good things to them that ask Him?
12. Therefore all things whatsoever ye would that men should do to you, do ye even so to them: for this is the law and the prophets."

I. How can we help "judging," and why should we not "judge"? The power of seeing into character is to be coveted and cultivated, and the absence of it makes simpletons, not saints. Quite true: but seeing into character is not what Jesus is condemning here. The "judging" of which He speaks sees motes in a brother's eye. That is to say, it is one-sided, and fixes on faults, which it magnifies, passing by virtues. Carrion flies who buzz with a sickening hum of satisfaction over sores, and prefer corruption to soundness, are as good judges of meat as such critics are of character. That Mephistophelean spirit of detraction in this day has wide scope. Literature and politics, as well as social life with its rivalries, are infested by it, and it finds its way into the church and threatens us all. The race of fault-finders we have always with us, blind as moles to beauties and goodness, but lynx-eyed for failings, and finding meat and drink in proclaiming them in tones of affected sorrow. How flagrant a breach of the laws of the kingdom this temper implies, and how grave an evil it is, though thought little of, or even admired as cleverness and a mark of a very superior person, Christ shows us by this earnest warning, imbedded among His fundamental moral teachings.

He points out first how certainly that disposition provokes retaliation. Who is the Judge that judges us as we do others? Perhaps it is best to say that both the Divine and the human estimates are included in the purposely undefined expression. Certainly both are included in fact. For a carping spirit of eager fault-finding necessarily tinges people's feelings towards its possessor, and he cannot complain if the severe tests which he applied to others are used on his own conduct. A cynical critic cannot expect his victims to be profoundly attached to him, or ready to be lenient to his failings.

If he chooses to fight with a tomahawk, he will be scalped some day, and the bystanders will not lament profusely. But a more righteous tribunal than that of his victims condemns him. For in God's eyes the man who covers not his neighbour's faults with the mantle of charity has not his own blotted out by Divine forgiveness.

This spirit is always accompanied by ignorance of one's own faults, which makes the man indulging it ludicrous. So our Lord would seem to intend by the figure of the mote and the beam. It takes a great deal of close peering to see a mote; but the censorious man sees only the mote, and sees it out of scale. No matter how bright the eye, though it be clear as a hawk's, its beauty is of no moment to him. The mote magnified, and nothing but the mote, is his object; and he calls this one-sided exaggeration "criticism," and prides himself on the accuracy of his judgment. He makes just the opposite mistake in his estimate of his own faults, if he sees them at all. We look at our neighbour's errors with a microscope, and at our own through the wrong end of a telescope. We see neither in their real magnitude, and the former fault is sure to lead to the latter. We have two sets of weights and measures: one for home use, the other for foreign. Every vice has two names; and we call it by the flattering and minimizing one when we commit it, and by the ugly one when our neighbour does it. Everybody can see the hump on his friend's shoulders, but it takes some effort to see our own. David was angry enough at the man who stole his neighbour's ewe lamb, but quite unaware that he was guilty of a meaner, crueller theft. The mote can be seen; but the beam, big though it be, needs to be "considered." So it often escapes notice, and will surely do so; if we are yielding to the temptation of harsh judgment of others, every man may be aware of faults of his own very much bigger than any that he can see in another. For each of us may fathom the depth of our own sinfulness in motive, and unspoken, unacted thought, while we can see only the surface acts of others.

Our Lord points out, in verse 4, a still more subtle form of this harsh judgment, when it assumes the appearance of solicitude for the improvement of others, and teaches us that all honest desire to help in the moral reformation of our neighbours must be preceded by earnest efforts at mending our own conduct. If we have grave faults of our own undetected and unconquered, we are incapable either of judging or of helping our brethren. Such efforts will be hypocritical, for they pretend to come from genuine zeal for righteousness and care for another's good, whereas their real root is simply censorious exaggeration of a neighbour's faults; they imply that the person affected with such a tender care for another's eyes has his own in good condition. A blind guide is bad enough, but a blind oculist is a still more ridiculous anomaly. Note, too, that the result of clearing our own vision is beautifully put, not as being ability to see, but ability to cure our fellows. It is only the experience of the pain of casting out a darling evil, and the consciousness of God's pitying mercy as given to us, that makes the eye keen enough, and the hand steady and gentle enough, to pull out the mote. It is a delicate operation, and one which a clumsy operator may make very painful, and useless, after all. A rough finger or a harsh spirit makes success impossible.

II. Verse 6 comes in singular juxtaposition with a warning against uncharitable judgments. Christ's calling men dogs and swine does not sound like obeying His own precept. But the very shock which the words give at first hearing is part of their value. There are men whom Jesus, for all His gentleness, has to estimate thus. His pitying eyes were not blind to truth. It was no breach of infinite charity in Him to see facts, and to give them their right names; and His previous precept does not bid us shut ours, or give up common sense. This verse limits the application of the preceding, and inculcates prudence, tact, and discernment of character, as no less essential to His servants than the sweet charity, slow to suspect and sorrowful to expose a brother's fault. The fact that His gentle lips used such words may well make us shudder as we think of the deforming of human nature into pure animalism, which some men achieve, and which is possible for all.

The inculcation of discretion in the presentation of the truth may easily be exaggerated into a doctrine of reserve which is more Jesuitical than Christian. Even when guarded and limited, it may seem scarcely in harmony with the commission to preach the gospel to every creature, or with the sublime confidence that God's word finds something to appeal to in every heart, and has power to subdue the animal in every man. But the divergence is only apparent. The most expansive zeal is to be guided by prudence, and the most enthusiastic confidence in the universal power of the gospel does not take leave of common sense. There are people who will certainly be repelled, and perhaps stirred to furious antagonism to the gospel and its messengers, if they are not approached with discretion. It is bad to hide the treasure in a napkin; it is quite as bad to fling it down without preparation before some people. Jesus Himself locked His lips before Herod, although the curious ruler asked many questions; and we have sometimes to remember that there are people who "will not hear the word," and who must first "be won without the word." Heavy rains run off hard-baked earth. It must first be softened by a gentle drizzle. Luther once told this fable: "The lion made a great feast, and he invited all the beasts, and among the rest, a sow. When all manner of costly dishes were set before the guests, the sow asked, 'Have you no bran?' Even so, said he, we preachers set forth the most dainty dishes,—the forgiveness of sins, and the grace of God; but they turn up their snouts, and grub for guilders."

This precept is one side of the truth. The other is the adaptation of the gospel to all men, and the obligation on us to preach it to all. We can only tell most men's disposition towards it by offering it to them, and we are not to be in a hurry to conclude that men are dogs and swine.

III. We have the bountiful law of Christ's giving. The connection with the previous verse is difficult. It may possibly be "You are not only givers, but have first to receive, and this is how you may receive." Notice first the condition on which we obtain the divine gift. The three words, "ask, seek, knock," are obviously a climax. We are perhaps not intended to press the difference between them, but still it seems improbable that there should be no meaning in the studied variety of expression. The first condition is desire, addressed to Him who can grant it. The second is effort in the direction of our desires. The third is persistent continuance of desire and effort. Experience seems to contradict such promises. Is there any region in which to ask is to have, to seek is to find, and in which every door flies open at our knock? Certainly not in the world of common life, where bitter disappointment, vain wishes, and bootless search are so common. Jesus Christ did not mean that His followers may have whatever they like. The way to spoil a child is to give it all it asks, and He does not mean to spoil us. Therefore He must thwart our wishes till they run parallel with His will, and are fixed on higher good than earth holds. So, of course, this promise is true only in the spiritual realm, or in regard to the development of the Christian character. We may have as much of God as we will. Christ puts the key of the treasure chamber into our hand, and bids us take all that we want. If a man is admitted into the bullion vault of a bank, and told to help himself, and comes out with one cent, whose fault is it that he is poor? Whose fault is it that Christian people generally have such scanty portions of the free riches of God?

This climax teaches us that prayers unaccompanied by effort are not answered. Many ask who do not seek. There are precious things which cannot be given to a mere wish. We have to seek, not as though we do not know where to find, but like gold-diggers, toiling on their claims, not because they do not know where the gold is, but because they do know that it is there. And there must be continuous desire and effort. That implies that the answers do not always come immediately. The best gifts grow slowly,—more than forty-and-six years is the temple of a Christ-like nature in building. Therefore patient continuance in waiting on the Giver is the final condition of receiving His highest gifts. Like Peter at the gate, we must "continue knocking." Many a man prays for spiritual gifts, and, like a rifleman who fires and does not wait to see whether his ball has struck the target, goes away before the signal can be made that his prayer is heard.

It may be a question whether, in verse 8, the emphasis is to be laid on "every one" or on "that asketh," or, in other words, whether it is an assurance that the universal law will be followed in our case, or a statement of the universal condition without which no receiving is possible, and, least of all, the receiving of the gifts of the kingdom by its subjects. In either case, this verse gives the reason for the preceding exhortation. Then follows the tender illustration in which the dim-sighted love of earthly fathers is taken as a parable of the all-wise tenderness and desire to bestow which move the hand of the giving God. There is some resemblance between an Eastern loaf and a stone, and some between a fish and a serpent. However imperfect a father's love, he will neither be cruel enough to cheat his unsuspecting child with what looks like an answer to his wish, but is useless or hurtful, nor foolish enough to make a mistake. All human relationships are in some measure marred by the faults of those who sustain them. What a solemn attestation of universal sinfulness is in these words of Christ's, and how calmly He separates Himself in His sinlessness from us! I do not know that there is anywhere a stronger scriptural proof of these two truths than this one incidental clause, "ye, being evil." I wonder whether the people who pit the Sermon on the Mount against evangelical Christianity are ready to take this bit of it into their creeds. It is noteworthy, also, that the emphasis is laid, not on the earthly father's willingness, but on his knowing how to give good gifts. Our Lord seems to think that He need not assure us of the plain truth, that of course our Father in heaven is willing, just because He is our Father, to give us all good; but He heartens us with the assurance that His love is wisdom, and that He cannot make any mistakes. There are no stones mingled with our bread, nor any serpents among the fish. He gives good, and nothing but good. What if a foolish child should ask for a stone, thinking that it was bread, or for a serpent, believing it to be a fish? Will our Father give these to us? Surely not. Therefore, in the region of earthly good, where our desires are often wrong, His love and wisdom will be shown by His disappointing our wishes, that He may satisfy our wants. So Luke, in His version of these words, explains "good thing" by "the Holy Spirit," the one certain good, which we may ask for and not be disappointed.

IV. The great precept which closes the lesson is not only to be taken as an inference from the immediately preceding context, but as the summing up of all the duties to our neighbours, on which Christ has been laying down the law of the kingdom from Matthew v. 17. This general reference of the "therefore" is confirmed by the subsequent clause, "this is the law and the prophets"; the summing up of the whole past revelation of the Divine will, and therefore in accordance with our Lord's previous exposition of the relation between His new law and that former one, the summing up of all His teaching. As Luther puts it in his vigorous, homely way, "With these words He now closes His instructions given in these three chapters, and ties it all up in a little bundle." But a connection may also be traced with the preceding paragraph. There our desires were treated as securing God's corresponding gifts. Here our desires, when turned to men, are regarded, not as securing their corresponding conduct, but as obliging us to action. By taking our wishes as the rule of our dealings with others, we shall be like God, who takes our wishes as the rule of His dealings with us. Our desires sent heavenward procure blessings for us; sent earthward, they prescribe our blessing of others. That is a startling turn to give to our claims on our fellows. It rests on the principle that every man has equal rights, therefore we ought not to look for anything from others which we are not prepared to extend to others. A should give B whatever A thinks B should give him. Our error is in making ourselves our own centre, and thinking more of our claims on others than of our obligations to them. Christ teaches us that these are one. Such a principle applied to our lives would wonderfully pull down our expectations and lift up our obligations. It is really but another way of putting the law of loving our neighbours as ourselves. If observed, it would revolutionise society. Nothing short of it is the law of the kingdom, and the duty of all who call themselves Christ's subjects.

This is the inmost meaning, says Jesus, of the law and the prophets. All the former revelations of the Divine will in regard to men's relations to men are summed in this. Of course, this does not mean, as some people would like to make it mean, that morality is to take the place of religion, but simply that all the precepts touching conduct to men are gathered up for the subjects of the kingdom in this one, " Love worketh no ill to his neighbour : therefore love is the fulfilling of the law."

LESSON XII.

Closing Warnings.

MATTHEW vii. 13-29.

13. "Enter ye in at the strait gate: for wide is the gate, and broad is the way, that leadeth to destruction, and many there be which go in thereat:

14. Because strait is the gate, and narrow is the way, which leadeth unto life, and few there be that find it.

15. Beware of false prophets, which come to you in sheep's clothing, but inwardly they are ravening wolves.

16. Ye shall know them by their fruits. Do men gather grapes of thorns, or figs of thistles?

17. Even so every good tree bringeth forth good fruit; but a corrupt tree bringeth forth evil fruit.

18. A good tree cannot bring forth evil fruit, neither can a corrupt tree bring forth good fruit.

19. Every tree that bringeth not forth good fruit is hewn down, and cast into the fire.

20. Wherefore by their fruits ye shall know them.

21. Not every one that saith unto Me, Lord, Lord, shall enter into the kingdom of heaven: but he that doeth the will of my Father which is in heaven.

22. Many will say to Me in that day, Lord, Lord, have we not prophesied in Thy name? and in Thy name have cast out devils? and in Thy name done many wonderful works?

23. And then will I profess unto them, I never knew you: depart from Me, ye that work iniquity.

24. Therefore whosoever heareth these sayings of Mine, and doeth them, I will liken him unto a wise man, which built his house upon a rock:

25. And the rain descended, and the floods came, and the winds blew, and beat upon that house; and it fell not: for it was founded upon a rock.

26. And every one that heareth these sayings of Mine, and doeth them not, shall be likened unto a foolish man, which built his house upon the sand:

27. And the rain descended, and the floods came, and the

winds blew, and beat upon that house; and it fell: and great was the fall of it.

28. And it came to pass, when Jesus had ended these sayings, the people were astonished at His doctrine:

29. For He taught them as one having authority, and not as the scribes."

WE have reached the close of the Sermon on the Mount, and the verses of this lesson are the concluding warnings and exhortations. They fall into three parts: the two ways; the test and end of false guides; the two houses, which represent the two lives of the true and the feigned disciple, and their fates.

I. The two ways. The metaphor of a path signifying a course of life is common to all languages and teachers, and needs no elucidation. "The Way" was one of the earliest designations for the Christian life, and its use may probably be traced back to these words. We read in the Psalms of "the way everlasting" and of "the way of the wicked" which "perishes." Similarly our Lord here contrasts the two courses of discipleship and of worldliness in four particulars—the entrance, the breadth of the way, the number of travellers, and the end. If we adopt the reading which retains the "for" at the beginning of verse 14, we have, first, the exhortation in verse 13, and then its enforcement by two co-ordinate reasons. This seems better than to suppose that the second "for" gives the reason in the character of the narrow way for the preceding character of the broad one; or, than the adoption of the other reading which substitutes the exclamation "how narrow" for the second "for."

The "gate" is simply the means of entrance on the path. It is refining too much to recall the other use of the figure, which sets Christ forth as the door. Such an interpretation would require to be applied to the other half of the contrast, and would land us in the monstrous explanation which is found in patristic commentaries, that the devil is the wide gate! The meaning is simply, it is easy enough to get into the road of worldly self-indulgence. That gate is open wide always. But the beginning of discipleship is not easy to flesh and blood. The entrance is through a narrow wicket, which can only be passed on condition of leaving a great deal outside that we do not like to part from. Nobody can get in there in a carriage and pair, nor carrying a high head, or bearing honours and possessions. These will catch on the lintels, and have to be dropped. In plain English, a man cannot be a Christian unless he is willing to be small, to give up self, and forsake the world. We see in some pre-historic houses on Scotch moors a low narrow entrance, a foot or so square, which can only be passed by lying down and squeezing through a dark, twisting passage. So the way into the kingdom is too tight to admit any who are not humbled by conscious sin, and ready to cease from self.

> " But easy is the way and passage plain
> To pleasure's palace; it may soon be spied,
> And day and night her doors to all stand open wide."

As are the gates, so are the ways. The one way is narrow, the other broad—that is to say, the course of conduct which belongs to the disciples or subjects of the kingdom is one of restraint, and limitation, constant self-denial, and abstinence, while the path of the worldly man is pleasant to the ignobler self, and permits him to go whithersoever his inclination carries him. "Do as you like" is a broad road. There is ample room to expatiate with such a charter. It is down hill too, and the down grade is always easy travelling. There is a pleasant swing when we shut off steam at the top of the incline, and let the train run down by its own weight, very unlike the laborious puffing of the locomotive on the up-track. Self-indulgence is an easy prescription for conduct, and self-denial is always hard to the worser self who is denied. It would be all very pleasant if the roads led nowhither; but what if the delightful descent stops short at the top of a cliff, and the whole rushing train is sure to go over? It will not be quite so pleasant then. So, our Lord puts the third contrast in regard to the respective ends. The narrow path goes up. That makes it hard, but it leads at last to the broad tablelands where God is the light, and life the possession of the dwellers. The other road is "a primrose way," going merrily down,—but to "the everlasting burning." Life and destruction are opposed. The nature of the one defines that of the other. Life is the blessed being of the spirit united to God, not mere existence. Destruction is the miserable being of the spirit separated from God—a living death.

Awful and strange, then, is the last point of contrast between the crowds on the one, and the few on the other way. The tragic fact that there are few who choose the harder path of duty and discipleship rather than the easier one of self-indulgence gives the real sombreness to life as seen by a thoughtful mind. It is not so much that men are miserable and mortal as that they choose to be sad, which makes their history such a bewilderment and mystery. That is true today—as it was when Christ looked with His sad heart on the multitudes torn and wandering like lost sheep. It should touch all Christian hearts with Christ-like pity ; it should stir them to efforts which would put to shame the feeble work of the Church as we know it. Above all, it should quicken to renewed diligence that we follow not the multitude to do evil, nor ever be ashamed to be in the minority which aspires and endures, and denies self for the kingdom of heaven's sake.

II. *The test and end of false guides.* The warning against the broad road naturally leads to a warning against guides who might tempt to it. By "prophets" is meant not merely predictors, but persons who assume to speak as Divine messengers ; that is (as Christ takes for granted without seeming to think the step a great one), persons who speak in His name. They look like sheep, in their meekness and apparent innocence, but at heart they are wolves, and their work is to tear the flock. Two things are said about them—that they are discovered by their fruits (verses 16-20), and that their end is to be rejected by Him (verses 21-23). The usual explanation of this section is that it refers to heretical teachers, and that conduct is given as the test of doctrine. But not to raise the question whether it is true that the lives of teachers who have departed from the line of orthodoxy have been so gross as to discredit their teachings—it must be observed that such an explanation makes the doctrines the trees, whereas obviously the teachers are the trees ; and also that, throughout the whole context, nothing is said about false doctrines, but, on the contrary, the false prophets are represented as saying, "Lord, Lord," and teaching in His name, and are condemned, not because their teachings are untrue, but because their lives are not in accordance with their teachings. The application of this test, therefore, comes nearer home to orthodox people than they imagine.

Put into plain words, it is that a teacher's life, like any other man's, is the revealer of his character. Good fruit comes from a good tree, evil from an evil. The failure to bear good fruits is as condemnatory as the fact of bearing bad, and leads to as certain destruction. Therefore all Christian teachers, preachers, writers, commentators, and the like are "false prophets," however pure their doctrine, if they are not good men. It is not a test to detect heretics, but to unmask hypocrites, and the worst kind of them, unconscious hypocrites. Many an eloquent preacher, or learned theologian, many a dragon of orthodoxy who used to apply these words complacently to "heretics," who were better men than himself, will find out some day that he would have been wiser to look at home, and see how they flashed a terrible light into the hollowness of his own religion. They are a warning to the flock as well as the shepherds, and bid them beware of any man however golden-mouthed and sound in the faith, who has not the credentials of a holy, fruitful, Christ-like life. It is a solemn thought that a man may be a "false prophet" and a "ravening wolf," while others think him, and he thinks himself, a minister of Christ, and a pillar of the Church. Each of us listening to such words should humbly say, "Lord, is it I?"

The end of the false guides is given in words terrible when we think what lips spoke then. Distinctly does our Lord claim in them to be the Judge of the world, whose knowledge of each heart pierces through all shows, whose sentence is final, from whom to be shut out is to perish. Do the admirers of "the pure morality of the Sermon on the Mount" take this part of it into their creeds? But, apart from that, observe that these solemn words distinctly describe not heretical, but hypocritical teachers. The weight of their condemnation is that, while proclaiming Christ's name, and calling Him Lord, and doing mighty deeds for Him, they had no real union with Him, that He never knew them with that knowledge which is friendship, although He knew them only too well, and that they are still perhaps even at that awful hour workers of iniquity.

So profound has been their self-deception that they appear before the Judge with confidence, and present the deeds which had won them credit among men as His messengers in evidence of their claim to acceptance. Is that wholly drapery, or may it not teach a lesson that may well make us all tremble, as to the possible surprises of that day?

III. The two houses and their fates. The principles laid down in the preceding words do not apply to teachers only, but to all the subjects of the kingdom, and to all who hear its laws. Therefore, Christ here closes the whole with the solemn extension of them to "every one . . . which heareth these sayings of Mine." The same contrast is still presented between the mere hearer and the doer. Obedience it still set forth as the only safety.

Consider first the house on the rock. We are all builders. Day by day we lay fresh courses of masonry. The houses we build are our characters, or, we may say, ourselves. There may be much beauty in the design, much convenience and grace in the building. We do well to spend pains and toil on it, but the underground work is the main thing in estimating stability. No house is stronger than its foundation. The rock may mean nothing more than the solid foundation laid for a life in obedience and submission of will to Christ's commands; but, when we remember the frequent use of the metaphor to signify Christ Himself, and take into account the passage in Isaiah, which gives form to our Lord's words here, and in which we read of the "sure foundation," the "precious corner stone," we can scarcely but give a deeper meaning to the emblem, and draw the lesson that real building on Christ means practical obedience to His commandments. Only such a life is firm whatever storm comes. The description of the tempest is singularly vivid, whether we refer it to the calamities of life, or to the last judgment regarded as a test of the stability of the structure. All parts of the building are assailed at once; as Bengel says, "Rain on the roof; flood against the foundation; winds on the walls." It stands, not because of the strength of the walls, but because of the immovable firmness of the foundation. "He that believeth shall not make haste." There shall be no need for him, at the last moment, while the storm is raging, to run from the tumbling ruin, to try to find some shelter elsewhere. That last judgment shall sift and try every man's work of what sort it is, and if ours stand, it will be because we built on Jesus, and, by faith which wrought obedience, reared on the God-laid foundation, other than which can no man lay, the structure of a holy life.

The dark contrasted picture is with solemn emphasis

given in almost the same words. The uniformity is broken by three differences, which by the uniformity are flung into startling prominence. The man is "foolish" —alas for those, whom the infinite wisdom must call by the name which He forbade us to use! (Matt. v. 22.) His foundation is "sand"—the loose foundation of a mere shifting profession which will all be swilled away when the flood comes. When the house is built, you cannot see the foundation. There are lives which look like true Christian lives, and are not. The houses stand in a row in the street, and nobody can detect which is which. But the man who built knows, if he will be honest, and take the trouble to examine. We can ascertain what our foundation is, if we will. Better to do it now, though it may involve pain and shame, than to have the discovery flashed upon our lazy self-complacency by the wild tempest. "It fell" is the last difference. One little "not" left out expresses the awful contrariety in the experience of the two men, whose houses, perhaps, stood side by side in the same row for years.

So the sermon ends. These two pictures are burned in on our imagination. May they sink into our hearts, and lead us all to build our else fleeting and unstable lives on the "living Stone," to whom coming, we also shall share in His nature and "as living stones" be "built up."

> "Lo! on the solid rock I stand,
> And all beside is shifting sand."

LESSON XIII.

The Centurion and the Captain of the Lord's Host.

Matt. viii. 5-13.

5. "And when Jesus was entered into Capernaum, there came unto Him a centurion, beseeching him,

6. And saying, Lord, my servant lieth at home sick of the palsy, grievously tormented.

7. And Jesus saith unto him, I will come and heal him.

8. The centurion answered and said, Lord, I am not worthy that Thou shouldest come under my roof: but speak the word only, and my servant shall be healed.

9. For I am a man under authority, having soldiers under me: and I say to this man, Go, and he goeth; and to another, Come, and he cometh; and to my servant, Do this, and he doeth it.

10. When Jesus heard it, He marvelled, and said to them that followed, Verily I say unto you, I have not found so great faith, no, not in Israel.

11. And I say unto you, That many shall come from the east and west, and shall sit down with Abraham, and Isaac, and Jacob, in the kingdom of heaven.

12. But the children of the kingdom shall be cast out into outer darkness: there shall be weeping and gnashing of teeth.

13. And Jesus said unto the centurion, Go thy way; and as thou hast believed, so be it done unto thee. And his servant was healed in the selfsame hour."

IN chapter iv. 23 Matthew sketches the work of Jesus in Galilee as "preaching the gospel of the kingdom, and healing all manner of sickness." The Sermon on the Mount is the example of the former, and the long procession of miracles in chapters viii. and ix. are, in like manner, specimens of the latter. They are nine in number, if we reckon the miracle of the raising of

Centurion and Captain of the Lord's Host.

Jairus' daughter, and that of the cure of the woman which is narrated in the middle of the account of it, as one. These nine are broken up into three groups of three each, separated by narratives of their effect on the bystanders. The present lesson is the second miracle of the first group. The key-note is the great word "faith," which is used here for the first time in the gospel.

I. Note the man and his faith. He was a foreigner and a heathen. The Herod who then ruled over Galilee had his troops officered by Romans, of whom this centurion was probably one, in command of a small garrison at Capernaum. If we put together the traits of character given by Matthew and Luke, we get a lovable picture of a man with a much tenderer heart than might be expected to beat beneath the armour of a mercenary soldier, set to overawe a sullen people. Like so many of the better spirits of that strange era, he had been drawn to "love our nation," certainly not because of their amiability, but because of the revelation which they possessed. By his own wealth, or by the exercise of his influence, he had built them a synagogue, and thereby expressed his adhesion to their worship, and won the confidence even of the suspicious elders. His solicitude for his servant bespeaks a nature from which neither the harshness of military life nor the natural carelessness about a slave's welfare had been able to banish the sweetness. The crowning trait of his character is his humility, which is manifest in Matthew, and even more conspicuous in Luke's version of the story, where he does not venture to approach the miracle-working Rabbi, but sends the elders to intercede for him. Such a character, springing up in heathenism like a rare flower on some waste unsheltered open, puts to shame the results of centuries of patient culture by the great husbandman as shown in the Jewish nation. One can scarcely help noticing the common type of character, in different degrees, shown in the centurions of the New Testament, this man, the anonymous one who stood by the cross, and was more open to its teachings than rulers and priests, Cornelius, and the kindly Julius who had Paul in charge on his voyage.

The centurion's appeal, as given by Matthew, does not say what he wants, but simply tells the tale of suffering, as if that were enough to move Christ's heart. He will not take upon him to prescribe by requesting, but casts himself, with his unspoken desire, on a compassion which he believed was ready to well up at the sight of sorrow, and needed no entreaty to move it to activity. The sad sisters at Bethany sent a like message to Jesus, but their confidence was the growth of years of close friendship. This man's was greater because its foundation was less.

Christ's answer is full of consciousness of power, as well as of willingness to meet the unbreathed prayer. He volunteers to come where He had not been asked. He refuses to go when His going seems made an indispensable condition of His miracle, as in the story of the healing of the "nobleman's" son at Capernaum, which some critics perversely make out to be the same as this incident. His wisdom may be trusted to decide when it is best to exceed and when to fall short of our wishes. In both cases our good determines His action. Here the promise to come is spoken to evoke the noble confession which follows, and so to give the centurion a higher blessing than his servant's healing, even a self-conscious and uttered faith.

That confession begins with humble acknowledgment of unworthiness, and rises to perhaps the clearest and deepest conception of Christ's authority over all the forces of the universe which was ever attained during His earthly life. The centurion had learned the omnipotence of the word of command. One syllable from the general, and the legion moved, as animated by one mind, and each man in its ranks was ready to "go," though it were to death. Prompt, unquestioning obedience is the redeeming virtue, which, amid all its devilishness, war promotes. His rough trade had become to this man, as he thought about it, a means of reaching this wonderful estimate of Christ. Even he himself, though but captain of a poor hundred, the sixtieth part of a legion, and having himself to obey, could secure compliance without a murmur with his orders. Is he drawing a parallel or a contrast between himself and Jesus? Does he think of Him as under authority, or as supreme? The Revised Version has replaced an omitted "also" in verse ix., which seems to make the former alternative the more probable. We could scarcely expect from the centurion, however profound his conception, the clear recognition of Christ's Divine sovereignty which His closest followers had not clearly grasped. It is much more in accordance with the probabilities of the case that he should have thought of Jesus, as, like himself, subordinate, and yet clothed with absolute power over His soldiers and servants, or, in other words, as a messenger of God, to whom had been given command over all physical agents. Nor does the clearest conception of our Lord's divinity forbid that view: for the Son is subject to the Father, and all power is given to Him. But the centurion's conception of the manner of exercising the power is the remarkable thing here. A word is enough; and here he anticipates the profoundest teaching of theology and science. "He spake, and it was done," is the full statement of God's way of working in creation, and in that preservation of creatures which is a continued creation. The mere forth-putting of the Divine will, without media or other Divine act, is adequate to produce and sustain the universe. This sign manual of deity is stamped on Christ's works. He rebukes diseases, and they cease. He speaks to howling tempests and roaring billows, and there is a great calm. He flings a word into the grave, and Lazarus stumbles out, dazzled, into the light. All creatures, all forces of the universe, are His soldiers; and at the bare word of that great "imperator" the embattled and ordered hosts move and act. No grander, truer thought of Christ's sway, its sweep and its manner, can be attained, than this heathen soldier had learned from the dreadful instrument of war as a part of which he was at once subordinate and authoritative.

II. The eulogium on faith. The confession is followed by praise from Christ's lips, which is praise indeed. Contrast His calm acceptance of the highest place which could be given Him with Elisha's "Am I God, to kill and to make alive?" or with Peter's "Why look ye so earnestly on us?" And remember that Jesus here does the very thing for which Moses was shut out from the land, and judge whether this demeanour is consistent with humility or reverence, except on one hypothesis of His nature. "He marvelled," as we read again that He did at the Jews' unbelief. We cannot thread the mysteries of His participation in our human limitations, but it is more profitable to note that His wonder was excited by the unbelief of those who had so much light, and by the swift and strong faith of him who had had so little. That all-important word is spoken for the first time now. Faith is the fruit which He had come seeking. What a pathetic tone of disappointed search echoes in the sad close of the sentence, " No, not in Israel "! That vine which had for so long been the husbandman's care, offers even to His loving eye but wild grapes, when He looked closely beneath the leaves of profession and ceremonial for grapes. This wild vine, left to grow as it would, has what the other lacks. Therefore is the centurion's faith praised as "great." It was great in the clearness of the belief which it included; great in the difficulties which it had overcome; great in the rapidity of growth on so slight a knowledge of Jesus; great in the firmness and completeness of its moral part, confidence great in the humility which it produced. Such faith, so self-distrustful, so clear in exaltation of His power, so child-like in its reliance on Him, is what He seeks for in us all; and where He finds it, He rejoices as a thirsty traveller who "finds grapes in the wilderness."

The centurion was, in some sense, the first-fruits of the Gentiles, and our Lord's sad prescience sees in him the forerunner of a long train who shall exercise a faith which puts the children of the kingdom to shame. It is remarkable that this early intimation of the transference of the kingdom to the Gentiles should not be found in Luke's Gospel, where we might have expected to meet it, and should be in Matthew's. But it was distinctly part of his purpose, as the evangelist who had most to say about the kingdom of heaven, to make sun-clear the condition of belonging to it, as being faith, and faith only. And these fateful prophecies were even more relevant to the scope of his Gospel than to that of Luke's.

Mark the use by our Lord of that "Come." Then He sits King at the head of the table, and to enter the kingdom is to come to Him. The metaphor of the feast was familiar to His hearers, as expressive of the satisfaction of all the hunger of the spirit, and of the glad companionship of the future days. It is no part of His purpose here to give the more fully developed teaching which He associated with it at a later period. But while He leaves untouched the when and the where, His reticent words are terribly distinct on the two points which Jewish pride and trust in their descent from Abraham needed to be driven into their unwilling ears. The Gentiles from every corner of the world shall be there, and recognised by Abraham as his children. Those to whom the kingdom was offered shall, some of them, not be there. What could be plainer, when taken in connection with the immediately preceding eulogium on the centurion's faith, than this teaching, that the one condition of entrance into the kingdom, whether in its imperfect manifestation on earth, or in its complete and final form hereafter, is just that which the centurion had, and Israel had not,—namely, faith in Him? This teaching is the complement, not the contradiction, of that in the last words of the Sermon on the Mount. There the condition was, "Not every one that saith unto Me, Lord, Lord; ... but he that doeth the will of My Father;" and, for doing that will, the first requisite is faith, without which there may be the formal acknowledgment of Jesus as Lord, but no obedience.

It does not become us to enlarge on the terror that lies half disclosed in the awful words which describe the fate of those who do not belong to the kingdom. The lighted banqueting-house is ringed round with darkness. It is darkness, because it is outside the circle of the light. The darkness is but, as it were, the externalising of the dispositions of those who are in it. Darkness reigned in them here, the darkness of sin; and now they dwell in darkness of sorrow, the creation of their own evil natures. They are "cast out"; therefore they were once in. If they were not members of the kingdom by the submission of their wills, and the glad acceptance of the King, they were in it, by being surrounded by invitations and offers of its blessings, and by being in close contact with its earthly form. The nearer a man is to that kingdom here, the further sunken will he be in the darkness hereafter. Out of the blackness come sounds of woe,—"the weeping," as the original has it, on which Bengel makes the pregnant remark, "The article emphatic. In this life sorrow is not yet sorrow." Nor is it only sorrow that broods there, but gnashing of teeth, the token of unavailing passion. The picture is darkly shaded. Let us remember who it was that spoke it, even one who "speaks that He knows," and whose every word throbbed with love; and let us take heed lest, in speculating about the duration and the manner of future retribution, we lose our sense of the certainty and awfulness of the fact.

III. The answer to faith. " Go thy way ; and as thou hast believed, so be it done unto thee." Christ delights to have His path marked out for Him by faith. When distrust prescribes His course, it is presumption ; when faith does, it is but putting Him in mind of His own character or promise. These great words of Christ's give the key of His storehouse into our hands, and lay down the law to which He rigidly adheres. Our faith is the measure of our reception. The more we trust, the more we can contain of His gift ; and the more we can contain, the more we shall surely possess. As St. Bernard beautifully says, "He puts the oil of His mercy into the vase of our trust,"—and the larger the vase, the fuller the stream which He pours into it. As long as we bring vessels, the blessing runs, like the oil into the widow's cruse. When we cease to hold up our emptiness to the fountain, it stays. "Ye have not, because ye ask not." If our Christian life be shrunken, and our graces feeble, it is only because we have not gone to Him for fresh supplies. Little faith means little grace.

Here Christ lets the man prescribe the very manner of His working. When the "nobleman" asked Him to come down ere his child died, He would not, because the request spoke of a low conception of His power which He elevated by the refusal. But the centurion's willingness to be content with a word showed a strong faith, which He confirms by demonstrating that it had not thought too loftily of Him. So He often disappoints our expectations of the manner of His working, when these are built on an unworthy or tremulous faith, but always does so in such a fashion as that our confidence in Him may be increased, if we duly consider His dealings with us. But He complies with the desires of a strong faith, which is ready to do without visible signs of His work, and does so in such a fashion as that we can always say, "I did not trust Him too much, nor think Him able to do what I find He cannot." The education of faith is His aim in all His dealings with us, and He disappoints, or answers, or over-answers it, in subordination to that great purpose.

LESSON XIV.

The Peace-bringer in the World of Nature.

MATTHEW viii. 18-27.

18. "Now when Jesus saw great multitudes about Him, He gave commandment to depart unto the other side.
19. And a certain scribe came, and said unto Him, Master, I will follow Thee whithersoever Thou goest.
20. And Jesus said unto Him, The foxes have holes, and the birds of the air have nests; but the Son of man hath not where to lay His head.
21. And another of His disciples said unto Him, Lord, suffer me first to go and bury my father.
22. But Jesus said unto Him, Follow Me: and let the dead bury their dead.
23. And when He was entered into a ship, His disciples followed Him.
24. And, behold, there arose a great tempest in the sea, insomuch that the ship was covered with the waves: but He was asleep.
25. And His disciples came to Him, and awoke Him, saying, Lord, save us: we perish.
26. And He saith unto them, Why are ye fearful, O ye of little faith? Then He arose, and rebuked the winds and the sea; and there was a great calm.
27. But the men marvelled, saying, What manner of man is this, that even the winds and the sea obey Him!"

WE have already pointed out that the three triads of miracles in this series are separated by paragraphs narrating their effects on the bystanders. This lesson includes the landing-place, if we may call it so, between the first and second group, and the first miracle of the second triplet. It falls, therefore, into two distinct portions, only connected in time with each other,—our Lord's apparently opposite treatment of two men, and the miracle of stilling the tempest.

I. We have Christ repelling the too willing, and drawing to Himself the half-reluctant. The miracles of the first group, and many others, done at the same time, but only mentioned in the gross, had caused a stir in the comparatively small town of Capernaum, to escape from which Christ bade His disciples get the boat ready to cross the lake. The prospect of His going affected these two men in opposite ways. It stirred the scribe to a too swift and lightly formed resolve. He could not bear the thought of losing Jesus from his sight, and so, in a fit of well-meaning and perfectly sincere emotion, he volunteered brave words, whose very unconditionalness showed that he did not know what he was promising so glibly. The other man, already a disciple, perhaps in the looser application of the word, shrinks from leaving home, especially after what Jesus had said to the scribe. He had a good reason, for his father lay dead, and surely a son's first duty was to lay his parent in his grave. Clearly the two men represent opposite types of character which result in discipleship imperfect in opposite ways. Apparently, too, the request of the second is closely connected with the prospect of a wandering life, opened by the reply of Jesus to the first. The former is a man of impulse, sanguine, enthusiastic in the bad sense, ready to promise more than he has weighed. The other is somewhat slow to move, deliberate, very conscious of duties which keep him from making the light vows of the other man, and influenced by ties which to himself seem of prior obligation. It would not be fair to say that he belonged to the great class who always say to every duty in turn, "Suffer me first to do something else, and then——" and so postpone for ever what, all the while, they fancy themselves intending to do. But he was on the road to join that useless band. Both men were sincere. They meant what they said. The one quite thought that he could follow anywhere; the other quite intended to come after Christ as soon as the stone was rolled to the door of his father's grave. We do them injustice, and lose the value of Christ's teaching, unless we recognise that.

But Jesus saw deeper than they did. He would not have poured cold water on enthusiasm which was fervent enough to burn on; nor have forbidden a son's heart the solace of laying his father's grey hairs in the grave, if that would have ended his preliminaries to discipleship. The scribe's offer is precisely what Jesus longs to hear from us all. A heart's devotion is too grateful to Him to be put aside, and His answer to the scribe is no refusal of His allegiance nor rebuke of His enthusiasm, but a sobering statement of what is involved in his offer, made, not to drive him away, but to dissipate the froth of his emotional vow, and to consolidate his lightly formed intention into a grave, fixed purpose. He tells him plainly what the conditions of His life are. The lower creatures have holes, and the birds roosting-places (not nests); but Jesus, who is the Son of man, whom Daniel the prophet saw as Messiah, and in whom humanity finds its ideal, has no home. It was literally true about His earthly life. He was born in a hired manger, He slept in others' houses, His head was laid in a borrowed grave. It is true in idea of all His followers. Man's prerogative among the creatures, each fitted for their environment, is to be a wanderer, smitten with the sense of disproportion between himself and his surroundings, and if he has not learned what that means, weighed upon and cursed with endless unrest. Christ's followers had to share His roaming life, when He was here. They have in all periods to be sojourners, declaring plainly that they seek a country. No man is fit for Christ's army who has not made up his mind to that sort of life. So this scribe had to be taught what he was vowing with so light a heart, and how much weary homeless wandering he was accepting by his " whithersoever " thou goest. Christ did not wish to send him away, but to knit him to Himself by this for ever. It is often the best way to draw men to a course, to put its difficulties plainly before them. The kindest treatment which a too easy resolve to high and noble life can receive is to cool it down; for cooling is condensation, and the fleeting vapour may thereby become water which shall flow musically through a life.

The other man in like manner got the treatment best suited to quicken his slowness into resolved surrender, and to deliver him from the unsuspected ties which held him back. Jesus would never have hindered his wish if there had not been something behind it, which, very probably, the man himself did not suspect. It is the " more than me " which lurks unseen in pure affections, that He wars against, because it wars against us. Therefore the sternness of the command, made still more severe by the comparison of physical death with the moral death of those who are not His disciples. Whoever is by the purest love or the most manifest earthly duty kept away from Jesus, had need ponder this command, and leave a father on his bier, or a bride at the altar, if they come between His Lord and him. Thus both these two cases, while opposite in defects and in mode of treatment, run up at last to the one principle, that the obligations of discipleship are of paramount stringency, calling on the one hand for the most sober, well-considered forsaking of all besides, and, on the other, for the most complete and immediate subordination of even the sacredest earthly duties, if these push themselves in before our surrender to Him.

II. The stilling of the tempest. The second group of miracles shows us Christ as the Prince of peace, and that in three regions—the material, the superhuman, and the moral. He stills the tempest, casts out demons, and forgives sins, thus quieting nature, spirit, and conscience.

Mountain-girdled lakes are exposed to sudden storms from the wind sweeping down the glens. Such a one comes roaring down as the little boat, probably belonging to James and John, is labouring across the six or seven miles to the eastern side. Matthew describes the boat as it would appear from shore, as being "covered," and lost to sight by the breaking waves. Mark, who is Peter's mouthpiece, describes the desperate plight as one on board knew it, and says the boat was "filling." It must have been a serious gale which frightened a crew who had spent all their lives on the lake.

Note Christ's sleep in the storm. His calm slumber is contrasted with the hurly-burly of the tempest and the fear of the crew. It was the sleep of physical exhaustion after a hard day's work. He was too tired to keep awake, or to be disturbed by the tumult. It is a sign of His true manhood, of His toil up to the very edge of His strength; a characteristic of His life of service, which we do not make as prominent in our thoughts as we should.

Peace-bringer in the World of Nature.

It is also a sign of His calm conscience and pure heart. Jonah slept through the storm because his conscience was stupefied; but Christ, as a tired child laying its head on its mother's lap.

That sleep may have a symbolical meaning for us. Though Christ is present, the storm comes, and He sleeps through it. Lazarus dies, and He makes no sign of sympathy. Peter lies in prison, and not till the hammers of the carpenters putting up the gibbet for to-morrow are heard, does deliverance come. He delays His help that He may try our faith and quicken our prayers. The boat may be covered with the waves, and He sleeps on, but He will wake before it sinks. He sleeps, but He never over-sleeps, and there are no too-lates with Him.

Note next the awaking cry of fear. The broken abruptness of their appeal reveals the urgency of the case in the experienced eyes of these fishermen. Their summons is a curious mixture of fear and faith. "Save us" is the language of faith; "we perish," is that of fear. That strange blending of opposites is often repeated by us. The office of faith is to suppress fear. But the origin of faith is often in fear, and we are driven to trust just because we are so much afraid. A faith which does not wholly suppress fear may still be most real; and the highest faith has ever the consciousness that unless Christ help, and that speedily, we perish.

So note next the gentle remonstrance. There is something very majestic in the tranquillity of our Lord's awaking, and, if we follow Matthew's order, in His addressing Himself first to the disciples' weakness, and letting the storm rage on. It can do no harm, and for the present may blow as it listeth, while He gives the trembling disciples a lesson. Observe how lovingly our Lord meets an imperfect faith. He has no rebuke for their rude awaking. He does not find fault with them for being "fearful," but for being "so fearful" as to let their fear cover their faith, just as the waves were doing the boat. He pityingly recognises the struggle in their souls, and their possession of some spark which He would fain blow into a flame. He shows them and us the reason for overwhelming fear as being the deficiency in our faith. And He casts all into the form of a question, thus softening rebuke, and calming their terrors by the appeal to their common sense. Fear is irrational if we can exercise faith. It is mere bravado to say "I will not be afraid," for this awful universe is full of occasions for just terror; but it is the voice of sober reason which says "I will trust, and not be afraid." Christ answers His own question in the act of putting it. Ye are of little faith, that is why ye are so fearful.

Note, next, the word that calms the storm. Christ yields to the cry of an imperfect faith, and so strengthens it. If He did not, what would become of any of us? He does not quench the dimly burning wick, but tends it and feeds it with oil—by His inward gifts and by His answers to prayer—till it burns up clear and smokeless, a faith without fear. Even smoke needs but a higher temperature to flame; and fear which is mingled with faith needs but a little more heat to be converted into radiance of trust. That is precisely what Christ does by this miracle. His royal word is all-powerful. We see Him rising in the stern of the fishing-boat, and sending His voice into the howling darkness, and wind and waves cower at His feet like dogs that know their master. As in the healing of the centurion's servant, we have the token of divinity in that His bare word is able to produce effects in the natural realm. As He lay asleep He showed the weakness of manhood; but He woke to manifest the power of indwelling divinity. So it is always in His life, where, side by side with the signs of humiliation and participation in man's weakness, we ever have tokens of His divinity breaking through the veil. All this power is put forth at the cry of timid men. The storm was meant to move to terror; terror was meant to quicken faith and lead to prayer; prayer was meant to bring the miracle—the result was complete and immediate. No after-swell disturbed the placid waters when the wind dropped. There had been "a great tempest," and now there was "a great calm," as they floated peacefully to their landing-place beneath the shadow of the hills. The wilder the tempest, the profounder the subsequent repose.

All this is a true symbol of our individual lives, as well as of the history of the Church. Storms will come, and He may seem to be heedless. He is ever awakened by our cry, which needs not to be pure faith to bring the answer, but may be strangely intertwined of faith and fear. "The Lord will help, . . . and that right early, . . . and the peace that He brings is peace indeed. So it may be with us amid the struggles of life. So may it be with us when "the voyage on this storm-tossed sea of time is done!" "They cry unto the Lord in their trouble. He maketh the storm a calm, so that the waves thereof are still. Then are they glad because they be quiet; so He bringeth them unto their desired haven."

LESSON XV.

The Peace-bringer in the World of Conscience.

MATTHEW ix. 1-8.

1. "And He entered into a ship, and passed over, and came into His own city.
2. And, behold, they brought to Him a man sick of the palsy, lying on a bed: and Jesus seeing their faith said unto the sick of the palsy; Son, be of good cheer; thy sins be forgiven thee.
3. And, behold, certain of the scribes said within themselves, This man blasphemeth.
4. And Jesus knowing their thoughts said, Wherefore think ye evil in your hearts?
5. For whether is easier, to say, Thy sins be forgiven thee; or to say, Arise, and walk?
6. But that ye may know that the Son of man hath power on earth to forgive sins, (then saith He to the sick of the palsy,) Arise, take up thy bed, and go unto thine house.
7. And he arose, and departed to his house.
8. But when the multitudes saw it, they marvelled, and glorified God, which had given such power unto men."

IN this miracle we have our Lord set forth as the Bringer of peace to the sin-laden conscience. It is the last and, in some sense, the highest of the three miracles of the second group, for it is a grander work to calm the agonised conscience than to still the tempest or bid demons flee. The most important part of the story is not the mere healing of the bodily disease, but the accompanying forgiveness. Our Lord Himself teaches us in it that His physical miracles are secondary, and that that work which He is ready to do to-day to all is far greater than they.

I. Note the apparently irrelevant answer which Christ gives to the unspoken petition of the paralytic and his friends; "Son, be of good cheer; thy sins be forgiven thee," seems miles away from their want. It was far from their wish, but yet the shortest road to it. Christ here goes straight to the heart of the need, when He passes by the disease and speaks pardon. Probably the palsy was the result of fast living,—"a sin of flesh, avenged in kind." Perhaps, too, whatever his friends may have wanted for him, the poor man himself dimly knew that forgiveness was his most pressing want. In his weary languor and idleness, sober thoughts drawing to penitence may have been busy. Christ would not thus abruptly have offered the pearl of pardon to an altogether unprepared heart.

So the first lesson of this incident is that pardon is man's deepest need. The most important relation is our relation to God. If it be wrong, all is wrong; if it be right, all is or will come right. Whatever be our surface diversities of culture, position, and the like, we are all alike at bottom in this, that we have sinned, and need forgiveness. There is the fountain of all the bitter sorrows that flow in every life. The bulk of our griefs come from our sins, and the remainder are needed because of our sins, in order to discipline and purify. Hence the profound wisdom of Christ in this incident, and in that wider work of which His dealing with this single poor cripple may be taken as a symbol. The gospel cures sorrow second, and sin first. It does not potter and peddle on the surface, but cuts deep down to the hidden ulcer. It lets secondary symptoms alone, and, like a wise physician, deals with the disease in its stronghold. Its remedies pierce to the centre, and work out towards the circumference. Grapes and easy beds are good, but a cholera patient needs something more. The first thing to do in order to heal men's misery is to make them pure; and the first thing to do in order to make them pure, is to assure them of the Divine forgiveness for the past impurity.

We must go a great deal deeper than the reformation of manners or the culture of the intellect or the taste, or than political or economical changes, before we touch the real reason of the misery that is in the world. One would not say a word even to seem to depreciate the value of such things, or to breathe a whisper against the enthusiasm of many earnest workers in these directions. The dismal swamp which threatens to engulf so much of our modern civilisation is formidable enough to call for many forms of attack and different ways of draining it, and Christianity should be full of ardent interest in them all. But whoever forgets, Christians should not forget that the fountain from which its bitter waters come is sin, and that we shall only effectually deal with the swamp when we drain off the sin. The true "saviour of society" is he who can go to his brother with the divine declaration of pardon on his lips. That will bring new energy into palsied limbs—and new hope into despairing hearts.

II. The next step in the story brings out that forgiveness is an exclusively Divine act.

A crowd of religious formalists of the first water were sitting by, collected together as a kind of ecclesiastical inquisition to scent heresy in Christ's teaching. They had no perception of the dewy pity in Christ's looks, nor

Less. XV.] **Peace-bringer in the World of Conscience.**

of the nascent hope glimmering in the paralytic's dim eye, but fastened upon this one thing, "This man blasphemeth,"—the blasphemy consisting, as the other evangelists explain, more in Christ's assuming authority to pardon, which they rightly regarded as belonging to God only. No people are so blind to the radiant beauty of lofty character, or so coldly insensible to the wants of sad humanity, as religious formalists, whose religion is mostly red tape, tied round men's limbs to keep them from getting at things they would like. But yet these scribes were perfectly right. Forgiveness is an exclusively Divine prerogative; for sin has to do with God only, and none but He against whom it has been committed can forgive it. The same deed may be a sin, a vice, and a crime, according as we regard its aspects towards God, towards morals, or towards law. As sin, God can forgive it; as a breach of ethical law, there is no forgiveness, for ethics cannot pardon; as a breach of the law of the land, the supreme power may remit penalties. That Divine forgiveness is more than merely remitting penalties, or shutting up some more or less material hell. It is, in its deepest meaning, the free flow of the Divine love, unchecked by the sinner's sin. Pardon is love rising above the ice dam which we have piled between us and it, and pouring over it into our hearts. When we forgive our child, what does it mean? Sometimes, not always, the remission of penalties, but always the remission of the worst penalty, the frown on the father's face, the sense of displeasure weighing on the child's heart, and the unimpeded flow of the parent's love. So God's pardon often leaves some of the natural consequences, which are the penalties of our sins, in order that we may hate and avoid the evil; but it brings the assurance that there is nothing in God's heart towards the sinner but pure and perfect love. All the barriers to its flow are removed by God's own act. None but God can do that.

And He can do it, though we hear now that forgiveness is impossible, because a man must reap what he has sown. It is true that the consequences of evil deeds considered as vice or as crime are not averted. It would be too bold to say, if we believe in a God, that He cannot avert them; but, as a matter of fact, they usually remain. But the consequences of evil considered as sin are averted, and of these the chiefest is the alienation from God, and the exposure to His righteous displeasure. Why such forgiveness as consists essentially in the restoration of a sinner to the Divine favour, and in the consequent abolition of the darkest results of his sin, and the modification into fatherly chastisement of such as remain, should be impossible, it would be difficult to say.

III. The next step in the narrative teaches us that Jesus Christ claims and exercises this Divine prerogative of pardon. Mark His answer to the cavillers. He admits their premises entirely. If Christ was only a man like us, standing in the same relation to God's forgiveness as other religious teachers do, and only declaring, as any man might, that God forgives, why, in the name of common sense and veracity, did He not turn round to these scribes, and say so? A devout and earnest man would have said, "I am not speaking blasphemies. You mistake my meaning. I know that God only can forgive sins; and I am only telling my poor brother here that God forgives his." But that is not His reply. In effect He says, "Yes, you are quite right. No man can forgive sins, but God only. I forgive sins; who, then, think you I am? It is easy to say, Thy sins be forgiven thee, far easier than to say, Take up thy bed and walk, because you can verify the accomplishment in the one case, and not in the other. The two sentences are equally easy to pronounce. The two things, pardoning and healing, are equally impossible for a man to do; but the difference between them is that you can see with your own eyes whether or not the one is done, and you cannot see the other. I will do the visible impossibility, and then you can judge whether I have the right to assert that I can do the invisible."

These words of our Lord's, then, bring us up to a sharp alternative. I know that it is not the best way of arguing to force an antagonist's position by a dilemma, but sometimes it is fair, and useful; and it is so here. We hear much talk about the beauty and lowly devoutness of Jesus from those who do not accept His Divinity. And it is worth while to insist that His claims to Divinity were urged in such a fashion that, if they are denied, it is impossible to save the beauty and lowliness of His character. Either the scribes were right, or Jesus was Divine. Either He was a blasphemer, or He was God manifest in the flesh. The whole context forbids us to take these words, "Thy sins be forgiven thee," as anything less than the act of Divine love wiping out transgressions; and if Jesus Christ claimed to do that, no hypothesis of His nature can save His character for the admiration of men, except that which sees in Him God revealed in humanity, the world's Judge, from whose hand the world may receive Divine forgiveness.

IV. Christ here brings visible facts into the witness-box, in attestation of His invisible powers. Of course, the miracle was such a witness in a special way. It is less than that which it witnesses. Christ's permanent work of forgiveness and sanctifying is higher than all signs and wonders, and these are honoured when they bear witness to that. But we may make a more general application of this principle of the visible evidences of invisible powers. Are not the results of every earnest effort to carry the message of forgiveness to men, in homes made Bethels, passions tamed, and lives elevated, witnesses of the reality of Christ's claim to exercise the Divine prerogative of forgiveness? All the difference between Christendom, imperfectly Christianised as it is, and heathendom, attests Him as the Fountain of the invisible good which has passed into visibility in the secondary results of the gospel, which the blindest can see, and the least spiritual can appraise. This rod has budded, at all events. Let the magicians do the same with their enchantments. The world takes its notions of the power of Christianity from the lives of Christians. They are the Bibles which most men read. So a solemn responsibility is laid on them to take care that they worthily represent the redeeming and ennobling power of their Master.

The greatest lesson of this narrative is, Do not waste time trying to purify the stream twenty miles down, but go to the Fountain-head. Our palsies and fevers, the impotence of our wills towards good, and our diseased ardour towards evil, with their consequent misery and restlessness in all regions of life, can never be cured till we go to Christ, the forgiving Christ, and let Him lay

Peace-bringer in the World of Conscience.

His hand upon us, and speak from His sweet and infallible lips the word that works as a charm, "Son, thy sins be forgiven thee." Then shall the eyes of the blind be opened; then shall the lame man leap as an hart; then limitations, sorrows, miseries, shall pass away, and forgiveness will bear fruit in joy and power, in health and peace.

LESSON XVI.

The Touch of Faith and the Touch of Christ.

MATT. ix. 18-31.

18. "While He spake these things unto them, behold, there came a certain ruler, and worshipped Him, saying, My daughter is even now dead: but come and lay Thy hand upon her, and she shall live.

19. And Jesus arose, and followed him, and so did His disciples.

20. And, behold, a woman, which was diseased with an issue of blood twelve years, came behind Him, and touched the hem of His garment:

21. For she said within herself, If I may but touch His garment, I shall be whole.

22. But Jesus turned Him about, and when He saw her, He said, Daughter, be of good comfort; thy faith hath made thee whole. And the woman was made whole from that hour.

23. And when Jesus came into the ruler's house, and saw the minstrels and the people making a noise,

24. He said unto them, Give place: for the maid is not dead, but sleepeth. And they laughed Him to scorn.

25. But when the people were put forth, He went in, and took her by the hand, and the maid arose.

26. And the fame hereof went abroad into all that land.

27. And when Jesus departed thence, two blind men followed Him, crying, and saying, Thou Son of David, have mercy on us.

28. And when He was come into the house, the blind men came to Him: and Jesus saith unto them, Believe ye that I am able to do this? They said unto Him, Yea, Lord.

29. Then touched He their eyes, saying, According to your faith be it unto you.

30. And their eyes were opened; and Jesus straitly charged them, saying, See that no man know it.

31. But they, when they were departed, spread abroad His fame in all that country."

THE three miracles included in the present lesson belong to the last group of this series. Those of the second group were all effected by Christ's word.

Those now to be considered are all effected by touch. The first two are intertwined. The narrative of the healing of the woman is embedded in the account of the raising of Jairus's daughter.

Mark the impression of calm consciousness of power and leisurely dignity produced by Christ's having time to pause, even on such an errand, in order to heal, by the way, the other sufferer. The father and the disciples would wonder at Him as He stayed His steps, and be apt to feel that priceless moments were being lost; but He knows His own resources, and can afford to let the child die while He heals the woman. The one shall receive no harm by the delay, and another will be blessed. Our Lord is sitting at the feast which Matthew gave on the occasion of His call, engaged in vindicating His sharing in innocent festivity against the cavils of the Pharisees, when the summons to the death-bed comes to Him from the lips of the father, who breaks in on the banquet with his imploring cry. Matthew gives the story much more summarily than the other evangelists, and does not distinguish, as they do, between Jairus's first words "at the point of death," and the message of her actual decease, which met them on the way. The call of sorrow always reaches Christ's ear, and the cry for help never is deemed by Him an interruption. So this "man gluttonous and a winebibber," as these Pharisees thought Him, willingly and at once leaves the house of feasting for that of mourning. How near together, in this awful life of ours, the two lie, and how thin the partition walls! Well for those whose feasts do not bar them out from hearing the weeping next door!

As the crowd accompanies Jesus, His hasting love is

for a moment, diverted by another sufferer. We never go on an errand of mercy but we pass a hundred other sorrowing hearts, so close packed lie the griefs of men. This woman is a poor shrinking creature, broken down by long illness (which had lasted for the same length of time as the joyous life of Jairus's child), made more timid by disappointed hopes of cure, and depressed by poverty to which her many doctors had brought her. She does not venture to stop this new rabbi-Physician, as He goes with the church dignitary of the town to heal his daughter, but lets Him pass before she can make up her mind to go near Him; and then she comes creeping up behind the crowd, puts out her wasted, trembling hand to the hem of His garment,—and she is whole.

The other evangelists give us a more extended account, but Matthew throws into prominence, in his condensed narrative, the essential points.

Notice her real but imperfect faith. There was unquestionable confidence in Christ's power, and very genuine desire for healing. But it was a very ignorant faith. She believes that her touch of the garment will heal without Christ's will or knowledge, much less His pitying love, having any part in it. She thinks that she may get her desire furtively, and may carry it away, and be none the wiser nor the poorer for the stolen blessing. What utter, blank ignorance of His character and way of working! What gross superstition! Yes, and withal what a hunger of desire, what absolute assurance of confidence that one finger-tip of His robe was enough! Therefore she had her desire, and her Healer recognized her faith as true, though blended with much ignorance of

Him. Her error was very like that which many Christians entertain with less excuse. To attach importance to external means of grace, rites, ordinances, sacraments, outward connection with Christian organisations, is the very same misconception in a slightly different form. Such error is always near us; it is especially rife in countries where there has long been a visible Church. It has received strange new vigour to-day, partly by reaction from extreme rationalism, partly by the growing cultivation of the æsthetic faculties. It is threatening to corrupt the simplicity and spirituality of Christian worship, and needs to be strenuously resisted. But the more we have to fight against it, the more do we need to remember that, along with this clinging to the hem of the garment instead of to the heart of its Wearer, there may be a very real trust, which might shame some of those who profess to hold a less sensuous form of faith. Many a poor soul clasping a crucifix clings to the cross. Many a devout heart kneeling at mass sees through the incense smoke the face of Christ.

This woman's faith was selfish. She wanted health; she did not care much about the Healer. She would have been quite contented to have had no more to do with Him, if she could only have stolen out of the crowd cured. She had had but little gratitude to the unconscious Giver of a stolen good. So many a Christian life, in its earlier stages, is more absorbed with its own deep misery, and its desire for deliverance, than with Him. Love comes after, born of the experience of His love. But faith precedes love, and the predominant motive impelling to faith at first is distinctly self-regard. That is all as it should be. The most purely self-absorbed wish to escape from the most rudely pictured hell is often the beginning of a true trust in Christ, which, in due time, will be elevated into perfect consecration. Some of our modern teachers who are shocked at Christianity because it lays the foundation of the most self-denying morality in such "selfishness" would be none the worse for going to school to this story, and learning from it how a desire, no nobler than to get rid of a painful disease, started a process which turned a life into a peaceful, thankful surrender of the cured self to the love and service of the mighty Healer.

Observe, next, how Christ answers the imperfect faith, and, by answering, corrects and confirms it. Matthew omits Christ's question as to who touched Him, the disciples' reply, His renewed asseverations that He was conscious of power having gone forth from Him. All that belongs to the loving method by which our Lord sought to draw forth an open acknowledgment. Womanly diffidence, enfeebled health, her special disease, all made her wish to hide herself. She wanted to steal away unnoticed, as she hoped that she had come. But Christ forces her to stand out before all the crowd, and there, with all eyes upon her,—cold, cruel eyes, some of them,—to conquer her shame, and tell all the truth. Strange kindness that; strangely contrasted with His ordinary desire to avoid notoriety, and with His ordinary tender consideration for shrinking weakness. He did it for her sake, not for His own. She is changed from timidity to courage. At one moment she stretches out her wasted finger, a tremulous invalid; at the next, she flings herself at His feet, a confessor. He would have us testify for Him, because faith unavowed, like a plant in the dark, is apt to become pale and sickly; but ere He bids us own His name, He pours into our hearts, in answer to our secret appeal, the health of His own life, and the blissful consciousness of that great gift which makes the tongue of the dumb sing.

His words to her are full of tenderness. She only receives the name of "daughter." Gently He encourages her timidity by that "Be of good cheer," and then He sets right her error: "Thy faith"—not thy finger—"hath made thee whole." There was no real connection between the touch of the robe and healing; but the woman thought that there was, and so Christ stooped to her childish thought, and allowed her to prescribe the road which His mercy should take. But He would not leave her with her error. The true means of contact between us and Him is not our outward contact with external means of grace, but the touch of our spirits by faith. That faith is nothing in itself, and heals only because it brings us into union with His power, which is the sole cause of our healing. Faith is the hand which receives the blessing. It may be a wasted and tremulous hand, like that which this woman laid lightly on His robe. But He feels its touch, though a universe presses on Him, and He answers. Not the garment's hem, but Christ's love is the cause of our salvation. Not an outward contact with it or with Him, but faith, is the condition on which His life, which knows no disease, pours into our souls. The hand of my faith lifted to Him will receive into its empty palm and clasping fingers the special blessing for my special wants.

The other evangelists tell us that, at the moment of His words to the woman, the messengers came bearing tidings of the child's death. How Jairus must have grudged the pause! A word from Christ, like the pressure of His hand, heartened him; and like a river turned from its course for a space, to fill some empty reservoir, His love comes back to its original direction. How abundant the power and mercy, to which such a work as that just done were but a parenthesis! The doleful music and the shrill shrieks of Eastern mourning, which met them as they entered Jairus's house, disturbed the sanctity of the hour, and were in strong contrast with the majestic calmness of Jesus. Not amid venal lamentations and excited cries will He do His work. He bids the noisy crowd forth with curt, almost stern, command, and therein rebukes all such hollow and tumultuous scenes, in the presence of the stillness of death, still more where faith in Him has robbed it of its terror, in robbing it of its perpetuity. It is strange that believing readers should have thought that our Lord meant to say that the little girl was not really dead, but only in a swoon. The scornful laughter of the flute-players and hired mourners understood Him better. They knew that it was real death, as men count death, and, as has often been the case, the laughter of His foes has served to establish the truth. That was not worthy to be called death from which the child was so soon and easily to be awaked. But, besides this special application to the case in hand, that great saying of our Lord's carries the blessed truth that, since He has come, death is softened into sleep for all who love Him. The euphemism is not peculiar to Christianity, but has a deeper meaning in it than when Greeks or Romans spoke of the eternal sleep. Others speak of death by any name rather than its own, because they fear it so much. The Christian does so, because he fears it so little,—and, as a matter of fact, the use of the word to imply merely the separation of soul and body by the physical act is exceptional in the New Testament.

This name of sleep, sanctioned thus by Christ, is the sweetest of all. It speaks of the cessation of connection with the world of sense, and "long disquiet merged in rest." It does not imply unconsciousness, for we are not unconscious when we sleep, but only unaware of externals. It holds the promise of waking when the sun comes. So it has driven out the ugly old name. Our tears flow less bitterly when we think of our dear ones as "sleeping in Jesus." Their bodies, like this little child's, are dead, but *they* are not. They rest, conscious of their own blessedness and of Him "in whom they live, and have their being," whether they "move" or no. Then comes the great deed. The crowd is shut out. For such a work silence is befitting. The father and mother, with His foremost three disciples, go with Him into the chamber. There is no effort, repeated and gradually successful, as when Elisha raised the dead boy; no praying, as when Peter raised Dorcas; but the touch of the hand in which life throbbed in fulness, and, as the other narratives record, two words, spoken strangely to, and yet more strangely heard by, the dull, cold ear of death. Their echo lingered long with Peter, and Mark gives us them in the original Aramaic. But Matthew passes them by, as he seems here to have desired to emphasise the power of Christ's touch. But touch or word, the real cause of the miracle was simply His will; and whether He used media to help men's faith, or said only "I will," mattered little. He varied His methods as the circumstances of the recipients required, and in order that they and we might learn that He was tied to none. These miracles of raising the dead are three in number. Jairus's daughter is raised from the bed, as just having passed away; the widow's son at Nain from his bier, having been for a little longer separated from his body; Lazarus from the grave, having been dead four days. A few minutes, or days, or four thousand years, are one to His power. These three are in some sense the first-fruits of the great harvest; the stars that shone out singly before all the heaven is in a blaze. For, though they died again, and so left to Him the precedence in resurrection, as in all besides, they are still prophetic of His power in the hour when they "that sleep in the dust" shall awake at His voice. Blessed they who, like this little maiden, are wakened, not only by His voice, but by His touch, and to find, as she did, their hand in His.

The third of these miracles, which Matthew seems to reckon as the second in the group, because he treats the two former as so closely connected as to be but one in numeration, need not detain us long. It is found only in this gospel. The first point to be observed in it is the cry of these two blind men. There is something pathetic and exquisitely natural in the two being together, as is also the case in the similar miracle, at a later period, on the outskirts of Jericho. Equal sorrows drive men together for such poor help and solace as they can give each other. They have common experiences which isolate them from others, and they creep close for warmth and companionship. All the blind men in the Gospels have certain resemblances. One is that they are all

Less. XVI.] Touch of Faith and Touch of Christ.

sturdily persevering, as perhaps was easier for them because they could not see the impatience of the listeners, and possibly because, in most cases, persistent begging was their trade, and they were used to refusals. But a more important trait is their recognition of Jesus as "Son of David." Blind as they are, they see more than the seeing. Thrown in upon themselves, they may have been led to ponder the old words, and by their affliction made more ready to welcome One who, if He were Messiah, was coming with a special blessing for them,—"to open the blind eyes." Men who deeply desire a good are quick to listen to the promise of its accomplishment. So these two followed Him along the road, loudly and perseveringly calling out their profession of faith, and their entreaty for sight.

The next point is our Lord's treatment. He let them cry on, apparently unheeding. Had, then, the two miracles just done exhausted His stock of power or of pity? Certainly His reason was, as it always was, their good. We do not know why it was better for them to have to wait, and continue their entreaty; but we may be quite sure that the reason for all His delays is the same,—the larger blessing which comes with the answer when it comes, and the large blessings which may be gathered while we wait its coming. Christ's question to them, when at last they have found their way even indoors, holds out more hope than they had yet received. By it, Christ established a close relation with them, and implied to them that He was willing to answer their cry. One can fancy how the poor blind faces would light up with a flush of eager expectation, and how swift would be the answer. The question is not cold or inquisitorial. It is more than half a promise, and a powerful aid to the faith which it requires.

There is something very beautiful and pathetic in the simple brevity of the unhesitating answer, "Yea, Lord." Sincerity needs few words. Faith can put an infinite deal of meaning into a monosyllable. Their eagerness to reach the goal made their answer brief. But it was enough. Again the hand which had clasped the maiden's palm is put out and laid gently on the useless eyes, and the great word spoken, "According to your faith be it unto you." Their blindness made the touch peculiarly fitting in their case, as bringing evidence of sense to those who could not see the gracious pity of His looks. The word spoken was, like that to the centurion, the declaration of the power of faith, which determines the measure, and often the manner, of His gifts to us. The containing vessel not only settles the quantity, but the shape assumed by the water, which is taken up in it from the sea. Faith, which keeps inside of Christ's promises (and what goes outside is not faith), decides how much of Christ we shall have for our very own. He condescends to run the molten gold of His mercies into the moulds which our faith prepares.

These two men, who had used their tongues so well in their persistent cry for healing, went away to make a worse use of them in telling everywhere of their cure. Jesus desired silence. Possibly He did not wish His reputation as a mere Worker of miracles to be spread abroad. In all His earlier ministry He avoided publicity, singularly contrasting therein with the evident desire to make Himself the centre of observation which marks its close. He dreaded the smoky flame of popular excitement. His message was to individuals, not to crowds. It was a natural impulse to tell the benefits they had received ; but truer gratitude and deeper faith would have made them obey His lightest word, and shut their mouths. We honour Christ most, not by taking our way of honouring Him, but by absolute obedience.

LESSON XVII.

The King's Ambassadors.

MATTHEW ix. 35-38; x. 1-8.

35. "And Jesus went about all the cities and villages, teaching in their synagogues, and preaching the gospel of the kingdom, and healing every sickness and every disease among the people.

36. But when He saw the multitudes, He was moved with compassion on them, because they fainted, and were scattered abroad, as sheep having no shepherd.

37. Then saith He unto His disciples, The harvest truly is plenteous, but the labourers are few;

38. Pray ye therefore the Lord of the harvest, that He will send forth labourers into His harvest.

1. And when He had called unto Him His twelve disciples, He gave them power against unclean spirits, to cast them out, and to heal all manner of sickness and all manner of disease.

2. Now the names of the twelve apostles are these; The first, Simon, who is called Peter, and Andrew his brother; James the son of Zebedee, and John his brother;

3. Philip, and Bartholomew; Thomas, and Matthew the publican; James the son of Alphæus, and Lebbæus, whose surname was Thaddæus;

4. Simon the Cananite, and Judas Iscariot, who also betrayed Him.

5. These twelve Jesus sent forth, and commanded them, saying, Go not into the way of the Gentiles, and into any city of the Samaritans enter ye not:

6. But go rather to the lost sheep of the house of Israel.

7. And as ye go, preach, saying, The kingdom of heaven is at hand.

8. Heal the sick, cleanse the lepers, raise the dead, cast out devils: freely ye have received, freely give."

THE first verse of this lesson is a verbatim repetition of Matthew iv. 23, which introduced the Sermon on the Mount. The whole of the intervening portion, therefore, including the sermon and the series of miracles, is set, as it were, in a frame, as a specimen of the teaching and works of the King, or, as we might say, of the laws and victories of the kingdom. Now we have the King sending out His servants and warriors. His personal work is no longer to be the sole agency for establishing his reign. A comparison of the other evangelists makes it probable that the apostles had been designated to their special position at an earlier period, but that they were sent forth now. Our lesson sets their mission in a touching light, as being the direct result of Christ's compassion, stirred by the sight of the multitudes.

Note first the King's pity. Apparently our Lord's miracles had drawn crowds after Him. As He looked on them, He saw in their outward appearance a symbol of their spiritual state. They were weary and worn with travel, and had flung themselves down in disordered masses, utterly exhausted, without leaders, a panting mob. The word rendered "scattered" is perhaps better given as "thrown down," and points rather to sheep lying huddled in helpless weariness than to the dispersion of what would then scarcely be called a "multitude." Jesus sees beneath the apparent. To His eye the spiritual condition was the most important, and, quick as He was to feel all sorrows, yet it appealed most strongly to His compassion. So should we look on men, not neglecting their physical and outward sufferings, but ever reminded by these of the deeper and sadder sorrows and cravings of the soul. Apart from Christ, men have no shepherd, whether we mean by the word a ruler or a teacher. Both ideas are included in it as used in the Old Testament. He is the King, and, if we serve not Him, there is none who can rule the will or subdue the passions; none who can set up a throne in the heart, or to whom it is honour and freedom to submit. Tyrants we may have, but no other Shepherd-King, who cares for, and guards and feeds as well as rules. We have teachers many, but, apart from Christ, none who bring certitude, and the final absolutely true word about God and ourselves. By common consent, it is Christ or no one. Either He is the King whose reign is righteousness, and the Teacher whose word is truth, or the race of men are left to grope as they may after duty and knowledge.

Apart from Christ, men are harassed, or, as the word literally means, "lacerated," like sheep, struggling in thorns or torn by enemies. They are worn out by long and vain search after green pastures and right roads, and too often fling themselves down panting, in a dreary despair of ever finding them. All great outbursts of moral earnestness have been followed by times of corruption and apathy. So these weary, footsore crowds that lay round Christ should stand to us as a picture of what the world is without Jesus, and Christ's way of looking on men should be our way.

His clear vision of the facts touched His heart at once with pity, and herein He was our Pattern, and, alas! our rebuke. He had the eye and the pity of a God, and the sympathy of a man. The result of His gaze was pity, not aversion, nor anger, nor curiosity, nor indifference, all of which are too often the results of our looking on men's miseries.

Note, next, the swift action that followed the compassionate look. There is a certain kind of lazy luxury, by no means unfamiliar to some of us, in contemplating men's griefs, and letting our emotions be tickled into not unpleasant action. But to excite emotion and give it no work to do is a dangerous proceeding, and sure to end in "hardening all within" and "petrifying the feeling." On the other hand, the most genuinely sympathetic work is apt to slide away from its true foundation, and, having begun in the spirit, to be carried on in the flesh, and to become mechanical and therefore weak. So, we have to learn from this close connection between knowledge, pity, and action, the intended law for our Christian service, and to give heed to keeping all three elements in close union, as the only means of keeping any of them in health.

Our Lord bade His disciples act by prayer. The condition of the people which moved His pity is regarded by Him, in the figure of the harvest waiting to be reaped, under a different point of view. Men's miseries apart from Him are part of their fitness for receiving Him. Among so many wandering sheep there must be many who will gladly hear of the Shepherd and the fold. So, we should regard the evils which afflict humanity, not with despair, but as hearing in them a summons to put in the sickle. Few indeed were the labourers in that field; hitherto, He had been the only one. Now, the pressure of men's need had determined Him to send forth others to toil. But before He sends out the twelve, He bids them and all the disciples pray that God would thrust out labourers into the field. What need for the prayer, if He was about to do this? The same need as there is for our asking any of the blessings which He has willed to give, on condition of our asking them. A man would have to know all about God, and about the relation of the Divine to the human will, in order to fashion a "philosophy of prayer" which should explain the Divine side of that need. Perhaps our ropes are not quite long enough, even in this system-spinning age, to let our buckets down to the bottom of that well. Jesus Christ has told us that prayer does move the hand of God, and possibly He knew as much about God as the wise men do who now assure us that it does not. They do not explain the difficulty by taking away all that needs explanation, and asserting that the influence of prayer on ourselves is its only influence. But we should not leave that side out of view either. Here, part of Christ's purpose was to impress on the disciples the sense of their large opportunities and responsibilities—to teach them and us that prayer to God is our best way of furthering His merciful purposes for a world of wanderers, and that they who honestly pray that God would thrust forth labourers must be ready to go when the lot falls on them.

So we come to the sending out of the twelve. We may observe that they were endowed with power the copy of His own. The language descriptive of these is plainly intended to recall the almost identical terms in which His miracles have been spoken of in verse 35. In like manner their message is the same as His, as at first reported. (Compare v. 7 with Matt. iv. 17.)

Note then, first, the broad fact that there is an order in the enumeration of the twelve. The number, of course, has reference to the twelve tribes, and proclaims that the kingdom of which they were the ministers is the true Israel. The list is divided into three groups of four each. In each group the same apostle is at the head in all the lists, Simon Peter being always the *doyen* of the first quaternion, Philip of the second, and James the son of Alphæus of the third. Clearly the most important come first, and probably the most important in each group heads it. They were brethren, and in some sense a pure specimen of a Christian democracy; and yet the men of weight came to the front, and there are degrees among them dependent on their force of goodness and consecration, as well as on natural endowment.

Note, too, the smaller groups within the circle. There were, at all events, two pairs of brothers, who constituted the four chief apostles. One theory makes a third pair in the persons of James and Judas, or Thaddæus as Matthew calls him. Philip and Bartholomew (that is, Nathanael) were friends. All the first six were closely connected before their discipleship. Further, Matthew and Luke—in both his lists—give the names in pairs; and Mark, who does not do so, mentions what was no doubt the reason for the pairs, that they were originally sent out by twos. So we learn the good of companionship in Christian service, which solaces, and checks excessive individuality, and makes men brave. One and one is more than two, for each man is more than himself by the companionship. We may note, too, the allowableness of special friendships among Christian workers, the consecration of friendship, and the beauty of the bonds of kindred and amity when they are heightened and sanctified by yoking us to Christ's plow. But these lists also teach us that Christ's service separates and dissolves natural ties. One of the twelve was Thomas Didymus, and his name in both languages means "a twin." Where was his twin brother?

Note, again, the variations in the order. Matthew belongs to the second group, and in his own Gospel stands last in it. The lowest place which he could take he modestly takes. In Mark's list (Mark iii. 16) He comes a place higher, as also in Luke's first (Luke vi. 14), but in Acts i. 13 he drops to eighth. Another little touch of lowliness lies in the fact that he, and he only, calls himself "the publican," and that in no other instance is the occupation of any of them mentioned. The list in Acts may be taken as giving the final positions of the apostles; and in it the pairs of brothers in the first group are parted, Peter and James being united, as probably the more active, while John, whose work was "to tarry," and Andrew, are placed together,—the latter being last, as certainly the least important of the four. Then, in the second division, Thomas comes up from the last place, which he occupies in Mark and Luke, and probably would have occupied in Matthew but for that apostle's modesty, and is coupled with Philip, whose companion Nathanael, whom he brought to Jesus, is now put third. So we may learn that our place in Christ's army is altered by our diligence and faithful use of opportunities. It used to be said that, in Napoleon's time, every French soldier carried a field-marshal's baton in his knapsack. Every Christian soldier has the possibility of high rank, and his advance will injure or hinder none of his fellows. The first may be last, and the last first.

We may note, too, the lessons of the last pair of names. Simon the zealot had been a member of that fierce party who were ready to draw the sword against Rome, and in whom hot passion masqueraded as holy zeal. The impure fire had been clarified, and turned into holy enthusiasm, by union with Christ, who alone has power to correct and elevate earthly passion into calm and permanent consecration and ardour. What a contrast He presents to the last name! A strangely assorted couple, these two: the zealot, and the cold-blooded, selfish betrayer, whose stagnant soul has never been moved by any breath of zeal for anything! The lessons of that name cannot be dealt with here. Enough to draw the warning that contact with Christ hurts where it does not help, and maddens to malignant hatred, if it does not soften to adoring love.

But perhaps not the least important lesson to be learned from these names, is that contained in the plain fact that of half of them we never hear again. None of them, except the three "who seemed to be pillars," appear to have been of much importance in the work of the Church. Surely, if they were the possessors of such extraordinary powers as the sacramentarian theory implies, it is odd that we should hear so little about them. As long as Christ was on earth, their office was to be with Him, to preach the kingdom when sent forth, and to work miracles. After His ascension, their office, according to Peter's notion of it, was to be witnesses "of His resurrection." The qualification for that was simply that they should "have companied with us all the time" of Christ's life. Miraculous gifts they had, but not as their peculiar possession. They could impart the Holy Spirit to believers, but so could Ananias at Damascus. Their simple task was witness-bearing, and there can be no apostolic succession for the sufficient reason that there is nothing to succeed to, except what cannot be transmitted, personal knowledge of Christ's resurrection.

Note, finally, our Lord's charge to these messengers of the kingdom. The first trial-mission is confined to Israel, according to the order ever observed, that to it the kingdom should be first brought. The yearning pity of Christ's heart, and the link between the apostles' mission and the sight of the fainting multitudes, is suggested by the echo of the former metaphor in "the lost sheep of the house of Israel." The message is, as we have noticed, the same as that of John, and of Christ at the beginning of His ministry. It is clearly a temporary one. Neither the message nor many of the instructions for this journey were meant for more than the time. The miraculous powers with which they are invested are the echo or reflection of His, and intended to be witnesses of the reality and specimens of the blessings of the kingdom. Ambassadors used sometimes to carry the king's signet-ring, and sometimes his sword as their credentials. These twelve bear the regalia of their Sovereign in these acts of mercy.

The great word with which this lesson closes is not part of the transitory instructions to the twelve. "Freely ye have received, freely give," contains the permanent law for Christ's kingdom. Do not sell what you did not buy. It is an appeal to chivalrous generosity. It touches on the solemn obligation arising from possession. To have, binds us to give. What should we say of a dweller in some waterless plain, who kept a well in his courtyard locked up, and let neighbours die of thirst? It touches on the even stronger motive arising from the way in which Christians have come into possession of their spiritual blessings. How delicately Christ just glances at the cost to Him, and the consequent weight of our obligations in that one word "freely"! He will not dilate on His sacrifice and pains. Enough is said when He points one finger, as it were, to what He has done, in order that this gift might be freely ours. The deepest ground of all on which the Christian duty of work for the salvation of others rests, is gratitude to Christ. Pity for men is less holy, and will prove less powerful, than thankfulness to Jesus. Christ's own example is here set before us as the pattern for our giving. His self-oblivion, His unwearied toil, His lowliness, His patient love, which refused to be put by, and answered all unkindness with gentleness, and refusal with renewed and more pressing beseechings, are meant not only for our trust, but for our imitation. The manner of Christian effort for others is prescribed in this command. Give as widely as you can to all whom your outstretched hand can reach. Give at the cost of sacrifice to yourselves, of money, time, and ease. Do not clog your gift with restrictions and shibboleths, nor compel the observance of needless conditions; but take pattern of the Master and of the Divine love which dwelt in Him bodily, and give to all, and that liberally, and without souring the sweetness of the offered salvation with the bitter flavour of upbraiding. Those who freely give are they who truly keep, and themselves most enjoy the gift, the highest result of which is that the receivers become like the Giver, and in their poor way echo His message and reflect the miracles of His healing power.

LESSON XVIII.

The King's Charge to His Ambassadors.

MATTHEW x. 32-42.

32. "Whosoever therefore shall confess Me before men, him will I confess also before My Father which is in heaven.

33. But whosoever shall deny Me before men, him will I also deny before My Father which is in heaven.

34. Think not that I am come to send peace on earth: I came not to send peace, but a sword.

35. For I am come to set a man at variance against his father, and the daughter against her mother, and the daughter in law against her mother in law.

36. And a man's foes shall be they of his own household.

37. He that loveth father or mother more than Me is not worthy of Me: and he that loveth son or daughter more than Me is not worthy of Me.

38. And he that taketh not his cross, and followeth after Me, is not worthy of Me.

39. He that findeth his life shall lose it: and he that loseth his life for My sake shall find it.

40. He that receiveth you receiveth Me, and he that receiveth Me receiveth Him that sent Me.

41. He that receiveth a propeht in the name of a prophet shall receive a prophet's reward; and he that receiveth a righteous man in the name of a righteous man shall receive a righteous man's reward.

42. And whosoever shall give to drink unto one of these little ones a cup of cold water only in the name of a disciple, verily I say unto you, he shall in no wise lose his reward."

THE first mission of the apostles, important as it was, was but a short flight to try the young birds' wings. The larger portion of this charge to them passes far beyond the immediate occasion, and deals with the permanent relations of Christ's servants to the world in which they live, for the purpose of bringing it into subjection to its true King. These solemn closing words, which make our present lesson, give us the duty and blessedness of confessing Him, the vision of the antagonisms which He excites, His demand for all-surrendering following; and the rewards of those who receive Christ's messengers, and therein receive Himself and His Father.

I. The duty and blessedness of confessing Him (vv. 32, 33). The "therefore" is significant. It attaches the promise which follows to the immediately preceding thoughts of a watchful, fatherly care, extending like a great invisible hand over the true disciple. Because each is thus guarded, each shall be preserved to receive the honour of being confessed by Christ. No matter what may befall His witnesses, the extremest disaster shall not come between them and their crown. They may be flung down from the house-tops where they lift up their bold voices, but He who does not let the sparrow fall to the ground uncared for, will give His angels charge concerning them who are so much more precious, and they shall be borne up on their outstretched wings, lest they be dashed on the pavement below. Thus preserved, they shall all attain at last to their reward. Nothing can come between Christ's servant and his crown. The tender providence of the Father, whose mercy is over all His works, makes sure of that. The river of the confessor's life may plunge underground, and be lost amid persecutions, but it will emerge again into the better sunshine on the other side of the mountains.

The confession which is to be thus rewarded, like the denial opposed to it, is, of course, not merely a single utterance of the lip. Judas Iscariot confessed Christ, and Peter denied Him. But it is the habitual acknowledgment by lip and life, unwithdrawn to the end. The context implies that the confession is maintained in the face of opposition, as the denial is a cowardly attempt to save one's skin at the cost of treason to Jesus. The temptation does not come in that sharpest form to us. Perhaps some cowards would be made brave if it did. It is perhaps easier to face the gibbet and the fire, and screw one's self up for once to a brief endurance, than to resist the more specious blandishments of the world, especially when it has been christened, and calls itself religious. The light laugh of scorn, the silent pressure of the low average of Christian character, the many associations in trade, literature, public and domestic life which Christians have with non-Christians, make many a man's tongue lie silent, to the sore detriment of his own religious life. "Ye have not yet resisted unto blood," and find it hard to fulfil the easier conflict to which you are called. The sun has more power than the tempest to make the pilgrim drop his garment. But the duty remains the same for all ages. Every man is bound to make the deepest springs of his life visible, and to stand to his convictions, whatever they be. If he do not, his convictions will disappear like a piece of ice hid in a hot hand, which will melt and trickle away. This obligation lies with infinitely increased weight on Christ's servants; and the consequences of failing to discharge it are more tragic in their cases, in the exact proportion of the greater preciousness of their faith. Corn hoarded is sure to be spoiled by weevils and rust. The bread of life hidden in our sacks will certainly go mouldy.

The King's Charge to His Ambassadors.

The reward and punishment of confession and denial come to them not as separate acts, but each as the revelation of the spiritual condition of the doers. Christ implies that a true disciple cannot but be a confessor, and that therefore the denier must certainly be one whom He has never known. Because, therefore, each act is symptomatic of the doer, each receives the congruous and correspondent reward. The confessor is confessed; the denier is denied. What calm and assured consciousness of His place as judge underlies these words! His recognition is God's acceptance; His denial is darkness and misery. The correspondence between the work and the reward is beautifully brought out by the use of the same word to express each. And yet what a difference between our confession of Him and His of us! And what a hope is here for all who have tremblingly, and in the consciousness of much unworthiness, ventured to say that they were Christ's subjects, and He their King, brother, and all! Their poor, feeble confession will be endorsed by His. He will say, "Yes, this man is mine, and I am his." That will be glory, honour, blessedness, life, heaven.

II. The vision of the discord which follows the coming of the King of peace. It is not enough to interpret these words as meaning that our Lord's purpose indeed was to bring peace, but that the result of His coming was strife. The ultimate purpose is peace; but an immediate purpose is conflict, as the only road to the peace. He is first King of righteousness, and after that also King of peace. But, if His kingdom be righteousness, purity, love, then unrighteousness, filthiness, and selfishness will fight against it for their lives.

The ultimate purpose of Christ's coming is to transform the world into the likeness of heaven; and all in the world which hates such likeness is embattled against Him. He saw realities, and knew men's hearts, and was under no illusions, such as many an ardent reformer has cherished, that the fair form of truth need only be shown to men, and they will take her to their hearts. Incessant struggle is the law for the individual and for society till Christ's purpose for both is realised.

That conflict ranges the dearest in opposite ranks. The gospel is the great solvent. As when a substance is brought into contact with some chemical compound, which has greater affinity for one of its elements than the other element has, the old combination is dissolved, and a new and more stable one is formed, so Christianity analyses and destroys in order to synthesis and construction. In verse 21 our Lord had foretold that brother should deliver up brother to death. Here the severance is considered from the opposite side. The persons who are "set at variance" with their kindred are here Christians. Perhaps it is fanciful to observe that they are all junior members of families, as if the young would be more likely to flock to the new light. But however that may be, the separation is mutual, but the hate is all on one side. The "man's foes" are of his own household; but he is not their foe, though he be parted from them.

III. Earthly love may be a worse foe to a true Christian than even the enmity of the dearest; and that enmity may often be excited by the Christian subordination of earthly to heavenly love. So our Lord passes from the warnings of discord and hate to the danger of the opposite—undue love.

He claims absolute supremacy in our hearts. He goes still farther, and claims the surrender, not only of affections, but of self and life to Him. What a strange claim this is! A Jewish peasant, dead eighteen hundred years since, fronts the whole race of man, and asserts His right to their love, which is strange, and to their supreme love, which is stranger still. Why should we love Him at all, if He were only a man, however pure and benevolent? We may admire, as we do many another fair nature in the past; but is there any possibility of evoking anything as warm as love to an unseen person, who can have had no knowledge of or love to us? And why should we love Him more than our dearest, from whom we have drawn or to whom we have given life? What explanation or justification does He give of this unexampled demand? Absolutely none. He seems to think that its reasonableness needs no elucidation. Surely never did teacher professing wisdom, modesty, and, still more, religion, put forward such a claim of right; and surely never besides did any succeed in persuading generations unborn to yield His demand, when they heard it. The strangest thing in the world's history is that to-day there are millions who do love Jesus Christ more than all besides, and whose chief self-accusation is that they do not love Him more. The strange, audacious claim is most reasonable, if we believe that Jesus is the Son of God, who died for each of us, and that each man and woman to the last of the generations had a separate place in His Divine human love when He died. It is meet to love Him, if that be true; it is not, unless it be. The requirement is as stringent as strange. If the two ever seem to conflict, the earthly must give way. If the earthly be withdrawn, there must be found sufficiency for comfort and peace in the heavenly. The lower must not be permitted to hinder the flight of the heavenly to its home. "More than Me" is a rebuke to most of us. What a contrast between the warmth of our earthly and the tepidity or coldness of our heavenly love! How spontaneously our thoughts, when left free, turn to the one; how hard we find it to keep them fixed on the other! How sweet service is to the dear ones here; how reluctantly it is given to Christ! How we long, when parted, to rejoin them; how little we are drawn to the place where He is! We have all to confess that we are "not worthy of" Him; that we requite His love with inadequate returns, and live lives which tax His love for its highest exercise, the free forgiveness of sins against itself. Compliance with that stringent law, and subordinating all earthly love to His, is the true elevating and ennobling of the earthly. It is promoted, not degraded, when it is made second, and is infinitely sweeter and deeper then than when it was set in the place of supremacy, where it had no right to be.

But Christ's demand is not only for the surrender of the heart, but for the giving up of self, and, in a very profound sense, for the surrender of life. How enigmatical that saying about taking up the cross must have sounded to the disciples! They knew little about the cross, as a punishment; they had not yet associated it in any way with their Lord. This seems to have been the first occasion of His mentioning it, and the allusion is so veiled as to be but partially intelligible. But what was intelligible was bewildering. A strange royal procession that, of the King with a cross on His shoulder, and all His subjects behind Him, with similar burdens! Through the ages that procession has marched, and it marches still. Self-denial for Christ's sake is the badge of all our tribe. Observe that word "take." The cross must be willingly and by ourselves assumed. No other can lay it on our shoulders. Observe that other word " His." Each man has his own special form in which self-denial is needful for him. We require pure eyes, and hearts kept in very close communion with Jesus, to ascertain what our particular cross is. He has them of many patterns, shapes, sizes, and materials. We can always make sure of strength to carry the one which He means us to carry, but not of strength to bear what is not ours.

But subordinated affections and continuous self-denial are not all which He wants from us. Life or self must be lost if it is to be found. That profound and comprehensive saying would afford material for many lessons. In each clause, finding life and losing it are used in two different senses. He that finds his life, in the sense of keeping, or being ready to keep, his bodily life by forsaking Christ, shall lose his truest life, which consists in union with Him, the Source of all life; and he who parts or is ready to part with that bodily life for the sake of keeping Christ, shall find that true life which is increased, and not destroyed, by the axe, or the fire of martyrdom. But the words are not only a lesson for times of persecution; they go down into the very depths of Christian experience. Death is the gate of life. To die to self is the path to living in Christ. We possess ourselves only when we give ourselves away to Him. We live by dying. We die in our true selves if we seek to live for and by ourselves. He only truly lives the motto of whose life is, "I live; yet not I, but Christ liveth in me."

IV. We have the rewards of those who receive Christ's messengers, and therein receive Him and His Father. Our Lord first identifies these twelve with Himself in a manner which must have sounded strange to them then, but have heartened them for their work by the consciousness of His mysterious oneness with them. The whole doctrine of Christ's unity with His people lay in germ in these words, though much more was needed, both of teaching and of experience, before their depth of blessing and strengthening could be apprehended. We know that He dwells in His true subjects by His Spirit, and that a most real union subsists between the head and the members of which the closest unions of earth are but faint shadows, so as that not only those who receive His followers receive Him, but, more wonderful still, His followers are received at the last by God Himself as joined to Him, and portions of His very self, and therefore "accepted in the Beloved." Our Lord adds to these words the thought that, in like manner, to receive Him is to receive the Father, and so implies that our relation to Him is in certain real respects parallel with His relation to the Father. We too are sent. He who sends abides with us, as the Son ever abode in God, and God in Him. We are sent to be the brightness of Christ's glory, and to manifest Him to men, as He to reveal the Father.

And then our Lord passes to speak, finally, of the rewards of receiving His messengers. Note the three types of character,—"prophet," "righteous man," and "these little ones." Are we to see intended gradation? and, if so, is this an ascending or a descending climax? At first sight, it seems that we go down from prophets, honoured with Divine words to speak, to righteous men, and from them to the humble disciples; but in reality the progress here is upwards. Righteousness is more than prophetic inspiration. Goodness is better than shining gifts. In Christ's classification, genius is less than purity; and if there could be a prophet who was not righteous, as in Balaam's case, he would be distinctly inferior to a righteous man, whose lips had never been touched with prophetic fire. So, above these highest types of the old covenant, our Lord here sets His disciples, the little ones who believe in Him. Faith in Him is better than genius, intellect, the poet's imagination, the philosopher's searching reason, and even the inspiration which makes men teachers of the thoughts of God. In like manner, there may be much beauty of character and rectitude of conduct apart from discipleship; but all that is on a lower level than the faith which grasps Christ.

Note also the variety of reward according to character. Each class is supposed to have, because each is capable of, a diverse reward. Here and now every course of conduct has satisfactions springing from it, which, of course, can only be realised in it. And so in the future, while we are not to conceive of heaven as given to "prophets" or "righteous men" who are not disciples, still presupposing faith, then according to the character and activity here will be the heaven hereafter. Note the sameness of reward to all who stand on the same level. To receive a prophet in the name of a prophet means to welcome him because he is such; or, in other words, it expresses recognition and sympathy. So in each of the other clauses. The power of appreciating a certain type of character indicates a partial possession of that character.

A man may be morally and spiritually on the prophet's level, though his stammering tongue has never been loosed. The widow of Sarepta had some spark of the prophetess in her, though Elijah's task was to beard Ahab and shake Israel, and hers was only to bake his bread. There must be some similarity for sympathy. There must be something of the poet in the man who feels the majesty of the organ music of "Paradise Lost," though he be but a "mute, inglorious Milton." So there is a likeness in the rewards, because there is a likeness in the men. All actions done from the same motive are alike in God's eyes. We are not all called to great service, but we are called to sympathetic interest in those who are so, and to help them as we may. It was a law in Israel: "As his part is that goeth down to the battle, so shall his part be that tarrieth by the stuff." It is the law of Christ's kingdom, in which motives, not deeds, and spiritual susceptibility, not the accidents of the mode of its expression, determine place, capacity of receiving, and therefore reward.

LESSON XIX.

John's Doubts of Jesus, and Jesus' Praise of John.

MATTHEW xi. 2-15.

2. "Now when John had heard in the prison the works of Christ, he sent two of his disciples.

3. And said unto Him, Art Thou He that should come, or do we look for another?

4. Jesus answered and said unto them, Go and show John again those things which ye do hear and see:

5. The blind receive their sight, and the lame walk, the lepers are cleansed, and the deaf hear, the dead are raised up, and the poor have the gospel preached to them.

6. And blessed is he, whosoever shall not be offended in Me.

7. And as they departed, Jesus began to say unto the multitudes concerning John, What went ye out into the wilderness to see? A reed shaken with the wind?

8. But what went ye out for to see? A man clothed in soft raiment? behold, they that wear soft clothing are in kings' houses.

9. But what went ye out for to see? A prophet? yea, I say unto you, and more than a prophet.

10. For this is He, of whom it is written, Behold, I send My messenger before Thy face, which shall prepare Thy way before Thee.

11. Verily, I say unto you, Among them that are born of women there hath not risen a greater than John the Baptist: notwithstanding he that is least in the kingdom of heaven is greater than he.

12. And from the days of John the Baptist until now the kingdom of heaven suffereth violence, and the violent take it by force.

13. For all the prophets and the law prophesied until John.

14. And if ye will receive it, this is Elias, which was for to come.

15. He that hath ears to hear, let him hear."

THIS lesson falls into two parts: the first, from verses 2-6 inclusive, giving us the faltering faith of the great witness, and Christ's gentle treatment of the waverer; the second, from verse 7 to the end of the lesson, giving the witness of Christ to John, exuberant in recognition, notwithstanding his momentary hesitation.

I. We do not believe that this message of John's was sent for the sake of strengthening his disciples' faith in Jesus as Messiah, nor that it was merely meant as a hint to Jesus to declare Himself. The question is John's. The answer is sent to him: it is he who is to ponder the things which the messengers saw, and to answer his own question thereby. The note which the evangelist prefixes to his account gives the key to the incident. John was "in prison," in that gloomy fortress of Machærus which Herod had rebuilt at once for "a sinful pleasure house," and for an impregnable refuge, among the savage cliffs of Moab. The halls of luxurious vice and the walls of defence are gone; but the dungeons are there still, with the holes in the masonry into which the bars were fixed to which the prisoners—John, perhaps, one of them—were chained. No wonder that in the foul atmosphere of a dark dungeon the spirit which had been so undaunted in the free air of the desert began to flag; nor that even he who had seen the fluttering dove descend on Christ's head, and had pointed to Him as the Lamb of God, felt that "all his mind was clouded with a doubt." It would have been wiser if commentators, instead of trying to save John's credit at the cost of straining the narrative, had recognised the psychological truth of the plain story of his wavering conviction, and had learned its lessons of self-distrust. There is only one Man with whom it was always high-water; all others have ebbs and flows in their religious life, and in their grasp of truth.

The narrative further gives the motive for John's embassy, in the report which had reached him of "the works of Christ." We need only recall John's earlier testimony to understand how these works would not seem to him to fill up the *rôle* which he had anticipated for Messiah. Where is the axe that was to be laid at the root of the trees, or the fan that was to winnow the chaff out? Where is the fiery spirit which He had foretold? This gentle Healer is not the theocratic judge of His warning prophecies. He is tending and nurturing, rather than felling, the barren trees. A nimbus of merciful deeds, not flashing "wrath to come," surrounds His path. So John began to wonder if, after all, he had been premature in his recognition. Perhaps this Jesus was but a precursor, as he himself was, of the Messiah. Evidently he continues firm in the conviction of Christ's being sent from God, and is ready to accept His answer as conclusive; but, as evidently, he is puzzled by the contrariety between Jesus' deeds and his own expectations. He asks, "Art Thou *He that cometh*,"—a well-known name for Messiah,—"or are we to expect another?" where it should be noted that the word for "another," means not merely a second, but a different kind of person, who should present the aspects of the Messiah as revealed in prophecy, and as embodied in John's own preaching, which Jesus had left unfulfilled.

We may well take to heart the lesson of the fluctuations possible to the firmest faith, and pray to be enabled to hold fast that we have. We may learn, too, the danger to right conceptions of Christ, of separating the two elements of mercy and judgment in His character and work. John was right in believing that the Christ must come to judge. A Christ without the fan in His hand is a maimed Christ. John was wrong in stumbling at the gentleness, just as many to-day, who go to the opposite extreme, are wrong in stumbling at the judicial side of His work. Both halves are needed to make the full-orbed character. We have not to "look for a different" Christ, but we have to look for Him, coming the second time, the same Jesus, but now with His axe in His pierced hands, to hew down trees which He has patiently tended. Let John's profound sense of the need for a judicial aspect in the Christ who is to meet the prophecies written in men's hearts, as well as in Scripture, teach us how one-sided and superficial are representations of His work which suppress or slur over His future coming to judgment.

Our Lord does not answer yes or no. To do so might have stilled, but would not have removed, John's misconception. A more thorough cure is needed. So Christ attacks it in its roots by referring him back for answer to the very deeds which had excited his doubt. In doing so, He points to, or indeed, we may say, quotes, two prophetic passages (Isa. xxxv. 5, 6; lxi. 1) which give the prophetic "notes" of Messiah. It is as if He had said, "Have you forgotten that the very prophets whose words have fed your hopes, and now seem to minister to your doubts, have said this and this about the Messiah?" Further, there is deep wisdom in sending John back again to think over the very deeds at which he was stumbling. It is not Christ's work which is wanting in conformity to the Divine idea; it is John's conceptions of that idea that need enlarging. What he wants is not so much to be told that Jesus is the Christ, as to grow up to a truer, because more comprehensive, notion of what the Christ is to be. A wide principle is taught us here. The very points in Christ's work which may occasion difficulty, will, when we stand at the right point of view, become evidences of His claims. What were stumbling-blocks become stepping-stones. Arguments against become proofs of the truth, when we look at them with clearer eyes, and from the proper angle. Further, we are taught here, that what Christ does is the best answer to the question who He is. Still He is doing these works among us. Darkened eyes are flooded with light by His touch, and see a new world, because they gaze with faith on Him. Lame limbs are endowed with strength, and can run in the way of His commandments, and walk with unfainting perseverance the thorniest paths of duty and self-sacrifice. Lepers are cleansed from the rotting leprosy of sin, and their flesh comes again, "as the flesh of a little child." Deaf ears hear the voice of the Son of God, and the dead who hear live. Good news is preached to all the poor in spirit, and whosoever knows himself to be in need of all things may claim all things as his own in Christ. He who through the ages has been working such works, and works them still, "needs not to speak anything" to confirm his claims, "neither is there salvation in any other." We look for no second Christ; but we look for that same Jesus to come the second time to be the Judge of the world of which He is the Saviour.

The benediction on him who finds none occasion of stumbling in Christ, is at once a beatitude and a warning. It rebukes in the gentlest fashion John's temper, which found difficulty in even the perfect personality of Jesus, and made that which should have been the " sure foundation" of his spirit a stone of stumbling. Our Lord's consciousness of absolute perfection of moral character, and of absolute perfectness in His office and work, is distinct in the words. He knows that "there is none occasion of stumbling in Him," and that whoever finds any, brings it or makes it. He knows and warns us that all blessedness lies for us in recognising Him for what He is—God's sure foundation of our hopes, our peace, our thoughts, our lives. He knows that all woe and loss are involved in stumbling on this stone, against which whosoever falls is broken, and by which, when it begins to move, and falls on a man, he is ground to powder, like the dust of the threshing-floor. What tremendous arrogance of assertion! Who is he who can venture on such words without blasphemy against God, and universal ridicule from men?

II. The witness of Christ to John. Praise from Jesus is praise indeed; and it is poured out here with no stinted hand on the languishing prisoner whose doubts had just been brought to Him. Such an eulogium at such a time is a wonderful instance of loving forbearance with a true-hearted follower's weakness, and of a desire which, in a man, we should call magnanimous, to shield John's character from depreciation on account of his message. The world praises a man to his face, and speaks of his faults behind his back. Christ does the opposite. Not till the messengers were departing does He begin to speak "concerning John." He lays bare the secret of the Baptist's power, and allocates his place as greatest in one epoch and as less than the least in another, with an authority more than human, and on principles which set Himself high above all comparison with men, whether the greatest or the least. The King places His subjects, and Himself sits enthroned above them all.

First, Christ praises John's great personal character in the dramatic and vivid questions which begin this section. He recalls the scenes of popular enthusiasm when all Israel streamed out to the desert preacher. A small man could not have made such an upheaval. What drew the crowds? Just what will always draw them; the qualities without which, either possessed in reality or in popular estimation, no man can be a power religiously. The first essential is heroic firmness. It was not reeds swaying in the wind by Jordan's banks, nor a poor feeble man like them, that the people flocked to listen to. His emblem was not the reed, but "an iron pillar." His whole career had been marked by decisiveness, constancy, courage. Nothing can be done worth doing in the world without a wholesome obstinacy and imperturbability, which keep a man true to his convictions and his task whatever winds blow in his teeth. The multitudes will not flock to listen to a teacher who does not speak with the accent of conviction, nor will truths feebly grasped touch the lips with fire. The first requisite for a religious teacher is that he shall be sure of his message and of himself. Athanasius has to stand "against the world" before the world accepts his teaching. "Though there were as many devils in Worms as there are tiles on the house-tops, go I will," said Luther. That is the temper for God's instruments.

The next requisite, which John also had, is manifest indifference to material ease. Silken courtiers do not haunt the desert. Kings' houses, and not either the wilderness or kings' dungeons, are the sunny spots where they spread their plumage. If the gaunt ascetic, with his girdle of camel's hair and his coarse fare, had been a self-indulgent sybarite, his voice would never have shaken a nation. The least breath of suspicion that a preacher is such a man ends his power, and ought to end it; for self-indulgence and the love of fleshly comforts eat the heart out of goodness, and make the eyes too heavy to see visions. John was the same man then as they had known him to be; therefore it was no impatience of the hardships of his prison that had inspired his doubts.

Our Lord next speaks of John's great office. He was a prophet. The dim recognition that God spoke in His fiery words had drawn the crowds, weary of teachers in whose endless jangle and jargon of casuistry was no inspiration. The voice of a man who gets his message at first hand from God has a ring in it which even dull ears detect as something genuine. Alas for the bewildering babble of echoes and the paucity of voices to-day!

So far Jesus had been appealing to His hearers' knowledge; He now goes on to add higher truth concerning John. He declares that he is more than a prophet, because he is His messenger before His face; that is, immediately preceding Himself. We cannot stay to comment on the remarkable variation between the original form of the quotation from Malachi and Christ's version of it, which, in its substitution of "thee" for "me," bears so forcibly on the divinity of Christ; but we may mark the principle on which John's superiority to the whole prophetic order is based. It is that nearness to

Jesus makes greatness. The closer the relation to Him, the higher the honour. In that long procession the King comes last; and of "them that go before Me, crying Hosanna to Him that cometh," the order of precedence is that the first are last, and the highest is he who walks in front of the Sovereign.

Next, we have the limitations of the forerunner and His relative inferiority to the least in the kingdom of heaven. Another standard of greatness is here from that of the world, which smiles at the contrast between the uncultured preacher of repentance and the mighty thinkers, poets, legislators, kingdom-makers, whom it enrolls among the great. In Christ's eyes greatness is nearness to Him, and understanding of Him and His work. Neither natural faculty nor worth is in question, but simply relation to the kingdom and the King. He who had only to preach of Him who should come after him, and had but a partial apprehension of Christ and His work, stood on a lower level than the least who has to look to a Christ who has come, and has opened the gates of the kingdom to the humblest believer. The truths which were hid from ages, and but visible as in morning twilight to John, are sunlit to us. The scholars in our Sunday-schools know familiarly more than prophets and kings ever knew. We "hold the gray barbarian lower than the Christian child"; and not merely he, but the wisest of the prophets, and the forerunner himself. The history of the world is parted into two by the coming of Jesus Christ, as every dictionary of dates tells, and the least of the greater is greater than the greatest of the less. What a place, then, does Christ claim! Our relation to Him determines greatness. To recognise

Him is to be in the kingdom of heaven. Union to Him brings us to fulfil the ideal of human nature; and this is life, to know and trust Him, the King.

Our Lord adds a brief characterisation of the effect of John's ministry. It was of mingled good and evil, and there is a tone of sadness perceptible in the ambiguous words. John had aroused great popular excitement, and had stirred multitudes to seek to enter the kingdom. So far was good. But had all the crowds understood what sort of kingdom it was? Had they not too often dragged down the lofty conception to their own vulgar level, and, with their dream of an outward sovereignty, thought to gain it for their own by violence instead of meekness, by arms and worldly force rather than by submission? The earnestness was good, but Christ's sad insight saw how much strange fire had mingled in the blaze, as if some earth-born smoky flame should seek to blend with the pure sunlight. Such seems the most natural interpretation of the words; but they are ambiguous, and may possibly mean by "the violent" those who had been roused to genuine earnestness by the clarion voice which rang in the ears of that slumbering generation.

Then follows the explanation of this new interest in the kingdom. "All the prophets and the law prophesied until John." The whole period till His coming was of preparation, and it all converged on the epoch of the forerunner. The eagerness to flock into the kingdom which characterised His time would have been impossible in the earlier days. He closes that order of things, standing, as it were, on the isthmus between prophecy and fulfilment, belonging properly to neither, but having affinities with both, and being the transition from the one to the other. Then our Lord closes His words concerning John with the distinct statement, which He expects His hearers to have difficulty in receiving, probably from the contradiction to it which John's present condition seemed to give, that in Him was fulfilled Malachi's prophecy of the sending of "Elijah the prophet before the . . . day of the Lord." The fiery Tishbite, gaunt and grim, ascetic and solitary, who bearded Ahab, and flamed across a corrupt age with a stern message of repentance or destruction, was repeated in the lonely ascetic who had his Ahab in Herod and his Jezebel in Herodias, and, like his prototype, knew no fear, but flashed out the lightnings of his words on every sin. The two men were brothers, and their voices answer each other across the centuries. Christ crowns His witness to John with thus pointing to the last swan song of ancient prophecy, and thereby at once sets John on a pinnacle of greatness, and advances a claim concerning Himself, all the more weighty because He leaves it to be inferred. "He that hath ears to hear, let him hear," suggests that He has spoken some deep truth, which needs reflection ere all its bearings are seen. If John was Elias, the day of the Lord was at hand, and "the Sun of Righteousness" was already above the horizon. Jesus' witness concerning John ends in witness concerning Himself.

LESSON XX.

Christ's Voice of Judgment, Thanksgiving, Self-attestation, and Invitation.

MATTHEW xi. 20-30.

20. "Then began He to upbraid the cities wherein most of His mighty works were done, because they repented not:

21. Woe unto thee, Chorazin! woe unto thee, Bethsaida! for if the mighty works, which were done in you, had been done in Tyre and Sidon, they would have repented long ago in sackcloth and ashes.

22. But I say unto you, It shall be more tolerable for Tyre and Sidon at the day of judgment, than for you.

23. And thou, Capernaum, which art exalted unto heaven, shalt be brought down to hell: for if the mighty works, which have been done in thee, had been done in Sodom, it would have remained until this day.

24. But I say unto you, That it shall be more tolerable for the land of Sodom in the day of judgment, than for thee.

25. And at that time Jesus answered and said, I thank Thee, O Father, Lord of heaven and earth, because Thou hast hid these things from the wise and prudent, and hast revealed them unto babes.

26. Even so, Father: for so it seemed good in Thy sight.

27. All things are delivered unto Me of my Father: and no man knoweth the Son, but the Father; neither knoweth any man the Father, save the Son, and he to whomsoever the Son will reveal Him.

28. Come unto Me, all ye that labour and are heavy laden, and I will give you rest.

29. Take My yoke upon you, and learn of Me; for I am meek and lowly in heart: and ye shall find rest unto your souls.

30. For My yoke is easy, and My burden is light."

MATTHEW has probably brought together, in this chapter, several incidents, which throw light on the strange variety of effects produced by our Lord's appearance. The verses included in this lesson are all closely connected by definite notes of time, but it is doubtful whether they are in their chronological place here, or in Luke's Gospel. However that may be, it is worth noticing how this whole chapter is occupied with showing how variously Jesus affected men. A gallery of swift sketches is hung in it,—John the doubting herald; the excitable multitude, with their eagerness too genuine for wholesale censure, though too smoky and carnal for unmixed praise; the cynical critics who, with inconsistent impartiality of censure, picked holes in John's asceticism and in Christ's freedom. Then follows our lesson, which gives us His lamentation over the impenitent, whom more light had made more guilty; and, in sharp contrast, His joy over the babes who welcomed His message, His claim to be the sole medium of the knowledge of God, and His blessed universal call, which is addressed to, and may be obeyed by, all these varieties of men, whose different attitudes towards the truth do not make the truth less truly meant for all.

I. The voice of sad upbraiding. The words (vv. 20-24) are weighed down with the sorrow of Christ's loving heart, and stern with denunciations of judgment. He weeps in pronouncing the dark doom, and the doom is pronounced that it may not be fulfilled. But it is false kindness to hide grim facts; and the gospel is a gospel because one of its elements is the proclamation of judgment. The grace poured into Christ's lips would not be the grace which we need, unless its tenderness left us in no doubt of the solemn fact of retribution. The full chord includes the deep bass note of loving threatening as well as the clear treble of lightsome promise.

Besides the weightier lesson of these verses, they suggest two thoughts regarding Christ's miracles. The one is, How small a sheaf of these has been harvested in the Gospels, compared with the large number unrecorded. Most of His mighty works were done in these cities, but Chorazin is only twice mentioned in Scripture, while a very small percentage of the narrated works are allocated to either of the other two places. The earth's path lay through a field of meteors; but only a few of them blaze still in our sky. The other thought is that our Lord rated highly the evidential and spiritual power of His miracles. In modern days we are too apt to dwell on sayings of His which subordinate their worth to that of the self-evidencing power of His personality and words. But that is one-sided. His miracles were signs, and they were powers not only in the physical realm, but in leading to the knowledge of Him.

The great lesson taught here is that degrees of judgment correspond to degrees of light. What a solemn thought it is that the long past generations of Sodom and Tyre were then living and waiting their trial! With what calm certitude of knowledge Christ declares what is to happen at that future day! Is not His voice like the voice of the King, who is to be the Judge? He sees all and says little. We, who see nothing, had best listen and make sure that we weigh and feel His words. That profound and mysterious "more tolerable" can be but dimly understood by us; but this we can understand, that it clearly indicates degrees in retribution, as infinite as the moral differences between men, who may all do the same thing, and yet be unequally guilty of the various conditions determining the amount of culpability. The measure of knowledge, against which the deed was done, is the most important. The glimmer which shed a twilight on Sodom was enough to warrant the fierce blaze of the destroying fire; but the light which shone from Jesus was so bright that, if neglected, a far more lurid flame must flash around its despisers. The most hopeless people are gospel-hardened formalists. Christ here claims to shed a clearer light for guidance than can be seen anywhere else; and, as He is the last and fullest revelation of the mercy of God, and the strongest motives for repentance are drawn from His work, so the consequences of insensibility to these are the most terrible. The brighter the summer sunshine, the louder the thunder. Indifference to Him is the sin of sins. The men of Chorazin had not actively opposed Him, but had simply not actively accepted. They had not been bestial in their profligacy, like the foul Sodomites. The deadliest poison may be colourless, and look quite innocent. So, not these long-dead men of the villages by the lake, but the respectable people of to-day, may learn that the worst sinners are not the doers of the worst things, but the sinners against the clearest light, who know all about Jesus, and care nothing for it all.

II. The solemn voice of thanksgiving. The vision of judgment which lay before Christ's inward eye drives Him, as a relief, to the contrasted thought of the humble souls who did receive Him. " He answered "—what? Apparently, not any word from others, but the emotions of His own heart at the sad foresight of the doom of the rejecters. Who are the two classes spoken of?

"The wise and prudent" were, no doubt, primarily the scribes and Pharisees; but the designation includes all who, like them, trust in their own superior enlightenment, and along with intellectual eminence, which is a good, have intellectual conceit, which is an evil. Just as Christ said that it was hard for the rich to enter the kingdom, and explained the saying, when misunderstood, by the varied form, "how hard is it for them that trust in riches to enter," so here, the possession of intellectual wealth is not a disqualification, nor is there any discord between true culture and Christianity, nor any natural affinity between ignorance and religion; but the exaggerated estimate of the value of culture, and the tone of mind produced by pluming one's self on it, and using it as the measure of all things, are fatal disqualifications. On the other hand, the "babes" are those conscious of their ignorance and need, self-distrustful, willing to obey, docile. These, whether they be wise or foolish, are fit to receive the light. A childlike receptivity will not look in vain. The reasons for the gospel's being hid from those and revealed to these lie in the very nature of the gospel. For what are its characteristics? It addresses itself to all men, not to classes, schools, or coteries. It appeals to beggars and millionaires, to scholars and to barbarians, with the same message. It knows no ranks nor distinctions. It treats all as utterly helpless, and offers to all redemption as their most pressing want, and demands from all submission and trust. That being so, they who see its beauty must be the persons who consent to its estimate of them, and are willing to accept its terms. Hence the disqualification of the "wise" necessarily results. Wisdom is no barrier in itself nor in its proper use. The organ for the reception of the gospel is the heart, not the head; and wisdom becomes a barrier because its possessors are accustomed to think it the master key, and do not care to go in at a door which it does not open. If the wise man will "cease to glory in his wisdom," and be content to be saved on the same terms as the poor simpleton who cannot read a line, his wisdom will cease to be a hindrance and become a help. "Let him become a fool, that he may be wise." The apparent harshness and exclusiveness of this saying melt away when steadily regarded, and it is seen to cover and be a consequence of the universal adaptation of the gospel, and of the simplicity of its conditions. It is "hid from the wise and prudent," just because it is "babes" to whom it is "revealed." There are no special entrance doors for the *élite* of the race; and if any set of men are so enamoured of their own intellectual or other qualifications that they want differently coloured tickets of admission, and a private entrance, they will have to stop outside. Not their superiority, but their insisting that it shall be recognised, keeps them out.

III. The majestic voice of self-attestation (ver. 27). Jesus turns now from prayer to witness, from heaven to earth. His spirit had passed from the woes of the rejecters to the contemplation of the gracious Divine purpose, which had appointed terms so possible to the humblest; and now He points all, be they wise or foolish, to Himself as the one revealer. The words sound like a verse of John's Gospel; and their occurrence here may serve to show that the side of our Lord's teaching which had the strongest affinities for John's deep mystical nature was not unknown to the other evangelists, though sparingly reproduced by them. What tremendous claims He here makes for Himself!—unlimited power, as universal in its sweep as unbounded in its sway. Intercommunion with the Father so deep that perfect knowledge (for the word rendered "know" is an emphatic form, and implies full and adequate knowledge) reciprocally substitutes between the Father and Him; a mystery in His being, of which the Father alone is fully cognizant; His own exclusive and complete revelation of the Father, without which every eye is dark, and by which any eye that He wills may be enlightened,—all this was said in the quietest tones by a Galilean peasant, who, in almost the same breath, said, in His next sentence, "I am meek and lowly in heart." Strange meekness! And stranger still that men have taken Him at His word, seen no contradiction between His claims and His humility, though that humility announced its own presence, and have joyfully found that He does all which He undertook, and shows them the Father. Who can fathom the depths of this saying? It pierces the primeval depths before time and "all things" were. It plunges into the Divine abysses, and lets us dimly see the eternal, ineffable impartation of the Father to the Son, and the absolute completeness of their communion. On these transcendent facts of the eternal, super-sensual world, it bases the exclusive power of the Son to reveal the Father; whereby the paradox comes to be true, that the Son is to us more of a mystery than the Father whom He reveals, and that He, though unknown with perfect knowledge by any but the Father, nevertheless imparts to us a knowledge of the Father which He parallels with His own, inasmuch as it is derived from Him, and He will not cease to declare God's name unto His brethren till we have learned all which He can teach. Is this insanity? If not, who and what is He who thus speaks?

IV. The pleading voice of universal invitation (vv. 28-30). A listener might have asked to whom the Son willed to reveal the Father. If He is the only Revealer, does His merciful desire to be such include "the wise and prudent" as well as "the babes," the sinners of Chorazin as well as the little group of followers? These final words answer all such questions. Thorwaldsen has filled the pediment of a great church with figures representing all varieties of human pains and woes, and set Him in the centre, calm and pure, with compassion and conscious power in His look, and outstretched arms expressing invitation, and dropping the benediction of rest. The artist has but embodied these wonderful words.

We may note in them the twofold designation of the persons invited. They are such as "labour and are heavy laden.' These two expressions cover the active and the passive sides of our need. The former refers to work which, by reason of excess in amount, or distastefulness in kind, has become wearisome toil. The latter points not so much to the burden of duties or tasks, as to the heavy and painful experiences which we all, sooner or later, have to carry,—the burdens of sorrow and care. Most men have to stagger under both these sorts of evils, and to toil and sorrow at the same time. But both have a deeper significance when viewed in relation to God's law of righteousness. There are painful and futile efforts to keep the law, which weary the doers; and there is the sore burden of failure, guilt, and habit, which bows down men's backs, always, whether they know it or no. So this twofold designation embraces every soul; and he to whom the Revealer wills to reveal the one Light is every man, whatever his culture or his sin. The call touches deep chords in every heart.

We may note the twofold invitation—" Come unto Me," and "Take My yoke upon you." The former is faith; the latter, practical obedience. The former is the call to all the weary; the latter is the further call, which they only who have come will obey. Faith is the true approach of the soul to Jesus. It has Him, not mere doctrines about Him, for its object. It is the movement of the whole man to Him. It has for its result our continual companionship by His side. It is the initial Christian act. On it follows "Take My yoke upon you, and learn of Me." The yoke is that which is laid on the neck of the draught ox, and enables it to draw the burden. The load, then, is the whole mass of duties and services, while the yoke is that which binds them on us: namely, His authority. Obedience, then, to His command, and a consequent active performance of all which He wills, is Christ's second merciful call to us all. It comes second, not first; but it does come. Our relation to Him is not exhausted in the faith which has recourse to Him for healing and comfort; it must pass on to include this other also. The whole sum of practical obedience is further set forth as "learning of Him." The imitation of Jesus, is the one commandment of Christian morals; but it should never be forgotten that such imitation is only possible when His Spirit dwells in us, and makes us like Him. There may be as much weariness and bondage in imitating Christ without His life in us, as in any other form of trying to work out our own righteousness.

We may note further the twofold rest. Perhaps the variation in the form of the promise in the two clauses is intended to carry a great lesson. "I will give you rest," seems more appropriate to describe the rest consequent on our first coming to Christ, which is simply and exclusively a direct bestowment, and "ye shall find rest" more fitted to describe a repose which is none the less His gift, though it is dependent on our practical obedience, in a way in which the former is not. There is an initial rest, the rest of faith, of pardon, of a quieted conscience, of filial communion with God,—a rest involved in the very act of trust, as of a child sleeping secure on its mother's breast. Nothing less than Divine power can give such a gift, and Christ offers it to all. But there is a further rest in bearing His yoke. Obedience delivers us from the unrest of self-will. To obey an authority which we love is repose. He that "hath ceased from his own works" and does Christ's, hath entered into rest. It brings rest from the tyranny of passion, from the weight of too much liberty, from conflicting desires. There is rest in Christ-likeness. He is meek and lowly; and they who wear His image find in meekness tranquillity, and some quieting from His deep calm hushes their spirits. Such rest is like God's rest, full of energy.

His yoke is easy, and His commandments are not grievous, not because He lowers the standard of duty, but because He alters the motives which enjoin it, and gives the power to do them. Christ's yoke is padded with love, so it rests lightly on the neck. His burden is light, because, as St. Bernard says, it carries the man who carries it. The true rest for every soul lies first in coming to Christ by faith, and then in yielding heart and will to Him, and carrying the burden of our lighter cross after and for the sake of Him, who has borne the heaviest cross for us.

> "Here giveth He the rest
> Which to His best belov'd doth still remain."

LESSON XXI.

The Pharisees' Sabbath, and Christ's.

MATTHEW xii. 1-14.

1. "At that time Jesus went on the Sabbath day through the corn; and His disciples were an hungred, and began to pluck the ears of corn, and to eat.

2. But when the Pharisees saw it, they said unto Him, Behold, Thy disciples do that which is not lawful to do upon the Sabbath day.

3. But He said unto them, Have ye not read what David did, when he was an hungred, and they that were with him;

4. How he entered into the house of God, and did eat the shewbread, which was not lawful for him to eat, neither for them which were with him, but only for the priests?

5. Or have ye not read in the law, how that on the Sabbath days the priests in the temple profane the Sabbath, and are blameless?

6. But I say unto you, That in this place is one greater than the temple.

7. But if ye had known what this meaneth, I will have mercy, and not sacrifice, ye would not have condemned the guiltless.

8. For the Son of man is Lord even of the Sabbath day.

9. And when He was departed thence, He went into their synagogue:

10. And, behold, there was a man which had his hand withered. And they asked Him, saying, Is it lawful to heal on the Sabbath days? that they might accuse Him.

11. And He said unto them, What man shall there be among you, that shall have one sheep, and if it fall into a pit on the Sabbath day, will he not lay hold on it, and lift it out?

12. How much then is a man better than a sheep? Wherefore it is lawful to do well on the Sabbath days.

13. Then saith He to the man, Stretch forth thine hand. And he stretched it forth; and it was restored whole, like as the other.

14. Then the Pharisees went out, and held a counsel against Him, how they might destroy Him."

WE have had frequent occasion to point out that this Gospel is constructed, not on chronological, but on logical lines. It groups together incidents related in subject, though separated in time. Thus we have the collection of Christ's sayings in the Sermon on the Mount, followed by the collection of doings in chapters viii. and xix., the collected charge to his ambassadors in chapter x., the collection of instances illustrative of the relations of different classes to the message of the kingdom and its King in chapter xi., and now in this chapter a series of incidents setting forth the growing bitterness of antagonism on the part of the guardians of traditional and ceremonial religion. This is followed, in the next chapter, with a series of parables.

The present lesson includes two Sabbath incidents, in the first of which the disciples are the transgressors of the sabbatic tradition; in the second, Christ's own action is brought into question. The scene of the first is in the fields, that of the second is the synagogue. In the one, Sabbath observance is set aside at the call of personal needs; in the other, at the call of another's calamity. So the two correspond to the old Puritan principle that the Sabbath law allowed of "works of necessity and of mercy."

1. The Sabbath and personal needs. This is a strange sort of King who cannot even feed His servants. What a glimpse into the penury of their usual condition the quiet statement that the disciples were hungry gives us, especially if we remember that it is not likely that the Master had fared better than they! Indeed, His reference to David and his band of hungry heroes suggests that "He was an hungred" as well as "they that were with Him." As they traversed some field path through the tall yellowing corn, they gathered a

few ears, as the merciful provision of the law allowed, and hastily began to eat the rubbed-out grains. As soon as they "began," the eager Pharisees, who seem to have been at their heels, call Him to "behold" this dreadful crime, which, they think, requires His immediate remonstrance. If they had had as sharp eyes for men's necessities as for their faults, they might have given them food which it was "lawful" to eat, and so obviated this frightful iniquity. But that is not the way of Pharisees. Moses had not forbidden such gleaning, but the casuistry which had spun its multitudinous webs over the law, hiding the gold beneath elaborate dirty net-work, decided that plucking the ears was of the nature of reaping, and reaping was work, and work was forbidden, *ergo*—which being settled, of course the inferential prohibition became more important than the law from which it was deduced. That is always the case with human conclusions from revelation; and the more questionable these are, the more they are loved by their authors, as the sickly child of a family is the dearest.

Our Lord does not question the authority of the tradition, nor ask where Moses had forbidden what His disciples were doing. Still less does He touch the sanctity of the Jewish Sabbath. He accepts His questioners' position, for the time, and gives them a perfect answer on their own ground. Perhaps there may be just a hint in the double "Have ye not read?" that they could not produce Scripture for their prohibition, as He would do for the liberty which He allowed. He quotes two instances in which ceremonial obligations give way before higher law. The first, that of David and his followers eating the shewbread, which was tabooed to all but priests, is perhaps chosen with some reference to the parallel between Himself, the true King, now unrecognised and hunted, with His humble followers, and the fugitive outlaw with his band. It is but a veiled allusion at most; but, if it fell on good soil, it might have led some one to ask, "If this is David, where is Saul, and where is Doeg, watching him to accuse him?" This example serves our Lord's purpose of showing that even a Divine prohibition which relates to mere ceremonial matter melts, like wax, before even bodily necessities. What a thrill of holy horror would meet the enunciation of the doctrine that such a carnal thing as hunger rightfully abrogated a sacred ritual proscription! The law of right is rigid; that of external ceremonies is flexible. Better that a man should die than that the one should be broken; better that the other should be flung to the winds than that a hungry man should go unfed. It may reasonably be doubted whether all Christian communities have learned the sweep of that principle yet, or so judge of the relative importance of keeping up their appointed forms of worship, and of feeding their hungry brother. The brave Abimelech, "the son of Ahitub," was ahead of a good many people of to-day.

The second example comes still closer to the question in hand, and supplies the reference to the Sabbath law, which the former had not. There was much hard work done in the temple on the Sabbath,—sacrifices to be slain, fires and lamps to be kindled, and so on. That was not Sabbath desecration. Why? Because it was done in the temple, and as a part of Divine service. The sanctity of the place, and the consequent sanctity

The Pharisees' Sabbath, and Christ's.

of the service, exempted it from the operation of the law. The question, no doubt, was springing to the lips of some scowling Pharisee, "And what has that to do with our charge against your disciples?" when it was answered by the wonderful next words, "In this place"—here among the growing corn, beneath the free heaven, far away from Jerusalem—"is one greater than the temple." Profound words, which could only sound as blasphemy or nonsense to the hearers, but which touch the deepest truths concerning His person and His relations to men, and which involved the destruction of all temples and rituals. He is all that the temple symbolised. In Him the Godhead really dwells; He is the meeting-place of God and man, the place of the oracle, the place of sacrifice. Then, where He stands is holy ground, and all work done with reference to Him is worship. These poor followers of His are priests; and if, for his sake, they had broken a hundred Sabbath regulations, they are guiltless.

So far our Lord has been answering His opponents; now He attacks. The quotation from Hosea is often on His lips. Here He uses it to unmask the real motives of His assailants. Their murmuring came not from more religion, but from less love. If they had had a little more milk of human kindness in them, it would have died on their lips; if they had grasped the real meaning of the religion they professed, they would have learned that its soul was "mercy"; that is, of course, man's gentleness to man—and that sacrifice and ceremony was but the body, the help, and sometimes the hindrance, of that soul. They would have understood the relative importance of disposition and of external worship, as end and means, and not have visited a mere breach of external order with a heat of disapprobation only warranted by a sin against the former. Their judgment would have been liker God's if they had looked at those poor hungry men with merciful eyes, and with merciful hearts, rather than with eager scrutiny, that delighted to find them tripping in a triviality of outward observance. What mountains of harsh judgment by Christ's own followers on each other would have been removed into the sea if the Spirit of these great words had played upon them!

The "for" at the beginning of verse 8 seems to connect with the last words of the preceding verse, "I call them guiltless, for," etc. It states more plainly still the claim already put forward in verse 6. "The Son of man," no doubt, is equivalent to "Messiah"; but it is more, as revealing at once Christ's true manhood and His unique and complete manhood, in which the very ideal of man is personally realised. It can never be detached from His other name, the Son of God. They are the obverse and reverse of the same golden coin. He asserts His power over the Sabbath, as enjoined upon Israel. His is the authority which imposed it. It is plastic in His hands. The whole order of which it is part has its highest purpose in witnessing of Him. He brings the true "rest."

II. The Sabbath, and works of beneficence. Matthew appears to have brought together here two incidents which were separated in time, according to Luke. The scene changes to a synagogue, perhaps that of Capernaum. Among the worshippers is a man with "a withered hand," who seems to have been brought there by the Pharisees as a bait to try to draw out Christ's compassion. What a curious state of mind that was,— to believe that Christ could work miracles, and to want one, not for pity's sake, nor for confirmation of faith, but to get material for accusing Him! And how heartlessly careless of the poor sufferer they are, when they use him thus! He for his part stands silent. Desire and faith have no part in evoking this miracle. Deadly hatred and calculating malignity ask for it, and for once they get their wish. Having baited their hook, and set the man with his shrunken hand full in view, they get into their corners, like hunters, and wait the event. Matthew tells us that they ask our Lord the question which Luke represents Him as asking them. Perhaps we may say that He gave voice to the question which they were asking in their hearts. Their motive is distinctly given here. They wanted material for a legal process before a local tribunal. The whole thing was an attempt to get Jesus within the meshes of the law. Again, as in the former case, it is the traditional, not the written law, which healing would have broken. The question evidently implies that, in the judgment of the askers, healing was unlawful. Talmudical scholars tell us that in later days the rabbis differed on the point, but that the prevalent opinion was, that only sicknesses threatening immediate danger to life could lawfully be treated on the Sabbath. The more rigid doctrine was obviously held by Christ's questioners. It is a significant instance of the absurdity and cruelty which are possible when once religion has been made a matter of outward observance. Nothing more surely and completely ossifies the heart and blinds common sense.

In His former answer Jesus had appealed to Scripture to bear out His teaching that Sabbath observance must bend to personal necessities. Here He appeals to the natural sense of compassion to confirm the principle that it must give way to the duty of relieving others. His question is as confident of an answer as the Pharisees' had been. But though He takes it for granted that His hearers could only answer it in one way, the microscopic and cold-blooded ingenuity of the rabbis, since His day, answers it in another. They say, "Don't lift the poor brute out, but throw in a handful of fodder, and something for him to lie upon, and let him be till next day." A remarkable way of making "thine ox and thine ass" keep the Sabbath! There is a delicacy of expression in the question; the owner of "one sheep" would be more solicitous about it than if he had a hundred; and our Shepherd looks on all the millions of His flock with a heart as much touched by their sorrow and needs as if each were His only possession. The question waits for no answer; but Christ goes on (as if there could be but one reply) to His conclusion, which He binds to His first question by another, equally easy to answer. Man's superiority to animals makes his claim for help more imperative. "You would not do less for one another than for a sheep in a hole, surely." But the form in which our Lord puts His conclusive answer to the Pharisees gives an unexpected turn to the reply. He does not say "It is lawful to heal," but "It is lawful to do well," thus at once showing the true justification of healing, namely, that it was a beneficent act, and widening the scope of His answer to cover a whole class of cases. "To do well" here means, not to do right, but to do good, to benefit men. The principle is a wide one: the charitable succour of men's needs, of whatever kind, is congruous with the true design of that day of rest. Have the churches laid that lesson to heart? On the whole, it is to be observed that our Lord here distinctly recognises the obligation of the Sabbath, that He claims power over it, that He permits the pressure of individual necessities, and of others' need of help, to modify the manner of its observance, and that He leaves the application of these principles to the spiritual insight of His followers.

The cure which follows is done in a singular fashion. Without a word of request from the sufferer or any one else, He heals him by a word. His command has a promise in it, and He gives the power to do what He bids the man do. "Give what Thou commandest," says St. Augustine, "and command what Thou wilt." We get strength to obey in the act of obedience. But beyond the possible symbolical significance of the mode of cure, and beyond the revelation of Christ's power to heal by a word, the manner had a special reason in the very cavils of the Pharisees. Not even they could accuse Him of breaking any Sabbath law by such a cure. What had He done? Told the man to put out his hand. Surely that was not unlawful. What had the man done? Stretched it forth. Surely that broke no subtle rabbinical precept. So they were foiled at every turn, driven off the field of argument, and baffled in their attempt to find ground for laying an information against Him. But neither His gentle wisdom nor His healing power could get to these hearts, made stony by conceit and pedantic formalism; and all that their contact with Jesus did was to drive them to intenser hostility, and to send them away to plot His death. That is what comes of making religion a round of outward observances. The Pharisee is always blind as an owl to the light of God and true goodness; keen-sighted as a hawk for trivial breaches of his cobweb regulations, and cruel as a vulture to tear with beak and claw. The race is not extinct. We all carry one inside, and need God's help to cast him out.

LESSON XXII.

Four Sowings and One Ripening.

MATTHEW xiii. 1-9.

1. "The same day went Jesus out of the house, and sat by the sea side.

2. And great multitudes were gathered together unto Him, so that He went into a ship, and sat; and the whole multitude stood on the shore.

3. And He spake many things unto them in parables, saying, Behold, a sower went forth to sow;

4. And when he sowed, some seeds fell by the way side, and the fowls came and devoured them up:

5. Some fell upon stony places, where they had not much earth: and forthwith they sprung up, because they had no deepness of earth:

6. And when the sun was up, they were scorched; and because they had no root, they withered away.

7. And some fell among thorns; and the thorns sprung up, and choked them:

8. But other fell into good ground, and brought forth fruit, some an hundredfold, some sixtyfold, some thirtyfold.

9. Who hath ears to hear, let him hear."

THE seven parables of the kingdom, in this chapter, are not to be regarded as grouped together by Matthew. They were spoken consecutively, as is obvious from the notes of time in vv. 36 and 53. They are a great whole, setting forth the "mystery of the kingdom" in its method of establishment, its corruption, its outward and inward growth, the conditions of entrance into it, and its final purification. The sacred number seven, impressed upon them, is the token of completeness. They fall into two parts: four of them being spoken to the multitudes from the boat, and presenting the more obvious aspects of the development of the kingdom; three being addressed to the disciples in the house, and setting forth truths about it more fitted for them. The first parable, which concerns us now, has been generally called the Parable of the Sower, but he is not the prominent figure. The subject is much rather the soils; and the intention is, not so much to declare anything about him, as to explain to the people, who were looking for the kingdom to be set up by outward means, irrespective of men's dispositions, that the way of establishing it was by teaching, which needed receptive spirits. The parable is both history and prophecy. It tells Christ's own experience, and it foretells His servants'. He is the great Sower, who has "come forth" from the Father. His present errand is not to burn up thorns or to punish the husbandmen, but to scatter on all hearts the living seed, which is here interpreted, in accordance with the dominant idea of this Gospel, as being "the word of the kingdom" (ver. 19). All who follow Him, and make His truth known, are sowers in their turn, and have to look for the same issue of their work. The figure is common to all languages. Truth, whether intellectual, moral, or spiritual, is seminal, and, deposited in the heart, understanding, or conscience, grows. It has a mysterious vitality, and its issue is not a manufacture, but a fruit. If all teachers, especially religious teachers, would remember that, perhaps there would be fewer failures, and a good deal of their work would be modified. We have here four sowings and one ripening,—a sad proportion! We are not told that the quantity of seed was in each case the same. Rather we may suppose that much

Four Sowings and One Ripening.

less fell on the wayside, and on the rocky soil, and among the thorns, than on the good ground. So we cannot say that seventy-five per cent. of it was wasted; but, in any case, the proportion of failure is tragically large. This sower was under no illusion as to the result of his work.

It is folly to sow on the hard footpath, or the rocky ground, or among thorns; but Christ and His servants have to do that, in endless hope that these unreceptive hearts may become good soil. One lesson of the parable is, Scatter the seed everywhere, on the most unlikely places.

I. Our Lord begins with the case in which the seed remains quite outside the soil, or, without metaphor, in which the word finds absolutely no entrance into the heart or mind. A beaten path runs by the end or perhaps through the middle of the cornfield. It is of exactly the same soil as the rest, but many passengers have trodden it hard, and the very foot of the sower, as he comes and goes in his work, has helped. Some of the seed, sown broadcast of course, falls there, and lies where it falls, having no power to penetrate the hard surface. As in our own English cornfields, a flock of bold, hungry birds watch the sower; and, as soon as his back is turned, they are down with a swift-winged swoop, and away goes the exposed grain. So there is an end of it; and the path is as bare as ever, five minutes after it has been strewed with seeds.

The explanation is too plain to be mistaken, but we may briefly touch its main features. Notice, then, that our Lord begins with the case in which there is least contact between His word and the soul, and that, as the contact is least in degree, so it is shortest in duration. A minute or two finishes it. Notice especially that the path has been made hard by external pressure. It is not rock, but soil, like the other parts of the field. It represents the case of men whose insensibility to the word is caused by outward things having made a thoroughfare of their natures, and trodden them into incapacity to receive the message of Christ's love. The heavy baggage-waggons of commerce, the light cars of pleasure, merry dancers, and sad funeral processions, have all used that way, and each footfall has beaten the once loose soil a little firmer. We are made insensitive to the gospel by the effect of innocent and necessary things, unless we take care to plow up the path along which they travel, and to keep our spirits susceptible by a distinct effort. How many hearers of every teacher are there, who never take in his words at all, simply because they are so completely preoccupied!

Notice what becomes of the seed that lies thus bare. "Immediately," says Mark, "Satan cometh." His agents are these light-winged thoughts that flutter round the hearer as soon as the sermon or the lesson is over. Talk of the weather, criticism of the congregation, or of the sower's attitude as he flung the seed, or politics, or business, drives away even the remembrance of the text, before many of our hearers are out of sight of the church. Then the whirl of traffic begins again, and the path is soon beaten a little harder. If the seed had got ever so little way into the ground, the sharp beaks of the thieves would not have carried it off so easily. Impressions so slight as Christ's word makes on busy men are quickly rubbed out. But if the seed sown vanishes thus swiftly,

Four Sowings and One Ripening.

the fault is not in it, but in ourselves. Satan may seek to snatch it away, but we can hinder him.

Our Lord uses a singular expression, "This is he that was sown by the way side," which appears to identify the man with the seed rather than with the soil. It has been suggested by some commentators that this expression is to be regarded as conveying the truth that the seed sown in the heart and growing up there becomes the life-spring of the individual, and that therefore we may speak of him or of it as bearing the fruit. But this explanation will not avail for the case where there is no entrance of the word into the heart, and so no new birth by the word. More probably we are to regard the expression simply as a conversational shorthand form of speech, not strictly accurate, but quite intelligible; unless, indeed, we suppose that "sown" is used in the same double sense in which we speak of a field as well as of seed being sown.

II. The next variety of soil differs from the preceding in having its hindrance deep seated. Many a hillside in Galilee—as in Scotland or New England—would show a thin surface of soil over rock, like skin stretched tightly on a bone. No roots could get through that, nor find nourishment in it; while the very shallowness of earth and the heat of the underlying stone would accelerate growth. Such premature and feeble shoots perish as quickly as they spring up; the fierce Eastern sun makes a speedy end of them, and a few days sees their springing and withering. It is a case of "lightly come, lightly go." Quick-sprouting things are soon-dying things. A shallow pond is up in waves under a breeze which raises no sea on the Atlantic, and it is calm again in a few minutes. Readily stirred emotion is transient. Brushwood catches fire easily, and burns itself out quickly. Coal takes longer to kindle, and is harder to put out. The persons meant are those of excitable temperament, whose feelings lie on the surface, and can be got at without first passing through the understanding or the conscience. Such people are easily played on by the epidemic influence of any prevalent enthusiasm or emotion, as every revival of religion shows. Their very "joy" in hearing the word is suspicious; for a true reception of it seldom begins with joy, but rather with "the sorrow which worketh repentance not to be repented of." Their immediate reception of it is suspicious, for it suggests that there has been no time to consult the understanding or to form a deliberate purpose; stable resolutions are slowly formed. It is the sunny side of religion which has attracted them. They know nothing of its difficulties and depths. Hence, as soon as they find out the realities of the course which they have embraced so lightly, they desert, like John Mark, running away as soon as home comforts at Cyprus were left behind. The Christian life means self-denial, toil, hard resistance to many fascinations. It means sweat and blood, or it means nothing. Whether there be "persecution" or no, there will be affliction, "because of the word," and all the joyful emotion will ooze out at the man's finger-ends. The same superficial excitability which determined his swift reception of the word will determine his hasty casting of it aside, and immediately he stumbles. All his acts will be done in a hurry, and none of his moods will last. Feeling is in its place down in the engine-room, but it makes a poor pilot. Very significant is that phrase "no root in himself." His roots are in the accidents of the moment. His religion has never really struck root in him, but only in the superficial layer of him. His conscience, will, understanding, are unpenetrated by its fibres. So it is easily pulled up, as well as soon withered. There is another profound truth in this picture. The hard, impenetrable rock lies right under the thin skin of soil. The nature which is over-emotional on its surface is utterly hard at its core. The most heartless people are those whose feelings are always ready to gush; the most unimpressible are those who are most easily brought to a certain degree of emotion by the sound of the word. This class is an advance on the former in that there has been a real contact with the word, which has lain longer in their hearts, and has had some growth. We may regard it as either better or worse than the former, according as we consider that it is better to accept and feel than not to accept at all, or that it is worse to have in some measure had and felt than not to have received the word of the kingdom.

III. In one part of the field was a patch where the soil was neither rammed solid, as on the foot-path, nor thin, as where the rock cropped out, but where there had been a tangle of thorns, which grow luxuriantly in Palestine. These had been cut down, but not stubbed up, as is plain from the very fact that the seed reached the ground, as also from the description of them as "springing up." The two growths advance together. In this case, the seed has a longer life than in the former. It roots and grows, and even, according to the other evangelist's version, fruits, though it does not mature its fruit. There is no question of "falling away" here. Only the hardier growth, which had the advantage of previous possession, and which pushes up its shoots above ground all round the more tender plant, gets the start of it, and smothers its green blades, overtopping it, and keeping it from sun and air, as well as drawing to itself the nourishment from the soil. The main point here is the two simultaneous growths. The man is, as James calls him, a "double-minded man." He is trying to grow both corn and thorn on the same soil. He has some religion, but not enough to make thorough work of it. He is endeavouring to ride on two horses at once. Religion says "either—or"; he is trying "both—and." The human heart has only a limited amount of love and trust to give, and Christ must have it all. It has enough for one,—that is, for Him; but not enough for two,—that is, for Him and the world. This man's religion has not been powerful enough to grub up the roots of the thorns. They were cut down when the seed was sown For a little while, at the beginning of his course, the new life in him seemed to conquer; but the roots lay hid, and, in due time, showed again above ground. "Ill weeds grow apace"; and these, as is their nature, grow faster than the good seed. So the only thing to do is to get them out of the ground to the last fibre.

Christ specifies what He calls thorns. We can all understand care being so called; but riches? Yes, they too have sharp prickles, as anybody will find who stuffs a pillow with them. But our Lord chooses His words to point the lesson that not outward things, but our attitude to them, make the barrenness of this soil. It is not "this world," but "the care of this world," not "riches," but "the deceitfulness of riches," that choke the word. These two seem opposites, but they are really the same

Less. XXII.] Four Sowings and One Ripening. 225

thing on two opposite sides. The man who is burdened with the cares of poverty, and the man who is deceived by the false promises of wealth, are really the same man. The one is the other turned inside out. We make the world our god, whether we worship it by saying "I am desolate without thee," or by fancying that we are secure with it. Note the effect that the issue in this case is —unfruitfulness. The man may, and I suppose usually does, keep up a profession of Christianity all his life. He very likely does not know that the seed is choked, and that he has become unfruitful. But he is a stunted, useless Christian, with all the sap and nourishment of his soul given to his worldly position, and his religion a poor pining thing, with blanched leaves and abortive fruit. How much of Christ's field is filled with plants of that sort!

IV. The parable tells us nothing about the comparative acreage of the path, rocky and thorny ground on the one hand, and of the fertile soil on the other. It is not meant to teach the proportion of success to failure, but to exhibit the fact that the reception of the word depends on men's dispositions. The good soil has none of the faults of the rest of the field. It is loose, and thus unlike the path; deep, and thus unlike the rocky bit; clean, and thus unlike the thorn brake. The interpretation given of it by our Lord seems at first sight incomplete. It is all summed up in one word, "understandeth." Then, did not the second and third classes, at all events, understand? They received the word, and it had some growth in them. The distinction between them and the good-soil hearer is surely of a moral nature, rather than of so purely intellectual a kind as "understanding" suggests. Hence, Luke's keep fast "in an honest and good heart" may seem a more adequate statement. But biblical usage does not regard "understanding" as a purely intellectual process, but rather as the action of the whole moral and spiritual nature. It knows nothing of dividing a man up into water-tight compartments, one of which may be full of evil, and the other clean and receptive of good. According to it, we "understand" religious truth by our hearts and moral nature in conjunction with the dry light of intellect. So the word here is used in a pregnant sense, and includes the grasp of the truth with the whole nature, the complete reception of the word of the kingdom not merely into the intellect, but into the central self, the undivided fountain from which flow the issues of life, whether these be called intellect, or affection, or conscience, or will. Only he who has thus become one with the word, and housed it deep in his inmost soul, "understands" it, in the sense in which our Lord here uses that expression. "Thy word have I hid in mine heart" exactly corresponds to the "understanding" which is here given as the distinctive mark of the good soil.

The result of that reception into the depths of the spirit is that he "verily beareth fruit." The man who receives the word is identified with the plant which springs from the seed which he receives. The life of a Christian is the result of the growth in him of a supernatural seed. He bears fruit, yet the fruit comes not from him, but from the seed sown. "I live; yet not I, but Christ liveth in me." Fruitfulness is the aim of the sower, and the test of the reception of the seed. If there is not fruit, manifestly there has been no real understanding of the word. A touchstone, that, which will produce surprising results in detecting spurious Christianity, if it be honestly applied!

There is variety in the degree of fruitfulness, according to the goodness of the soil; that is to say, according to the thoroughness and depth of the reception of the word. The great Husbandman does not demand uniform fertility. He is glad to get a hundredfold, but He accepts sixty, and does not refuse thirty, only He arranges them in descending order, as if He would fain have the highest rate from all the plants, and, not without disappointment, gradually stretches His merciful allowance to take in even the lowest. He will accept the scantiest fruitage, and will lovingly "purge" the branch "that it may bring forth more fruit."

No parable teaches everything. Paths, rocks, and thorns cannot change. But men can plow up the trodden ways, and blast away the rock, and root out the thorns, and, with God's help, can open the door of their hearts, that the Sower and His seed may enter in. We are responsible for the soil, else His warning were vain, "Take heed therefore how ye hear."

LESSON XXIII.

Various Aspects of the Kingdom.

MATTHEW xiii. 31-33, 44-52.

31. "Another parable put He forth unto them, saying, The kingdom of heaven is like to a grain of mustard seed, which a man took, and sowed in his field:

32. Which indeed is the least of all seeds: but when it is grown, it is the greatest among herbs, and becometh a tree, so that the birds of the air come and lodge in the branches thereof.

33. Another parable spake He unto them; The kingdom of heaven is like unto leaven, which a woman took, and hid in three measures of meal, till the whole was leavened.

44. Again, the kingdom of heaven is like unto treasure hid in a field; the which when a man hath found, he hideth, and for joy thereof goeth and selleth all that he hath, and buyeth that field.

45. Again, the kingdom of heaven is like unto a merchant man, seeking goodly pearls:

46. Who, when he had found one pearl of great price, went and sold all that he had, and bought it.

47. Again, the kingdom of heaven is like unto a net, that was cast into the sea, and gathered of every kind:

48. Which, when it was full, they drew to shore, and sat down, and gathered the good into vessels, but cast the bad away.

49. So shall it be at the end of the world: the angels shall come forth, and sever the wicked from among the just,

50. And shall cast them into the furnace of fire: there shall be wailing and gnashing of teeth.

51. Jesus saith unto them, Have ye understood all these things? They say unto Him, Yea, Lord.

52. Then said He unto them, Therefore every scribe which is instructed unto the kingdom of heaven is like unto a man that is an householder, which bringeth forth out of his treasure things new and old."

THE parables already considered might suggest that the kingdom was destined to partial and shaded success. The first spoke of three parts of the seed as coming to nothing, and the second of the fourth part as growing up amid tares. The listeners might say, " Is this all?" Therefore, in the next two, our Lord sets forth a brighter aspect of the future of the kingdom, exhibiting in the former its growth from small beginnings to great magnitude, and in the second its transforming influence on the mass in which it is deposited. They make a pair, and finish His instructions as to the kingdom, addressed to the crowds. The remaining three parables, spoken to the disciples in the house, consist of a pair, setting forth the supreme preciousness of the kingdom, and the wisdom of acquiring it at all costs, and of a single parable, which repeats, with a difference, the lesson of the separation of wheat and tares.

I. The twin parables illustrating the development of the kingdom from small and hidden beginnings. The parable of the little mustard seed still takes the process of vegetation as emblem of the growth of the kingdom; but the sower barely appears, though His agency is still part of the essence of the representation, and the field is " His field." But the seed is now the kingdom itself, and the only points brought into notice are the contrasted smallness of the commencement and bulk of the growth at the end. We need not spend time in discussing the correctness of the statements as to the smallness of the mustard seed and the size of the shrub. Jesus does not speak as a botanist, but in popular language; and it is enough to know that the mustard seed was a common proverbial illustration of extreme minuteness, and that the herb was a miracle of height and substance as compared with its tiny origin. The application is too plain to need any interpretation. It strikes home at once to the many among the first listeners, who had recoiled from the (as it seemed to them) dreadful down-come from the long-cherished national hopes to this obscure Galilean peasant and His handful of followers. He stole into the world in a despised corner of a despised land. He gathered a few believers, spoke some gentle words, laid his hands on a few sick folk, and then died. What proud incredulity would have curled the lips of the men of influence and culture in that day, if they had been pointed to Him and His disciples, and bidden to see there the mightiest force, destined to universal dominion! The lesson is not less needed now than then. God's great things have ever small beginnings, even as the seed of the "big trees" in California is smaller than that of many a much humbler conifer. The world's great things begin large, and dwindle fast. Enterprises launched with much drum-beating have an ugly habit of collapsing rapidly. We have to learn reverence for the smallest seed which has vitality, and confidence that the quantity, and still more the quality, of the life in the little black packet of latent possibility is not measured by its size. So we shall not be led away by vulgar admiration of the big, which we mistake for the great and divine, nor discouraged and impatient if a heritage be not "gotten hastily at the beginning." The parable brings the small seed into sharp contrast with the large result, and implies the world-wide spread of the kingdom. The picturesque touch of the birds lighting on the branches is probably an allusion to Ezekiel xvii. 23, and a definite prophecy of the coming of the nations to partake in its blessings. The fowls of the heaven sing among the branches. Souls weary of flight fold their tired wings, and find rest, shelter, and joy there.

The parable of the leaven completes the picture of the growth of the kingdom by describing its inward operation, as the former does its outward growth. It spreads in space, and increases in bulk; but it transforms inert matter into its own nature and thus grows by assimilation. The eccentric interpretation of the leaven as the emblem of evil is disposed of by observing that it is the kingdom, and not its corruption, which "is like unto leaven," and by remembering that the meal is improved, not spoiled, by it. No meaning is to be attached to the "woman," nor is it safe to find the three parts of human nature, body, soul, and spirit; nor the three divisions of the human race springing from Noah's sons; nor the three forms of society, the family, the church, and the state, in the number, which probably was chosen simply as the quantity most usually leavened at once, or as the definite number most commonly put for an indefinite. All such trifling hides the main lessons. These lie, first, in the addition of the leaven to the meal, teaching that the quickening influence comes from without; that, in a word, if human society is ever to contain a kingdom of heaven, and be transformed thereby, it must be imported, not developed. They lie, second, in the hiding of the leaven, by which is taught the same truth of secret beginnings as in the former parable. They lie, third, in the manner of the leaven's working, which is fermentation. So the gospel stirs up movement in the dead mass. Christ comes to bring peace at the end, but He must first bring a sword. Leaven works from within outwards. The gospel is planted in the depths of the individual spirit, and gradually permeates the whole being. It works underground in society, and only remodels institutions as the result of having remodelled men. The lesson lies further in the assimilative power of the leaven, which changes each particle of the meal, and, by means of each in turn, transmits transforming power to the outer unleavened particles. It lies, finally, in the hopes suggested by that "till the whole was leavened," which foretells the permeating of the mass with quickening influence, and the complete assimilation of the individual to it.

II. The second pair of parables begins the short series of three, addressed to the disciples, and appropriately deals with the supreme worth of the kingdom and the condition of attaining it. Observe the contrast with the group addressed to the multitude, in which the action of the sower is prominent, and simple receptivity is the condition of becoming a child of the kingdom, while in this pair of parables the human condition is emphatically insisted upon as being energetic action and self-surrender. There are four salient points in the two stories which run parallel to each other, but with significant differences. First, note man's true treasure. The kingdom of heaven means most simply the order or community in which God reigns, and loving obedience is rendered to His will. Its possession by the individual is the same as being a child of the kingdom, or, in other words, as the personal possession of salvation. This condition of loving obedience is, subjectively, our highest good and our true wealth. Objectively, God in Christ is our treasure. This alone meets our deepest poverty, and brings the riches of pardon, the wealth of mercy, which cleanses while it forgives. Nothing else meets this deep need, without the supply of which we are miserable and wretched and poor. It is our treasure, because it is wealth for all our nature, while all other possessions but satisfy a part and leave the rest hungry, as in a menagerie at feeding-time, one cage is quiet because it has its meal, and all the others growling unfed; it is so, because it is all wealth in one. The travelling jeweller had a bag full of small pearls; but when he saw the one great one, he knew it was worth far more. We need unity in what is to stay the soul. The one is more than the many. One sun gives more light than a million stars. Life wants one all-sufficient portion, one refuge, one aim, to simplify and ennoble it, one love for the heart. It is so because it is enduring wealth. All that remains outside of us is subject to circumstance and change. It often leaves us, and we have to leave it at last. But the true treasure is inwrought with the substance of the soul; and he only is rich who can say of his wealth, "I shall not lose thee, though I die."

The second point is the hiding of the treasure. The farmer's man, in the first parable, had often walked across the field, and never knew that there was anything in it but clods. A thin film of soil hid the glittering store. The merchantman, on the other hand, had a trained eye, and as soon as he saw the pearl he knew its value. So the combination of both pictures teaches that the worth of the kingdom is an open secret. Much ingenuity has been expended on assigning a meaning to "the field," but with small success. It is better to rest in the general thought that the gospel is presented in such a form as to veil its inward glories from dull, sense-bound eyes; or if we seek a more specific interpretation, we may perhaps find it in Paul's words, "In whom are all the treasures of wisdom and knowledge hidden." The lowly form of the king was a stumbling-block then, and, in some measure, has continued to be so. But, without pressing this suggestion, one has only to look around and see the thousands to whom the outward form of the gospel is so familiar that its spirit and power are undreamed of, to understand how the treasure was hid, while, on the other hand, it is an open secret, and its preciousness is plain to every instructed eye.

The next point is the two ways of discovering the true wealth. The rustic was not looking for it. A shower of rain, or a chance stroke of his spade, moved a little earth, and there it lay before his unexpectant, astonished eye. He is the type of those of whom the Divine Love says, "I was found of them that sought me not." Of such were Saul on the Damascus road, Philip the apostle, the woman of Samaria, and many more. We may not be seeking God, but He is seeking us. We may have no sense of need, no dreams nor wishes to find the treasure which we know not that we have lost; but He seeks the coin which *He* has lost, and lights a candle, and sweeps the house, and seeks diligently till He finds it. Thank God! the kingdom is found by many who seek it not. But the travelling jeweller, who has spent his life in the search for fair pearls, represents the better class of souls which cherish aspirations after truth, virtue, wisdom, and whatsoever things are lovely. It is a noble quest, but misdirected so long as it looks for many separate beauties and preciousnesses. The "one entire and perfect chrysolite," Jesus Christ, is the only adequate satisfaction for such souls, and in Him they will find embodied all which they have vainly sought.

The last point is the one way of obtaining the treasure. However discovered, there is but one method of possessing it, and between the recognition of its worth, and the making it our very own, is a deep gulf, over which the only bridge is "sell all that thou hast, and buy." We sell all that we have, when we recognise that all is worthless, and abandon it for the sake of the higher preciousness. Self is all that we have. We sell self when we forsake all self-reliance and self-righteousness. We buy the kingdom when we give away rags for a robe, sin for righteousness, ourselves for Christ. That purchase is without money or price. It is but the same self-surrender in conscious poverty, which is faith. It is a glad surrender, for the rustic was moved by his joy to part with all. It is a reasonable requirement, and they who comply with it are wise, however their action may look like folly; for they lose only what it is death to keep, and they gain what it is life to win.

III. The parable of the draw-net is, at first sight, identical with that of the tares, but a closer examination shows differences which are all that we need touch on. Before doing so, however, note the picturesque beauty of the representation of this restless, stormy life as a sea, contrasted with the fertile, stable shore of eternity, where the toilers sit. Note, too, the peculiar force of the parable as addressed to those whose calling had already been taken by Christ as an emblem of their apostolic work. Observe, also, that the net is cast once and drawn once, so that it is not to be taken as a figure of the work of the ministry, but as representing the historical founding of the kingdom by Christ, its continuance in human society, and its final withdrawal to the eternal world. Note further the size of the net, which is a great seine, or draw-net, implying the wide sweep of the kingdom.

As compared with the parable of the tares, this one has little to say about the period of intermingling, which makes the greater part of that. The points of view of the two are different. The one has for its theme principally the earthly form of the kingdom; and the other, the perfect form. The one deals with its development, and the other with its completion. We have nothing here corresponding to the conversation of the servants with the householder, nor to his command of forbearance; but the whole stress lies on that leisurely and careful separation of the evil from the good. Again, the destiny of the righteous is passed over lightly, while the fate of the corrupt and unwholesome fish is emphasised. These characteristics at once suggest the nature of the difference between the parables. That of the tares was, as we have seen, addressed to the multitudes, and gave them instruction in the form and growth of the kingdom as a power in the world. It was meant mainly to correct the false ideas of Christ's mission, as if He was to begin with a process of separation. But this parable, addressed to the disciples, was, like the two preceding, which were also meant for their ears, mainly intended to exhort them to the conduct required of those who would be His followers; and, as the hidden treasure and the pearl inculcated the need of utter self-surrender, so this impresses the necessity of moral purity as the indispensable characteristic of the true children of the kingdom. It is a warning to all who are held within the sweep of the

Various Aspects of the Kingdom.

net, that no outward connection with the kingdom, nothing but righteousness, ensures their standing within it. Therefore the dark side of that judgment is put forward here, that all professing Christians may lay to heart that "they are not all Israel, which are of Israel," and "give diligence" that they may be "found in peace, without spot and blameless."

LESSON XXIV.

Mingled in Growth, separated in Maturity.

MATTHEW xiii. 24-30.

24. "Another parable put He forth unto them, saying, The kingdom of heaven is likened unto a man which sowed good seed in his field:

25. But while men slept, his enemy came and sowed tares among the wheat, and went his way.

26. But when the blade was sprung up, and brought forth fruit, then appeared the tares also.

27. So the servants of the householder came and said unto him, Sir, didst not thou sow good seed in thy field? from whence then hath it tares?

28. He said unto them, An enemy hath done this. The servants said unto him, Wilt thou then that we go and gather them up?

29. But he said, Nay; lest while ye gather up the tares, ye root up also the wheat with them.

30. Let both grow together until the harvest: and in the time of harvest I will say to the reapers, Gather ye together first the tares, and bind them in bundles to burn them: but gather the wheat into my barn."

THE first four parables contained in this chapter were spoken to a miscellaneous crowd on the beach, the last three to the disciples in the house. The difference of audience is accompanied with a diversity of subject. The former group deals with the growth of the kingdom, as it might be observed by outsiders, and especially with aspects of the growth on which the multitude needed instruction; the latter, with topics more suited to the inner circle of followers. Of these four, the first three are parables of vegetation; the last, of assimilation. The first two are still more closely connected, inasmuch as the person of the sower is prominent in both, while he is not seen in the others. The general scenery is the same in both, but with a difference. The identification of the seed sown with the persons receiving it, which was hinted at in the first, is predominant in the second. But while the former described the various results of the seed, the latter drops out of sight the three failures, and follows its fortunes in honest and good hearts, showing the growth of the kingdom in the midst of antagonistic surroundings. It may conveniently be considered in three sections: the first teaching how the work of the sower is counterworked by his enemy; the second, the patience of the sower with the thick-springing tares; and the third, the separation at the harvest.

I. The work of the sower counter-worked by his enemy, and the mingled crops. The peculiar turn of the first sentence, "the kingdom of heaven is likened unto a man that sowed," etc., suggests that the main purpose of the parable is to teach the conduct of the king in view of the growth of the tares. The kingdom is concentrated in Him, and the "likening" is not effected by the parable, but, as the tenses of both verbs show, by the already accomplished fact of His sowing. Our Lord veils His claims by speaking of the sower in the third person; but the hearing ear cannot fail to catch the implication throughout that He Himself is the sower and the Lord of the harvest. The field is "His field," and His own interpretation tells us that it means "the world." Whatever view we take of the bearing of this parable on purity of communion in the visible Church, we should not slur over Christ's own explanation of the field, lest we miss the lesson that He claims the whole world as His, and contemplates the sowing of the seed broadcast over it all. The kingdom of heaven is to be developed on, and to spread through, the whole earth. The world belongs to Christ not only when it is filled with the kingdom, but before the sowing. The explanation of the good seed takes the same point of view as in the former parable. What is sown is "the word"; what springs from the seed is the new life of the receiver. Men become children of the kingdom by taking the gospel into their hearts, and thereby receive a new principle of growth, which in truth becomes themselves. Side by side with the sower's beneficent work the counter working of "His enemy" goes on. As the one, by depositing holy truth in the heart, makes men "children of the kingdom," the other, by putting evil principles therein, makes men "children of evil." Honest exposition cannot eliminate the teaching of a personal antagonist of Christ, nor of His continuous agency in the corruption of mankind. It is a glimpse into a mysterious region, none the less reliable because so momentary. The sulphurous clouds that hide the fire in the crater are blown aside for an instant, and we see. Who would doubt the truth and worth of the unveiling because it was short and partial? "The Devil is God's ape." His work is a parody of Christ's. Where the good seed is sown, there the evil is scattered thickest. False Christs and false apostles dog the true like their shadows. Every truth has its counterfeit. Neither institutions, nor principles, nor movements, nor indi-

Mingled in Growth.

viduals, bear unmingled crops of good. Not merely creatural imperfection, but hostile adulteration, marks them all. The purest metal oxidises, scum gathers on the most limpid water, every ship's bottom gets foul with weeds. The history of every reformation is the same: radiant hopes darkened, progress retarded, a second generation of dwarfs, careless or unfaithful guardians of their heritage.

There are, then, two classes of men represented in the parable, and these two are distinguishable without doubt by their conduct. Tares are said to be quite like wheat until the heads show, and then there is a plain difference. So our Lord here teaches that the children of the kingdom and those of evil are to be discriminated by their actions. We need not do more than point in a sentence to His distinct separation of men (where the seed of the kingdom has been sown) into two sets. Jesus Christ holds the unfashionable, "narrow" opinion that, at bottom, a man must either be His friend or His enemy. We are too much inclined to weaken the strong line of demarcation, and to think that most men are neither black nor white, but grey.

The question has been eagerly debated whether the tares are bad men in the church, and whether, consequently, the mingled crop is a description of the church only. The following considerations may help to an answer. The parable was spoken, not to the disciples, but to the crowd. An instruction to them as to church discipline would have been signally out of place; but they needed to be taught that the kingdom was to be "a rose amidst thorns," and to grow up among antagonisms which it would slowly conquer, by the methods which the next two parables set forth. This general conception, and not directions about ecclesiastical order, was suited to them. Again, the designation of the tares as "the children of evil" seems much too wide, if only a particular class of evil men—namely, those who are within the church—are meant by it. Surely the expression includes all, both in and outside the church, who "do iniquity." Further, the representation of the children of the kingdom, as growing among tares in the field of the world, does not seem to contemplate them as constituting a distinct society, whether pure or impure; but rather as an indefinite number of individuals, intermingled in a common soil with the other class. "The kingdom of heaven" is not a synonym for the church. Is it not an anachronism to find the church in the parable at all? No doubt, tares are in the church, and the parable has a bearing on it; but its primary lesson seems to me to be much wider, and to reveal rather the conditions of the growth of the kingdom in human society.

II. We have the patience of the husbandman with the quick-springing tares. The servants of the householder receive no interpretation from our Lord. Their whole conversation is silently passed by in His explanation. Clearly then, for some reason, He did not think it necessary to say any more about them; and the most probable reason is, that they and their words have no corresponding facts, and are only introduced to lead up to the Master's explanation of the mystery of the growth of the tares, and to His patience with it. The servants cannot be supposed to represent officials in the church, without hopelessly destroying the consistency of the parable; for surely all the children of the kingdom, whatever their office, are represented in the crop. Many guesses have been made,—apostles, angels, and so on. It is better to say, "The Lord hath not showed it me." The first question expresses, in vivid form, the sad, strange fact that, where good was sown, evil springs. The deepest of all mysteries is the origin of evil. Explain sin, and you explain everything. The question of the servants is the despair of thinkers in all ages. Heaven sows only good; where do the misery and the wickedness come from? That is a wider and sadder question than, How are churches not free from bad members? Perhaps Christ's answer may go as far towards the bottom of the bottomless as those of non-Christian thinkers, and, if it do not solve the metaphysical puzzles, at any rate gives the historical process, which is all the explanation of which the question is susceptible. The second question reminds us of "Wilt Thou that we command fire . . . from heaven, and consume them?" It is cast in such a form as to put emphasis on the householder's will. His answer forbidding the gathering up of the tares is based, not upon any chance of mistaking wheat for them, nor upon any hope that, by forbearance, tares may change into wheat, but simply on what is best for the good crop. There was a danger of destroying some of it, not because of its likeness to the other, but because the roots of both were so interlaced that one could not be pulled up without dragging the other after it.

Is this prohibition, then, meant to forbid the attempt to keep the church pure from unchristian members? The considerations already adduced are valid in answering this question, and others may be added. The crowd of listeners had, no doubt, many of them, been influenced by John the Baptist's fiery prophecies of the King who should come, fan in hand, to purge His floor, and were looking for a kingdom which was to be inaugurated by sharp separation and swift destruction. Was not the teaching needed then, as it is now, that that is not the way in which the kingdom of heaven is to be founded and grow? Is not the parable best understood when set in connection with the expectations of its first hearers, which are ever floating anew before the eyes of each generation of Christians? Is it not Christ's *apologia* for His delay in filling the *rôle* which John had drawn out for him? And does that conception of its meaning make it meaningless for us? Observe, too, that the rooting up which is forbidden is, by the proprieties of the emblem, and by the parallel which it must necessarily afford to the final burning, something very solemn and destructive. We may well ask whether excommunication is a sufficiently weighty idea to be taken as its equivalent. Again, how does the interpretation which sees ecclesiastical discipline here comport with the reason given for letting the tares grow on? By the hypothesis in the parable, there is no danger of mistake; but is there any danger of casting out good men from the church along with the bad, except through mistake? Further, if this parable forbids casting manifestly evil men out of the church, it contradicts the divinely appointed law of the church as administered by the apostles. If it is to be applied to church action at all, it absolutely forbids the separation of any man, however notoriously unchristian, and that, as even the strongest advocates of comprehension admit, would destroy the very idea of the church. Surely, an interpretation which lands us in such a conclusion cannot be right. We conclude, then, that the intermingling which the parable means is that of good men and bad in human society, where all are so interwoven that separation is impossible without destroying its whole texture; that the rooting up, which is declared to be inconsistent with the growth of the crop, means removal from the field, namely, the world; that the main point of this second part of the parable is to set forth the patience of the Lord of the harvest, and to emphasise this as the law of the growth of His kingdom; that it is amidst antagonism, and that its members are interlaced by a thousand rootlets with those who are not subjects of their King. What the interlacing is for, and whether tares may become wheat, are no parts of its teaching. But the lesson of the householder's forbearance is meant to be learned by us. While we believe that the scope of the parable is wider than instruction in church discipline, we do not forget that a fair inference from it is that, in actual churches, there will ever be a mingling of good and evil; and, though that fact is no reason for giving up the attempt to make a church a congregation of faithful men, and of such only, it is a reason for copying the Divine patience of the sower in ecclesiastical dealings with errors of opinion and faults of conduct.

III. The final separation at the harvest. The period of development is necessarily a time of intermingling, in which, side by side, the antagonistic principles embodied in their representatives work themselves out, and beneficially affect each other. But each grows towards an end, and, when it has been reached, the blending gives place to separation. John's prophecy is plainly quoted in the parable, which verbally repeats his "gather the wheat into his barn," and alludes to his words in the other clause about burning the tares. He was right in his anticipations; his error was in expecting the King to wield His fan at the beginning, instead of at the end of the earthly form of His kingdom. At the consummation of the allotted era, the bands of human society are to be dissolved, and a new principle of association is to determine men's place. Their moral and religious affinities will bind them together or separate them, and all other ties will snap. This marshalling according to religious character is the main thought of the solemn closing words of the parable and of its interpretation, in which our Lord presents Himself as directing the whole process of judgment by means of the "angels" who execute His commands. They are "His angels," and whatever may be the unknown activity put forth by them in the parting of men, it is all done in obedience to Him. What stupendous claims Jesus makes here! What becomes of the tares is told first in words awful in their plainness, and still more awful in their obscurity. They speak unmistakably of the absolute separation of evil men from all society but that of evil men; of a close association, compelled, and perhaps unwelcome. The tares are gathered out of "His kingdom,"—for the field of the world has then all become the kingdom of Christ. There are two classes among the tares: men whose evil has been a snare to others (for the "things that offend" must, in accordance with the context, be taken to be persons), and the less guilty, who are simply called "them that do iniquity."

Perhaps the "bundles" may imply assortment according to sin, as in Dante's circles. What a bond of fellowship that would be! "The furnace," as it is emphatically called by eminence, burns up the bundles. We may freely admit that the fire is part of the parable, but yet let us not forget that it occurs not only in the parable, but in the interpretation; and let us learn that the prose reality of "everlasting destruction," which Christ here solemnly announces, is as awful and complete. For a moment He passes beyond the limits of the parable, to add that terrible clause about "weeping and gnashing of teeth,"—the tokens of despair and rage. So spoke the most loving and truthful lips. Do we believe His warnings as well as His promises?

The same law of association according to character operates in the other region. The children of the kingdom are gathered together in what is now "the kingdom of My Father"; the perfect form of the kingdom of Christ, which is still His kingdom, for "the throne of God and of the Lamb," the one throne on which both sit to reign, is "in it." Freed from association with evil, they are touched with a new splendour, caught from Him, and blaze out like suns; or so close is their association that their myriad glories melt as into a single great light. Now amid gloom and cloud, they gleam like tiny tapers far apart; then, gathered into one, they flame in the forehead of the morning sky, "a glorious church, not having spot, nor wrinkle, nor any such thing."

LESSON XXV.

The Martyrdom of John.

MATT. xiv. 1-12.

1. "At that time Herod the tetrarch heard of the fame of Jesus,
2. And said unto his servants, This is John the Baptist; he is risen from the dead; and therefore mighty works do shew forth themselves in him.
3. For Herod had laid hold on John, and bound him, and put him in prison for Herodias' sake, his brother Philip's wife.
4. For John said unto him, It is not lawful for thee to have her.
5. And when he would have put him to death, he feared the multitude, because they counted him as a prophet.
6. But when Herod's birthday was kept, the daughter of Herodias danced before them, and pleased Herod.
7. Whereupon he promised with an oath to give her whatsoever she would ask.
8. And she, being before instructed of her mother, said, Give me here John Baptist's head in a charger.
9. And the king was sorry: nevertheless for the oath's sake, and them which sat with him at meat, he commanded it to be given her.
10. And he sent, and beheaded John in the prison.
11. And his head was brought in a charger, and given to the damsel: and she brought it to her mother.
12. And his disciples came, and took up the body, and buried it, and went and told Jesus."

THE singular indifference of the Bible to the fate of even its greatest men is exemplified in the fact that the martyrdom of John is only told incidentally, in explanation of Herod's alarm. But for that he would apparently have dropped out of the narrative, as a man sinks in the sea, without a bubble or a ripple. Christ is the sole theme of the Gospels, and all others are visible only as His light falls on them.

It takes a long time for news of Christ to reach the ears of Herod. Peasants hear of Him before princes whose thick palace walls and crowds of courtiers shut out truth. The first thing to note is the alarm of the conscience-stricken king. We learn from the other evangelists that there was a difference of opinion among the attendants of Herod—not very good judges of a religious teacher—as to who this new miracle-working rabbi might be, but the tetrarch has no hesitation. There is no proof that Herod was a Sadducee; but he probably thought as little about a resurrection as if he had been, and, in any case, did not expect dead men to be starting up again one by one and mingling with the living. His conscience made a coward of him, and his fear made that terrible which would else have been thought impossible. In his terror he makes confidants of his slaves, overleaping the barriers of position in his need of some ears to pour his fears into. He was right in believing that he had not finished with John, and in expecting to meet him again with mightier power to accuse and condemn. "If 'twere done when 'tis done," says Macbeth; but it is not done. There is a resurrection of deeds as well as of bodies, and all our buried badnesses will front us again, shaking their gory locks at us, and saying we did them.

Instead of following closely the narrative, we may best gather up its lessons by taking the actors in the tragedy.

I. We have in Herod the depths of evil possible to a weak character. The singular double which he, Herodias, and John present to Ahab, Jezebel, and Elijah, has been often noticed. In both cases a weak king is drawn opposite ways by the stronger-willed temptress at his side, and by the stern ascetic from the desert. How John had found his way into "kings' houses" we do not know; but, as he carried thither his undaunted boldness of plain-spoken preaching of morality and repentance, it was inevitable that he should soon find his way from the palace to the dungeon. There must have been some intercourse between Herod and him before his imprisonment, or he could not have shaken the king's conscience with his blunt denunciations. From the account in Mark, it would appear that, after his imprisonment, he gained great influence over the tetrarch, and led him some steps on the way of goodness. But Herod was "infirm of purpose," and a beautiful fiend was at his side, and she had an Iron will sharpened to an edge by hatred, and knew her own mind, which was murder. Between them, the weaker nature was much perplexed, and, like a badly steered boat, yawed in its course, now yielding to the impulse from John, now to that from Herodias. Matthew attributes his hesitation in killing John to his fear of the popular voice, which, no doubt, also operated. Thus he, "let I dare not, wait upon I would," and had not strength of mind enough to hold to the one and despise the other of his discordant counsellors. He was evidently a sensual, luxurious, feeble-willed, easily frightened, superstitious and cunning despot; and, as is always the case with such, he was driven farther in evil than he meant or wished. He was entrapped into an oath, and then, instead of saying, "Promises which should not be made should not be kept," he weakly consents, from weak fear of what his guests will say of him, and unwillingly, out of pure imbecility, stains his soul for ever with blood. In this wicked world, weak men will always be wicked men; for it is less trouble to consent than to resist, and there are more siren voices to whisper "Come" than prophets to thunder, "It is not lawful." Strength of will is needful for all noble life.

We may learn from this man, also, how far we may go on the road of obedience to God's will, and yet leave it at last. What became of all his eager listening, of his partial obedience, of his care to keep John safe from Herodias's malice? All vanished like early dew. What became of his conscience-stricken alarms on hearing of Christ? Did they lead to any deep convictions? They faded away, and left him harder than before. Convictions not followed out ossify the heart. If he had sent for Christ, and told Him his fears, all might have been well. But he let them pass, and, so far as we know, they never returned. He did meet Jesus at last, when Pilate sent him the Prisoner, as a piece of politeness, and in what mood?—childish pleasure at the chance of seeing a miracle. How did Jesus answer his torrent of frivolous questions? "He answered him nothing." That sad silence speaks Christ's knowledge that now even His words would be vain to create one ripple of interest on the Dead Sea of Herod's soul. By frivolity, lust, and neglect he had killed the germ of a better life, and silence is the kindest answer which perfect love can give him.

He shows us, too, the intimate connection of all sins. The common root of every sin is selfishness, and the shapes which it takes are protean and interchangeable.

Lust dwells hard by hate. Sensual crimes and cruelty are closely akin. The one vice which he would not surrender, dragged after it a whole tangle of other sins. No sin dwells alone. There is none "barren among them." They are gregarious, and a solitary sin is more seldom seen than a single swallow. Herod is an illustration, too, of a conscience fantastically sensitive, while it is dead to real crimes. He has no twinges for his sin with Herodias, and no effective ones at killing John, but he thinks it would be wrong to break his oath. The two things often go together; and many a brigand in Calabria, who would cut a throat without hesitation, would not miss mass, or rob without a little image of the Virgin in his hat. We often make compensation for easy indulgence in great sins by fussy scrupulosity about little faults, and, like Herod, had rather commit murder than not be polite to visitors.

II. The next actors in the tragedy are Herodias and her daughter. What a miserable destiny to be gibbeted for ever by half a dozen sentences! One deed, after which she no doubt "wiped her mouth, and said, I have done no harm," has won for the mother an immortality of ignominy. Her portrait is drawn in few strokes, but they are enough. In strength of will and unscrupulous carelessness of human life, she is the sister of Jezebel, and curiously like Shakespeare's awful creation, Lady Macbeth; but she adds a stain of sensuous passion to their vices, which heightens the horror. Her first marriage was with her full uncle; and her second, if marriage it can be called when her husband and Herod's wife were both living, was with her step-uncle, and thus triply unlawful. John's remonstrance awoke no sense of shame in her, but only malignant and murderous hate. Once resolved, no failures made her swerve from her purpose. Hers was no passing fury, but cold-blooded, deliberate determination. Her iron will and unalterable persistence were accompanied by flexibility of resource. When one weapon failed, she drew another from a full quiver. And the means which are finally successful show not only her thorough knowledge of the weak man she had to deal with, but her readiness to stoop to any degradation for herself and her child to carry her point. "A thousand claims to abhorrence meet in her, as mother, wife, and queen." Many a shameless woman would have shrunk from sullying a daughter's childhood by sending her to play the part of a shameless dancing-girl before a crew of half-tipsy revellers, and from teaching her young lips to ask for murder. But Herodias sticks at nothing, and is as insensible to the duty of a mother as to that of a wife. If we put together these features in her character, her hot animal passions, her cool inflexible revenge, her cynical disregard of all decency, her deadness to natural affection for her child, her ferocity and her cunning, we have a hideous picture of corrupted womanhood. We cannot but wonder whether, in after days, remorse ever did its merciful work upon Herodias. She urged Herod to his ruin at last by her ambition, which sought for him the title of king, and, with one redeeming touch of faithfulness, went with him into dreary exile in Gaul. Perhaps there, among strangers, and surrounded by the wreck of her projects, and when the hot fire of passion had died down, she may have remembered and repented her crime.

The criminality of the daughter largely depends upon

her age, of which we have no knowledge. Perhaps she was too mere a child to understand the degradation of the dance, or the infamy of the request which her, we hope, innocent and panting lips were tutored to prefer. But, more probably, she was old enough to be her mother's fellow-conspirator, rather than her tool, and had learned only too well her lessons of impurity and cruelty. What chance had a young life in such a sty of filth? When the mother becomes the devil's deputy, what can the daughter grow up to be, but a worse edition of her? This poor girl, so sinning, and so sinned against, followed in Herodias's footsteps, and afterwards married, according to the custom of the Herods, her uncle, Philip the tetrarch. She inherited and was taught evil; that was her misfortune. She made it her own; that was her crime. As she stands there, shameless and flushed, in that hideous banqueting-hall, with her grim gift dripping red blood on the golden platter, and wicked triumph gleaming in her dark eyes, she suggests grave questions as to parents' responsibility for children's sins, and is a living symbol of the degradation of art to the service of vice, and of the power of an evil soul to make hideous all the grace of budding womanhood.

III. There is something dramatically appropriate in the silent death in the dungeon of the lonely forerunner. The faint noise of revelry may have reached his ears, as he brooded there, and wondered if the coming King would never come for his enlargement. Suddenly a gleam of light from the opened door enters his cell, and falls on the blade of the headsman's sword. Little time can be wasted, for Herodias waits. With short preface the blow falls. The King has come, and set His servant free, sending him to prepare His way before Him in the dim regions beyond. A world where Herod sits in the festal chamber, and John lies headless in the dungeon, needs some one to set it right. When the need is sorest, the help is nearest. Truth succeeds by the apparent failure of its apostle. Herodias may stab the dead tongue, as the legend tells that she did, but it speaks louder after death than ever. Herod kept his birthday with drunken and bloody mirth; but it was a better birthday for his victim.

IV. It needed some courage, for John's disciples to come to that gloomy, blood-stained fortress, and bear away the headless trunk which scornful cruelty had flung out to rot unburied. When reverent love and sorrow had done their task, what was the little flock without a shepherd to do? The possibility of their continued existence as a company of disciples was at an end. They show by their action that their master had profited from his last message to Jesus. At once they turn to Him, and, no doubt, the bulk of them were absorbed in the body of His followers. Sorrowful and bereaved souls betake themselves naturally to His sweet sympathy for soothing, and to His gentle wisdom for direction. The best thing any of us can do is to "go and tell Jesus" our loneliness, and let it bind us more closely to Him.

END OF VOL. I.

Printed by Hazell, Watson, & Viney, Ld., London and Aylesbury.

THE EXPOSITOR'S BIBLE.

EDITED BY REV.
W. ROBERTSON NICOLL, M.A., LL.D.

FIRST SERIES.

Price 7s. 6d. each Volume.

THE BOOK OF GENESIS.

By the Rev. Professor *MARCUS DODS, D.D.*

SIXTH EDITION.

THE FIRST BOOK OF SAMUEL.
THE SECOND BOOK OF SAMUEL.

By the Rev. Professor *W. G. BLAIKIE, D.D., LL.D.*

FOURTH EDITION, TWO VOLS.

"Very full of suggestive thought."—*English Churchman.*
"A solid and able piece of work."—*Academy.*

THE GOSPEL OF ST. MARK.

By the Very Rev. *G. A. CHADWICK, D.D.*, Dean of Armagh.

FOURTH EDITION.

"This exposition is original, full of life, striking, and relevant. He has given us the fruit of much careful thought."—*British Weekly.*

THE EPISTLES TO THE COLOSSIANS AND PHILEMON.

By the Rev. *ALEXANDER MACLAREN, D.D.*

FIFTH EDITION.

"In nothing Dr. Maclaren has written is there more of beauty, of spiritual insight, or of brilliant elucidation of Scripture. Indeed, Dr. Maclaren is here at his best."—*Expositor.*

THE EPISTLE TO THE HEBREWS.

By the Rev. Principal *T. C. EDWARDS, D.D.*

FOURTH EDITION.

"There is abundant evidence of accurate scholarship, acute criticism, patient thought, and faculty of lucid exposition. However thoroughly any one has studied the Epistle here explained, he will certainly find in Dr. Edwards' volume fresh suggestions."—*Dr. Marcus Dods.*

THE EXPOSITOR'S BIBLE.

SECOND SERIES.

Price 7s. 6d each Volume.

THE BOOK OF ISAIAH.
Vol. I. Chapters I.-XXXIX.
By the Rev. *GEORGE ADAM SMITH, M.A.*

SIXTH EDITION.

"This is a very attractive book. Mr. George Adam Smith had evidently such a mastery of the scholarship of his subject that it would be a sheer impertinence for most scholars, even though tolerable Hebraists, to criticise his translations. . . . A lucid, impressive, and vivid study of Isaiah."—*Spectator.*

THE EPISTLE TO THE GALATIANS.
By the Rev. Professor *G. G. FINDLAY, B.A.*

THIRD EDITION.

"In this volume we have the mature results of broad and accurate scholarship, exegetical tact, and a firm grasp of the great principles underlying the Gospel of Paul presented in a form so lucid and attractive that every thoughtful reader can enjoy it."—*Dr. Beet.*

THE EPISTLES OF ST. JOHN.
By the Right Rev. *W. ALEXANDER, D.D., D.C.L.,* Lord Bishop of Derry and Raphoe.

SECOND EDITION.

"Full of felicities of exegesis. . . . Brilliant and valuable."—*Literary Churchman.*

FIRST EPISTLE TO CORINTHIANS.
By the Rev. Professor *MARCUS DODS, D.D.*

THIRD EDITION.

"Dr. Dods' writings are always excellent, and the one before us is no exception to the rule."—*Record.*

THE BOOK OF REVELATION.
By the Rev. Professor *W. MILLIGAN, D.D.*

SECOND EDITION.

"Dr. Milligan's scholarly and attractive exposition."—*Aberdeen Free Press.*

THE PASTORAL EPISTLES.
By the Rev. *ALFRED PLUMMER, D.D.,* Durham.

THIRD EDITION.

"The treatment is throughout scholarlike, lucid, thoughtful."—*Guardian.*

THE EXPOSITOR'S BIBLE.

THIRD SERIES.

Price 7s. 6d. each Volume.

THE GOSPEL OF ST. MATTHEW.

By the Rev. *J. MONRO GIBSON, D.D.*

Second Edition.

"This running commentary upon St. Matthew's Gospel sets before the reader our Lord's words, deeds, and sufferings as recorded by that Evangelist in a vivid light."—*Guardian.*

THE BOOK OF EXODUS.

By the Very Rev. *G. A. CHADWICK, D.D.*

Second Edition.

"This is, to a great extent, a model of what an expository commentary should be. To exhibit the Old Testament in the light of the New, and to point out the spiritual and permanent truth under the type by which it was in that early age expressed, and through which it still shines, cannot fail to render a commentary extremely valuable."—*Literary Churchman.*

JUDGES AND RUTH.

By the Rev. *R. A. WATSON, M.A.,* Author of "Gospels of Yesterday."

"This is an unusually attractive volume. His pages will give many a valuable hint to the preacher."—*Literary Churchman.*

THE GOSPEL OF ST. LUKE.

By the Rev. *HENRY BURTON, M.A.*

"His chapters are full of vivid illustration, and fresh, bright exposition. —*Record.*

THE PROPHECIES OF JEREMIAH.

With a Sketch of His Life and Times.

By the Rev. *C. J. BALL, M.A.,* Chaplain of Lincoln's Inn.

"The critical portion will be prized most, as it exhibits deep learning breadth of view, and clear insight into the prophet's meaning."—*Manchester Examiner.*

THE BOOK OF ISAIAH.

Vol. II. By the Rev. *GEORGE ADAM SMITH, M.A.*

Second Edition.

"The results of thorough scientific study are here presented, not as the bare and wintry stem which too often repels, but rich and attractive, with the foliage and fruit which sound criticism yields."—*Dr. Marcus Dods.*

THE EXPOSITOR'S BIBLE.

FOURTH SERIES.

Price 7s. 6d. each Volume.

THE GOSPEL OF ST. JOHN. VOL. I.

By the Rev. *MARCUS DODS, D.D.*, Professor of Exegetical Theology, New College, Edinburgh.

"An excellent contribution to the series. Dr. Dods has the gift of lucidity of expression."—*Guardian.*

THE EPISTLES OF ST. JAMES AND ST. JUDE.

By Rev. *A. PLUMMER, D.D.*, Master of University College, Durham.

"It is even a better piece of work than his former volume on the Pastoral Epistles. It contains everything that the student can desire by way of introduction to the two Epistles, while for those who read with an eye to the manufacture of sermons, or for their own edification, the doctrinal and moral lessons are developed in a style redolent of books, yet singularly easy and unaffected. Points of interest abound."—*Saturday Review.*

THE BOOK OF ECCLESIASTES.

With a New Translation.

By the Rev. *SAMUEL COX, D.D.*

"The most luminous, original, and practical exposition of Ecclesiastes which is within the reach of ordinary English readers."—*Speaker.*

THE BOOK OF PROVERBS.

By the Rev. *R. F. HORTON, M.A.*, Hampstead.

"In each of these lectures will be found much strong and vigorous thought, firm and logical reasoning, and the results of high culture and ability."—*Literary Churchman.*

THE BOOK OF LEVITICUS.

By the Rev. *S. H. KELLOGG, D.D.*, Author of "The Light of Asia and the Light of the World."

"He has certainly succeeded in investing with fresh interest this old book of laws, with whose spirit he seems so heartily in sympathy."—*Scotsman.*

THE ACTS OF THE APOSTLES. VOL. I.

By the Rev. Professor *G. T. STOKES, D.D.*

"A very valuable addition to Biblical literature."—*British Weekly.*

THE EXPOSITOR'S BIBLE.

FIFTH SERIES, 1891—92.

Price 7s. 6d. each Volume.

THE BOOK OF JOB.

By the Rev. *R. A. WATSON, D.D.*, Author of "Gospels of Yesterday," etc.

[*Ready.*

THE EPISTLES TO THE THESSALONIANS.

By the Rev *JAMES DENNEY, B.D.*

[*Ready.*

THE PSALMS. VOL. I.

By the Rev. *ALEXANDER MACLAREN, D.D.*

[*Preparing.*

THE ACTS OF THE APOSTLES. VOL. II.

By the Rev. Professor *G. T. STOKES, D.D.*

[*In the Press.*

THE EPISTLE TO THE EPHESIANS.

By the Rev. Professor *G. G. FINDLAY, B.A.*

[*Preparing.*

THE GOSPEL OF ST. JOHN. VOL. II.

By the Rev. Professor *MARCUS DODS, D.D.*

[*Preparing.*

The Foreign Biblical Library.

NOW COMPLETE.
Price 7s. 6d. each Volume.

BY PROFESSOR DELITZSCH, D.D.

I.
A BIBLICAL COMMENTARY ON THE PROPHECIES OF ISAIAH.

Authorised Translation from the Third Edition by the Rev. *JAMES DENNEY, B.D.*

In Two Volumes.

II.
A BIBLICAL COMMENTARY ON THE PSALMS.

Translated by Rev. *DAVID EATON, M.A.*, from the Latest Edition revised by the Author.

In Three Volumes.

"We heartily welcome this accurate translation of an indispensable work. Delitzsch's revised editions are so full of minute and interesting corrections and additions that his exegetical masterpieces deserve to be retranslated."—*Academy*.

SELECTED SERMONS OF SCHLEIERMACHER.

With a Biographical Sketch.

Translated by *MARY F. WILSON.*

In One Volume.

"The twenty-seven sermons chosen include fine examples of Schleiermacher's power."—*Manchester Examiner*.

The Foreign Biblical Library.

CONTINUED.

Price 7s. 6d. each Volume.

BY RICHARD ROTHE.
STILL HOURS.

With Introductory Essay by Rev. *J. MACPHERSON, M.A.*
Translated by *J. T. STODDART.*

In One Volume.

"It is a book of the first order, full of Rothe himself, and of which one wearies as little as of the face of a friend."—*Dr. Marcus Dods.*

BY PROFESSOR KURTZ.
CHURCH HISTORY.

Authorised Translation from the Latest Revised Edition, by the Rev. *JOHN MACPHERSON, M.A.*

In Three Volumes.

"The complete work of Professor Kurtz is now translated, and it really shows itself so improved in form, so much fuller in substance—in fact, so much changed in mind, body, and state, that it may claim to be a new history altogether."—*Scotsman.*

BY PROF. BERNHARD WEISS, Ph.D.
A MANUAL OF INTRODUCTION TO THE NEW TESTAMENT.

Translated by *A. J. K. DAVIDSON.*

In Two Volumes.

"As a thoroughly complete and satisfactory introduction from the point of view of a fairly conservative criticism, no book can compete with Weiss. It is throughout full of knowledge, of sense, and of vigour."—*Expositor.*

THE CLERICAL LIBRARY.

Price 6s. each Volume.

I.

THREE HUNDRED OUTLINES OF SERMONS ON THE NEW TESTAMENT.

"Will come as a godsend to many an overworked preacher."—*Ecclesiastical Gazette.*

II.

OUTLINES OF SERMONS ON THE OLD TESTAMENT.

"Excellently well done. The discourses of the most eminent divines of the day are dissected, and their main thoughts presented in a very compact and suggestive form."—*Methodist Recorder.*

III.

PULPIT PRAYERS BY EMINENT PREACHERS.

"The prayers are, in all cases, exceedingly beautiful, and cannot fail to be read with interest and profit, apart from the special purpose in view."—*Rock.*

IV.

OUTLINE SERMONS TO CHILDREN.

With Numerous Anecdotes.

"Nearly a hundred sermons, by twenty-nine eminent men. They are remarkably well written, and most interesting."—*Rock.*

V.

ANECDOTES ILLUSTRATIVE OF NEW TESTAMENT TEXTS.

"This is one of the most valuable books of anecdote that we have ever seen. There is hardly one anecdote that is not of first-rate quality."—*Christian Leader.*

VI.

EXPOSITORY SERMONS ON THE OLD TESTAMENT.

"Sermons of very unusual merit, requiring from us emphatic praise."—*Literary Churchman.*

THE CLERICAL LIBRARY.
Price 6s. each Volume.

VII.
EXPOSITORY SERMONS ON THE NEW TESTAMENT.

"These sermons, collected together from the best sources, represent the ablest among our public orators."—*Irish Ecclesiastical Gazette.*

VIII.
PLATFORM AIDS.

"Just the book to give to some overworked pastor."—*Christian.*

IX.
NEW OUTLINES OF SERMONS ON THE NEW TESTAMENT.
By *EMINENT PREACHERS.*
Hitherto unpublished.

"They have a freshness and vivacity which are specially taking."—*Sword and Trowel.*

X.
ANECDOTES ILLUSTRATIVE OF OLD TESTAMENT TEXTS.

"An excellent selection, likely to prove most useful to preachers."—*English Churchman.*

XI.
NEW OUTLINES OF SERMONS ON THE OLD TESTAMENT.

"Not only are they excellent specimens of condensed sermons, but hardly without exception they are striking, vigorous, and fresh in treatment and in thought."—*Literary World.*

XII.
OUTLINES OF SERMONS FOR SPECIAL OCCASIONS.
By *EMINENT PREACHERS.*

"Sermons from such miscellaneous sources could hardly fail to be varied and comprehensive as these undoubtedly are, nor could they fail to exhibit eloquence, originality, or spirituality." *Rock.*

THE ESSENCE OF THE BEST HOMILETIC LITERATURE
OF THIS GENERATION.

THE SERMON BIBLE.

Each Volume containing upwards of Four Hundred Sermon Outlines, and Several Thousand References.

Strongly bound in half buckram. Price 7s. 6d. each Volume.

VOLUME I. **GENESIS TO 2 SAMUEL.**

,, II. **1 KINGS TO PSALM LXXVI.**

,, III. **PSALMS LXXVII. TO THE SONG OF SOLOMON.**

,, IV. **ISAIAH TO MALACHI.**

,, V. **ST. MATTHEW I. TO XXI.**

,, VI. **ST. MATTHEW XXII. TO ST. MARK XVI.**

,, VII. **ST. LUKE I. TO ST. JOHN III.**

,, VIII. **ST. JOHN IV. TO ACTS VI.**

,, IX. **ACTS VI. TO 1 CORINTHIANS.**

THE SERMON BIBLE.

OPINIONS OF THE PRESS.

"A very complete guide to the sermon literature of the present day."—*Scotsman.*

"The most practically useful work of its kind."—*Literary Churchman.*

"An excellent guide to the best English sermons of recent time."—*Methodist Recorder.*

"Admirable epitomes of the best homiletic literature."—*London Quarterly Review.*

"Beyond question the richest treasury of modern homiletics."—*Christian Leader.*

"Rich in variety, and thorough without being overloaded."—*Rock.*

"A rich mine of homiletical wealth."—*Christian.*

"A truly valuable book for preachers."—*Church Bells.*

"Of unique excellence as a pulpit help."—*Baptist.*

"The editor of this work has rendered a valuable service by his keen and logical analysis of the sermons, his succinct statement of their main points, and his effective presentation of their more striking and essential thoughts."—*Baptist Magazine.*

"The plan has been carried out with such admirable impartiality, and such excellent taste, that the student who wishes to ascertain how a given text has been handled by the ablest English-speaking pulpit expositors of the day can hardly fail to find here what he seeks presented in the briefest form possible."—*Manchester Examiner.*

The Theological Educator.

Fcap. 8vo, 2s. 6d. each Volume.

AN INTRODUCTION TO THE OLD TESTAMENT.

By the Rev. *C. H. H. WRIGHT, D.D.*

"The work is of brief compass, and covers a vast field of study, but the necessary compression has been done with the skill of one experienced in the needs of students."—*Scotsman.*

THE WRITERS OF THE NEW TESTAMENT.

Their Style and Characteristics.

By the Rev. *WILLIAM HENRY SIMCOX, M.A.*

"One of the choicest productions of English scholarship in recent years."—*Manchester Examiner.*

THE LANGUAGE OF THE NEW TESTAMENT.

BY THE SAME AUTHOR.

"The most living grammar of the New Testament we have."—*Expositor.*

OUTLINES OF CHRISTIAN DOCTRINE.

By the Rev. *H. C. G. MOULE, M.A.*

AN INTRODUCTION TO THE NEW TESTAMENT.

By the Rev. Professor *MARCUS DODS, D.D.*

"Dr. Marcus Dods has packed away an immense amount of information in a very small space."—*Methodist Recorder.*

THE TEXTUAL CRITICISM OF THE NEW TESTAMENT,

An introduction to.

By the Rev. Professor *B. B. WARFIELD, D.D.*

"A masterly survey of the whole subject."—*Expositor.*

The Theological Educator.

Price 2s. 6d. each Volume.

A MANUAL OF CHURCH HISTORY.

By the Rev. *A. C. JENNINGS, M.A.*

In Two Volumes.

Vol. I.— From the First to the Tenth Century.
Vol. II.—From the Eleventh to the Nineteenth Century.

"They are small, but they include 'infinite riches in little room.'"—*Globe.*

A MANUAL OF CHRISTIAN EVIDENCES.

By the Rev. Prebendary *C. A. ROW, M.A.*

"A veritable *multum in parvo*, clear, cogent, and concise."—*Saturday Review.*

A MANUAL OF THE BOOK OF COMMON PRAYER.

Showing its History and Contents. For the use of those Studying for Holy Orders and others.

By the Rev. *CHARLES HOLE, B.A.*, King's College, London.

"It is not overloaded with detail, and yet supplies in an admirably compact shape all essential information."—*British Weekly.*

A HEBREW GRAMMAR.

By the Rev. *W. H. LOW, M.A.*, Joint Author of "A Commentary on the Psalms," etc., etc.

"A brief and masterly sketch of Hebrew grammar."—*Literary Churchman.*

AN EXPOSITION OF THE APOSTLES' CREED.

By the Rev. *J. E. YONGE, M.A.*, late Fellow of King's College, Cambridge.

"An able treatise."—*Church Times.*
"A handy book for divinity students, which will give them all the information they want for examination for Orders on the subject which it handles."—*Saturday Review.*

The Household Library of Exposition.

THE GALILEAN GOSPEL.
By Professor *A. B. BRUCE*, D.D.

Third Thousand.

Price 3s. 6d.

"We heartily commend this little volume as giving an outline ably drawn of the teaching of Christ."—*Spectator.*

THE SPEECHES OF THE HOLY APOSTLES.
By *DONALD FRASER*, D.D.

Second Thousand.

Price 3s. 6d.

"Exceedingly well done."—*Scottish Review.*

THE LAMB OF GOD.
Expositions in the Writings of St. John.

By *W. ROBERTSON NICOLL*, M.A., LL.D.

Price 2s. 6d.

"A volume of rare beauty and excellence."—*New York Independent.*

THE LORD'S PRAYER.
By *CHARLES STANFORD*, D.D.

Third Thousand.

Price 3s. 6d.

"For spiritual grasp and insight, for wealth of glowing imagery, and for rare felicity of style, it will hold a first place in this valuable series of expository monographs."—*Christian.*

THE LAST SUPPER OF OUR LORD,
And His Words of Consolation to the Disciples.

By *J. MARSHALL LANG*, D.D., Barony Church, Glasgow.

Third Thousand.

Price 3s. 6d.

"With a rare power of insight—the result, doubtless, of much inward experience—Dr. Lang has entered into the very inmost spirit of the scenes and incidents, the words and feelings, which make up the history of that night."—*Scotsman.*

The Household Library of Exposition.

THE LAW OF THE TEN WORDS.
By *J. OSWALD DYKES*, D.D.
Crown 8vo. Price 3s. 6d.
"His style is a singular combination of strength and beauty."—*Literary World.*

THE LIFE OF DAVID.
As Reflected in His Psalms.
By *ALEXANDER MACLAREN*, D.D., of Manchester.
SEVENTH EDITION.
Price 3s. 6d.
"Just the book we should give to awaken a living and historical interest in the Psalms."—*Guardian.*

THE TEMPTATIONS OF CHRIST.
By *G. S. BARRETT*, M.A.
Price 3s. 6d.
"Marked alike by careful language and sober thought."—*Guardian.*

THE PARABLES OF OUR LORD.
As Recorded by St. Matthew.
By *MARCUS DODS*, D.D.
SEVENTH THOUSAND.
Price 3s. 6d.
"There is certainly no better volume on the subject in our language."—*Glasgow Mail.*

THE PARABLES OF OUR LORD.
As Recorded by St. Luke.
By *MARCUS DODS*, D.D.
SIXTH THOUSAND.
Price 3s. 6d.
"An original exposition, marked by strong common sense and practical exhortation."—*Literary Churchman.*

ISAAC, JACOB, AND JOSEPH.
By *MARCUS DODS*, D.D.
SIXTH THOUSAND.
Price 3s. 6d.
"The present volume is worthy of the writer's reputation. He deals with the problems of human life and character which these biographies suggest in a candid and manly fashion."—*Spectator.*

The Sunday Afternoon Library for Young People.

Crown 8vo, elegantly bound in cloth, 3s. 6d. each; or the Four Vols., in case, 12s.

TALKING TO THE CHILDREN.

By the Rev. ALEXANDER MACLEOD, D.D.

"An exquisite work. Divine truths are here presented in simple language, illustrated by parable and anecdote at once apt and beautiful."—*Evangelical Magazine.*

THE GENTLE HEART.

By the SAME AUTHOR.

"We have been fascinated with the originality and beauty of its thought, charmed with the simplicity and elegance of its language, and enriched with the store of its illustration."—*Mr. Spurgeon.*

THE CHURCHETTE.

A Year's Sermons and Parables for the Young.

By the Rev. J. REID HOWATT.

"Mr. Howatt has learned the knack of speaking to young people. Short, simple, cheery, colloquial, imaginative, impressive, the sermons yield abundant evidence that, as he says, his 'aim has been to speak to children in the sunshine.'"—*Literary World.*

"As breezy and refreshing as the breath of the ocean."—*Nonconformist.*

THE CHILDREN'S PORTION.

By the Rev. ALEXANDER MACLEOD, D.D.

"As a preacher to children, Dr. Macleod has, perhaps, no living equal. In these delightful chapters he seems to us to be at his best."—*Christian.*

"This is a collection of short sermons addressed to children. They are well adapted to strike the fancy and touch the heart of the young."—*Record.*

THE CRITICAL AND EXPOSITORY BIBLE CYCLOPÆDIA.

By the Rev. *A. R. FAUSSET, D.D.*, Canon of York, Joint Author of "The Critical and Experimental Commentary."

Illustrated by Six Hundred Woodcuts.

Cheap Edition, Unabridged. Eighth Thousand. 7s. 6d., *cloth, red edges.*

"This is a work of prodigious research, labour, and minute painstaking. The book is a rich and full storehouse of Scripture knowledge."—*Guardian.*

"I am glad to bear testimony to its accuracy and value. It accomplishes the purpose of putting the results of modern scholarship in a popular form."—*Rev. Alex. Maclaren, D.D.*

THE NEWBERRY BIBLE.

Comprising the
English-Hebrew Bible and the English-Greek Testament.

Designed to give as far as practicable the Accuracy, Precision, and Certainty of the Original Hebrew and Greek Scriptures on the page of the Authorised Version. Adapted both for the Biblical Student and for the Ordinary English Reader.

Edited by *THOMAS NEWBERRY.*

LARGE TYPE HANDY REFERENCE EDITION.

21s., 25s., 35s., *and a very superior Edition, in best Levant Yapp kid lined, silk sewn,* 60s. *Portable Edition,* 18s., 28s., 35s.

Among the Prominent Features are the following:—

AUTHORISED VERSION arranged in Paragraphs.
Leading Words and Emphatic Pronouns in distinctive type.
Poetical Portions arranged in parallels.
Parallel passages connected and references given.
Imperfect translations emended. Original Hebrew and Greek words inserted in margin.
Divine titles distinguished and explained.
Singular, dual, and plural numbers distinguished.
Important words traced to their Hebrew and Greek roots.
Hebrew and Greek tenses marked by simple and uniform signs.
The use and force of the letter "vau" or conjunction "and" shown.
Words translated by two or more words connected by a hyphen.
The signs employed are of the simplest possible character.

WORKS BY DR. R. W. DALE, of Birmingham.

FELLOWSHIP WITH CHRIST,

And other Discourses Delivered on Special Occasions.

Third Thousand.

Crown 8vo, cloth, price 6s.

"These are certainly among the most massive, and, as a consequence, most impressive sermons of the day. Each is a sort of miniature theological treatise, but the theology is alive—as it were, heated through and through by the fires of a mighty conviction, which has become a passion to convince. . . . In these sermons there is a fine universalism; they might be addressed to any audience—academic, professional, commercial, artisan. And to hear them would be to feel that religion is a thing to be believed and obeyed."—*Speaker.*

THE LIVING CHRIST AND THE FOUR GOSPELS.

Fifth Thousand.

Crown 8vo, cloth, price 6s.

"As a man of culture and eloquence he has put the case strongly and well, and it will not be surprising if his book, which is not written, he tells us, for Masters of Arts, but in the first instance for members of his own congregation, and then for all ordinary people who take an interest in such matters, should be the means of convincing many that the assumptions sometimes made about late origin of the Gospels, etc., are utterly unfounded."—*Scotsman.*

LAWS OF CHRIST FOR COMMON LIFE.

Fifth Thousand.

Crown 8vo, price 6s.

"Sound sense and wholesome Christian teaching conveyed in pure, idiomatic, and forcible English."—*Scotsman.*

"A storehouse of wise precepts, a repository of loving counsels—shrewd, practical, and fully cognisant of difficulties and drawbacks; but informed by such sympathy and a sense of Christian brotherhood as should do much to make it acceptable and effective."—*Nonconformist.*

WORKS BY DR. R. W. DALE.

NINE LECTURES ON PREACHING.

Sixth Edition. Crown 8vo, price 6s.

"Admirable lectures, briefly written, earnest and practical."—*Literary Churchman.*

"Dr. Dale's lectures are full of practical wisdom and intense devotion."—*The Expositor.*

THE JEWISH TEMPLE AND THE CHRISTIAN CHURCH.

A Series of Discourses on the Epistle to the Hebrews.

Eighth Edition. Crown 8vo, price 6s.

"Wholsomer sermons than these it is almost impossible to conceive. Mr. Dale's preaching has always been remarkable for moral energy and fervour, but here this characteristic rises to its highest power."—*Expositor.*

THE EPISTLE TO THE EPHESIANS.

Its Doctrines and Ethics.

Sixth Edition. Crown 8vo, price 7s. 6d.

"The terse and vigorous style, rising on occasion into a manly and impressive eloquence, of which Mr. Dale is known to be a master, gives lucid expression to thought that is precise, courageous, and original."—*Spectator.*

WEEK-DAY SERMONS.

Fifth Edition. Crown 8vo, price 3s. 6d.

"Dr. Dale is certainly an admirable teacher of Christian ethics. He is, perhaps, the greatest living successor of the Apostle James. In this volume he appears at his best."—*Christian.*

THE TEN COMMANDMENTS.

Sixth Edition. Crown 8vo, price 5s.

"Full of thought and vigour."—*Spectator.*

IMPRESSIONS OF AUSTRALIA.

Crown 8vo, cloth, price 5s.

"Dr. Dale's articles ... constitute one of the most sensible books about Australia. ... The book is readable, and indeed excellent."—*Athenæum.*

THE NEW EVANGELICALISM AND THE OLD.

Cloth, price 1s.

"It has more in it than many an elaborate treatise; it suggests by every sentence; it is throughout succinct, pregnant, masterly."—*British Weekly.*

MISSIONARY BIOGRAPHIES.

Popular Edition.   Complete in one Volume.
JOHN G. PATON, D.D.,
Missionary to the New Hebrides.
An Autobiography.
Edited by His Brother, the Rev. *JAMES PATON, B.A.*
Sixth Thousand.   Crown 8vo, cloth, price 6s.
" One of the best autobiographies we have ever read."—*Daily Chronicle.*

The Life of Mackay for Boys.
THE STORY OF THE LIFE OF MACKAY OF UGANDA.
Told for Boys.
By HIS SISTER.
With Portrait and Illustrations.
Fifth Thousand.   Handsomely bound, price 5s.
" A veritable romance of noble self-sacrifice."—*Times.*
" Should be one of the most popular boy's books of the season."—*Record.*
" Full of interest from beginning to end."—*Daily Chronicle.*

A. M. MACKAY,
Pioneer Missionary of the Church Missionary Society to Uganda.
By HIS SISTER.
With Etched Portrait.
Eleventh Thousand.   Crown 8vo, cloth, price 7s. 6d.
" It is a pleasant thing, after all the horrors we have lately been hearing in connection with Africa, to come across such a very bright episode in its history as is contained in the life of Alexander Mackay."—*Spectator.*

Medical Missions.
THE LIFE OF JOHN KENNETH MACKENZIE,
Medical Missionary to China; with the Story of the First Chinese Hospital.
By Mrs. *BRYSON,* Author of " Child Life in Chinese Homes," etc.
With Portrait in Photogravure.
Second Edition.   Crown 8vo, cloth, price 6s.
" The volume contains much that is fresh and interesting bearing on Chinese customs and manners."—*Scotsman.*

WORKS BY REV. PROF. MARCUS DODS, D.D.

ERASMUS, AND OTHER ESSAYS.

Crown 8vo, cloth, price 5s.

"Professor Marcus Dods is a theologian, and much more. The essays in this volume show him, not for the first time, as a man of much reading, of broad and genial sympathies, refined but liberal judgment, possessed of no little literary culture, and keenly appreciative of literary and mental power in other men even when they do not happen to belong to his own school."—*Scotsman.*

MOHAMMED, BUDDHA, AND CHRIST.

SIXTH THOUSAND.

Crown 8vo, cloth, price 3s. 6d.

THE PRAYER THAT TEACHES TO PRAY.

SEVENTH EDITION.

Crown 8vo, price 2s. 6d.

"It is highly instructive, singularly lucid, and unmistakably for quiet personal use."—*Clergyman's Magazine.*

ISRAEL'S IRON AGE.
Sketches from the Period of the Judges.

SIXTH EDITION.

Crown 8vo, price 3s. 6d.

"Powerful lectures. This is a noble volume, full of strength."—*Nonconformist.*

WORKS BY DR. W. M. TAYLOR, of New York.

THE PARABLES OF OUR SAVIOUR.
Expounded and Illustrated.

THIRD EDITION.

Crown 8vo, cloth, price 7s. 6d.

"We have many books on the Parables of our Lord, but few which so thoroughly as this condense within their covers the best teaching contained in the various commentaries written to elucidate their meaning."—*English Churchman.*

THE MIRACLES OF OUR SAVIOUR
Expounded and Illustrated.

By the Same Author.

Crown 8vo, cloth, price 7s. 6d.

"Dr. Taylor takes up each miracle separately, sets forth in a vivid and graphic manner the circumstances attending it, and then proceeds to draw out in impressive language the lessons it suggests."—*Scotsman.*

WORKS BY THE REV. DR. FAIRBAIRN.

I.

THE CITY OF GOD.

A Series of Discussions in Religion.

By the Rev. *A. M. FAIRBAIRN, D.D.*, Principal of Mansfield College, Oxford.

THIRD EDITION.

Price 7s. 6d.

CONTENTS :—Faith and Modern Thought —Theism and Science —Man and Religion—God and Israel —The Problem of Job— Man and God—The Jesus of History and the Christ of Faith— Christ in History—The Riches of Christ's Poverty—The Quest the Chief Good—Love of Christ—The City of God.

" We find in the discourses which form this volume much able statement and much vigorous thought, and an admirable comprehension of the great questions which are being discussed in our day with eagerness and bated breath."—*Scotsman.*

II.

STUDIES IN THE LIFE OF CHRIST.

FIFTH EDITION.

Demy 8vo, price 9s.

CONTENTS :—The Historical Conditions—The Narratives of the Birth and Infancy—The Growth and Education of Jesus—His Personality—The Baptist and the Christ—The Temptation of Christ—The New Teacher—The Kingdom of Heaven—Galilee, Judea, Samaria—The Master and the Disciples—The Earlier Miracles—Jesus and the Jews—The Later Teaching—The Later Miracles—Jericho and Jerusalem—Gethsemane—The Betrayer— The Chief Priests—The Trial—The Crucifixion—The Resurrection.

"There is ample room for Professor Fairbairn's thoughtful and brilliant sketches. Dr. Fairbairn's is not the base rhetoric often employed to hide want of thought or poverty of thought, but the noble rhetoric which is alive with thought and imagination to its utmost and finest extremities.' —*Expositor.*

WORKS BY THE REV. PROF. A. B. BRUCE, D.D.

THE MIRACULOUS ELEMENTS IN THE GOSPELS.

Second Edition. 8vo, cloth, price 12s.

"It displays minute acquaintance with the modern literature of the subject, and all forms of attack to which Christian belief in the supernatural has been subjected. The defence is able all round; and the closing chapters—in which the miracle implied in the character of Jesus is dwelt on, and where the defence is for a moment changed into attack—are full of spirit and fire."—*Methodist Recorder*.

THE CHIEF END OF REVELATION.

Third Edition. Crown 8vo, cloth, price 6s.

"Dr. Bruce has given us a contribution of very great value. Like everything else that has come from his pen, this series of lectures has the conspicuous excellence of boldness, vigour, breadth, and moral elevation." - *Professor Salmond*.

THE PARABOLIC TEACHING OF CHRIST:

A Systematic and Critical Study of the Parables of Our Lord.

Fourth Edition. 8vo, cloth, price 12s.

"Professor Bruce brings to his task the learning and the liberal and finely sympathetic spirit which are the best gifts of an expositor of Scripture. His treatment of his subject is vigorous and original."—*Spectator*.

THE GALILEAN GOSPEL.

Third Edition. Price 3s. 6d.

"The product of a rich, imaginative mind, marked by scholarly analysis, subtle insight, and the suggestiveness of an original and unconventional thinker." - *Glasgow Herald*.
"We heartily commend this little volume."—*Spectator*.

THE LIFE OF WILLIAM DENNY,

Shipbuilder, Dumbarton.

With Portrait.

Second Edition. 8vo, cloth, price 12s.

"A most interesting biography."—*Academy*.
"Mr. Bruce has done his work exceedingly well, and with admirable reserve and good taste... In every popular library the 'Life of William Denny' ought to find a place by the side of Helps' 'Life of Brassey.'"—*Manchester Guardian*.

DR. THAIN DAVIDSON'S BOOKS FOR YOUNG MEN.

I.
A GOOD START.

FOURTH THOUSAND.

Crown 8vo, cloth, price 3s. 6d.

"Books which are confessedly and designedly 'improving,' without being dull, are not very common. Such books Dr. Davidson has already proved his capacity to write, and these 'homely talks' with young men are not inferior to his previous efforts."—*Academy.*

"At once winning and stimulating."—*Christian.*

II.
SURE TO SUCCEED.

SIXTH THOUSAND.

Crown 8vo, cloth, price 3s. 6d.

"An excellent present for a youth just going into business or coming up to London. It consists of twenty pithy and practical lectures to young men."—*Record.*

III.
FOREWARNED—FOREARMED.

SEVENTH THOUSAND.

Crown 8vo, cloth, price 3s. 6d.

"Weighty counsels. Dr. Davidson is remarkably at home in talks with young men. His words glow with an intense earnestness which demands and obtains attention from his readers."—*Sword and Trowel.*

IV.
THE CITY YOUTH.

SIXTH THOUSAND.

Crown 8vo, cloth, price 3s. 6d.

"A volume well worthy to rank with his previous works on kindred subjects. Dr. Davidson's matter and manner are alike excellent."—*Globe.*

V.
TALKS WITH YOUNG MEN.

THIRTEENTH THOUSAND.

Crown 8vo, cloth, price 3s. 6d.

"For sterling common-sense combined with true spiritual feeling, they have not been surpassed for many a day. The addresses bristle with telling metaphors and illustrations, and the book can be read from cover to cover with profitable interest."—*Literary World.*

www.ingramcontent.com/pod-product-compliance
Lightning Source LLC
Chambersburg PA
CBHW031332230426
43670CB00006B/328